Anti-Fascists

Jim McNeill and his mates in the Spanish Civil War

Anti-Fascists
Jim McNeill and his mates in the Spanish Civil War

Michael Samaras
Foreword by Rodney Cavalier

Connor Court Publishing

Published in 2025 by Connor Court Publishing Pty Ltd

Copyright © Michael Samaras

All rights reserved. No part of this book may be reproduced or transmitted in any form or by any means, electronic or mechanical, including photo copying, recording or by any information storage and retrieval system, without prior permission in writing from the publisher.

Connor Court Publishing Pty Ltd
PO Box 7257
Redland Bay QLD 4165
sales@connorcourt.com
www.connorcourt.com

ISBN: 9781923224575

Cover Design by Maria Giordano

Front Cover Photo: State Library of Western Australia b2377462-6

Printed in Australia

The International Brigade is in some sense fighting for all of us – a thin line of suffering and often ill-armed human beings standing between barbarism and at least comparative decency.

George Orwell, 31 July 1937

Contents

Foreword	9
Introduction	13
1 – With the air of a martyr	15
2 – Despair entered your mind!	27
3 – Get into it	39
4 – I believe in it enough to fight for it	55
5 – All into action now	67
6 – How much they hated us	77
7 – The slaughter yards	87
8 – What a man!	101
9 – From Corrimal to Catalonia	129
10 – Stuck like flies	151
11 – A deferred casualty	171
12 – You are legend	175
13 – A noble stand	189
14 – The future will raise monuments	197
15 – A reactionary, imperialist war	213
16 – Soldiers of democracy	223
17 – The great democratic traditions of Australia	239
18 – Afterlife	275
Appendix 1 – The Ripoll photograph	287
Appendix 2 – The *Maloja* photograph	296
Appendix 3 – Another one	305
Acknowledgements	312
List of illustrations	314
Bibliography	317
Index	329

Foreword

Michael Samaras is blessed with curiosity. A chance remark, a chance sighting, encountering life's passing parade, they will arouse an interest that does not ebb readily. A writing project may begin as an essay, it may first appear as an essay. Having accomplished some part of his original purpose, Michael knows when he needs to write more in order to achieve a comprehensive understanding for the reader and for himself.

Hence, in considering the generosity of a Wollongong identity to the city art gallery, Michael found cause to be suspicious about the donor's activities during the Second World War. Anchoring his inquiry in purposeful research, Michael unmasked a Nazi war criminal. Michael is not an investigative journalist on salary, he is not an academic in secure employment. Throughout the time he expended on this work, he was employed in a job that demanded all his attention during working hours.

The story of Jim McNeill was one Michael encountered because of his fascination with those Australians who perceived the dangers of fascism to the existence of a free society and to civilisation. A story of one man was a story rich in itself. Michael's research went beyond one man and one conflict. This book contains many stories.

Those stories include work, trade unions, solidarity and membership of a very young Australian Communist Party. When a civil war broke out in Spain, Jim McNeill and his comrades were not motivated by a sense of adventure. Their world view was built on militancy, the harsh realities of working in furnaces making steel in Port Kembla, a sense of what was right and wrong.

By the time that the civil war broke out, these Australian anti-fascists had built a coherent ideology based on the belief that struggle was essential to achieve a better society. Though the other side may control capital, the state and the armed forces, those opposed to their control had an obligation to contest its exercise.

Spain was a cockpit to the world war ahead, to employ George Orwell's evocative description. McNeill and comrades, in this account of their lives and growing conviction, could not but have responded to the call to arms in Spain. Being motivated to be involved and actually reaching the front, that was the stuff of adventure. The journey is traced in caring detail in these pages.

The Australian cricket side, captained by D.G. Bradman, on their way to England to keep the Ashes, likely had no knowledge of the mission of their fellow voyagers. Researching passenger manifests is one example of how Michael Samaras is able to provide the reader with such treats. Michael will track down every available clue and discover so much that was not available.

Battles in a losing cause make depressing reading. Deaths of comrades change possibilities. What happened in the Spanish years affected all who were there for their remaining days. Survivors had to go on living, find jobs and a purpose. The outbreak of the Second World War afforded McNeill and friends a second cause to fight fascism.

In spite of the Nazi-Soviet Non-Aggression Pact and the shameful decision of Australia's communist party to curse both the Nazis and the British, McNeill was an early recruit. Frontline fighting was beyond men of his age. Michael tracks the important work of these soldiers in forestry.

The Communist Party, having been so shameful at the outset of the War, were no less shameless in the Cold War that followed in their embrace of McNeill because of his usefulness in the play for moral advantage that characterised their strategy to win the support of the mass of working people.

McNeill was prepared to serve the party, driven by a need to be useful. Continuous activism guaranteed surveillance by ASIO when the Commonwealth Government legislated a domestic security regime. Effort expended on aging activists, men and women in no danger of occasioning danger, is the stuff of satire if it had not been so potentially ruinous to those under watch.

In a world that is receding into memory and photographs, we find it hard to recognise that on all four corners of the main streets of our big cities there were newsstands and men selling newspapers, usually in good voice. Among them was Jim McNeill trying to sell *Tribune*, the CPA weekly. At night was CPA branch activity until Czechoslovakia. The schism caused by the Soviet invasion of Czechoslovakia severed friendships. The Australian party could no longer accept that Moscow was guided by an all-knowing wisdom. McNeill had to cope with the death of a god.

How these events continue to matter is a central concern of this book. The book builds on a heritage of recent times when memoirs and letters were being published of events a half-century earlier. Spain is not forgotten because of the scholarship of people like Michael Samaras.

Michael has placed Spain and the presence of Australians in a wider context. The fight against fascism continues.

Rodney Cavalier

Introduction

The Australians who fought against Franco in the Spanish Civil War were men and women of conscience. They were prescient in their understanding of fascism's threat and convinced that taking up arms against it was the right thing to do. At least 16 of them died, while others returned with severe physical and psychological wounds.

Jim McNeill was one these anti-fascist volunteers. He was a man of strong political convictions. It was this commitment that led him to fight fascism at home and abroad. Firstly, during the Depression, he fought the New Guard on the streets of Sydney. Next, in 1938, he stowed away on a meat ship to Europe where he joined the International Brigades and fought Franco's fascists in Spain. Then, at the outbreak of the Second World War, he enlisted in the 2nd Australian Imperial Force and returned to Europe to defend Britain from the threat of Nazi invasion.

McNeill knew many of the Australians who went to Spain. He was friends with men like the charismatic Ted Dickinson, the conscientious Bill Morcom, the musical Jack Franklyn and the life-hardened Joe Carter. They became part of McNeill's life. Their stories form part of his story and are told here with his.

Those who went to Spain were the first Australians to confront the military forces of Nazi Germany and fascist Italy, as well as those of the Spanish fascists who rose in insurrection against the democratically elected government of Spain. These Australian anti-fascists are not honoured in the Australian War Memorial. The Australian government did not send them to fight and it did not welcome them home. Fighting fascism in Spain did not make them eligible to receive the health benefits, pensions and support provided to other veterans and their families.

The reasons for this different treatment are not hard to discern. These Australians ignored their government's directives and travelled across the world to fight fascism, while at the same time their government's policy was to appease the fascist regimes of Hitler and Mussolini. After the Second World War, the Australian veterans of the Spanish Civil War were an awkward reminder that during the 1930s not everyone had been an appeaser, or an open admirer, of the dictators. Throughout the years of the Cold War, the fact that the volunteers in Spain were members of the broad left, with many being card-carrying members of the Communist Party of Australia, made it even harder for the Australian government to acknowledge the correctness of their cause. It was not until after the Cold War ended and the Communist Party had disappeared that a memorial to the Australian volunteers, funded not by the Australian government but by public subscription, was finally erected.

The aim of this book is to ensure that the memory of the Australians who went to Spain, and demonstrated the courage of their anti-fascist convictions, is not forgotten.

This is the story of Jim McNeill, his mates and comrades. They were Australia's pioneers against fascism.

1

With the air of a martyr

In February 1939, 200 people gathered in Adelaide's Rechabite Hall to honour a contingent of Australian veterans from the Spanish Civil War. Jim McNeill, one of the returning soldiers, stood and spoke of the heroism shown by his friend, Ted Dickinson,[1] who had served with the British Battalion of the International Brigades at Jarama, a critical battle between the Republican army and Franco's fascist forces.

McNeill described how a group of men from the Battalion's machine gun company was captured by the enemy. It was an emotional account of a tragic moment. The Adelaide newspapers reported that many in the audience were powerfully moved by McNeill's description of Dickinson's "act of resolute bravery" as he defiantly proclaimed to his captors: 'To hell with you! If we had 20,000 Australian bushmen here, we'd sweep you into the sea." In McNeill's words:

> Dickinson was placed against a tree and as his murderers took aim, he said to his comrades, "Keep your chins up! Salud!" He died as he lived – undaunted to the end.[2]

McNeill and Dickinson were great friends and both were committed anti-fascists. In going to Spain and joining the International Brigades, McNeill had followed in Dickinson's footsteps. Dickinson's death was reported in the media and mourned in those circles that supported the cause of the Spanish Republic. As the years passed it was McNeill who worked to ensure that Dickinson's memory did not slip into the obscurity that was the fate of many other brave International Brigaders.

---

[1] Dickinson's name has often been misspelt. The corrected version of Dickinson is used throughout.
[2] *Mail*, 11 February 1939, p. 2; *Workers' Weekly Herald*, 17 February 1939, p. 3.

Jim McNeill

James Vincent (Jim) McNeill was born on 8 January 1900 to the Scot-Irish Catholic family of Mary Ann Esther McNeill (née Hughes) and William James McNeill, who was said to have instilled a hatred of tyranny into his son.³ McNeill was one of nine children, with three of his brothers dying as infants. The family lived in Balmain and Jim received a primary school education at the local Catholic school, St Augustine's.

In the first decades of the twentieth century, Balmain was an industrial working-class suburb with a busy waterfront, coal mine, power station and other industries. It had a thriving political culture. People worked where they lived, trade unions were part of daily life and it was in Balmain that the first branch of the Australian Labor Party was established. Raised in this environment, McNeill traced his political thinking to the lectures and open-air meetings that took place during the anti-conscription campaign of the Great War and the general strike of 1917.⁴

While the Australian working class was strongly opposed to conscription, it did not lack martial spirit and McNeill, at 18, enlisted in the Australian Imperial Force in 1918. His enlistment papers recorded him as being employed as a labourer, height five feet ten inches, weight 126 pounds, with dark hair and brown eyes. One contemporary described him as "the type our sculptors and painters chose as the typical Digger. Lanky, lean, he did not talk much, but the antennas were out all the time."⁵ He had already undergone some basic military training, having spent four years as a cadet in the Universal Service Scheme, which had been introduced in the years before the Great War to provide compulsory military training for boys and young men.⁶

In joining up he took the place of his older brother, Edward, who had

---

³ Amirah Inglis, *Australians in the Spanish Civil War*, North Sydney, 1987, p. 122.
⁴ RGASPI 545/6/68/190.
⁵ *Tribune*, 25 August 1976, p. 6.
⁶ *Children and WW1* on the website of the State Library of South Australia: https://guides.slsa.sa.gov.au/c.php?g=410371&p=2794665.

been seriously injured on the Western Front with a bullet fracturing his femur. On 4 November, McNeill passed his medical examination and, one week later, was enlisted on what turned out to be Armistice Day. With the war over and no need to leave Australia, McNeill spent the summer months at a training camp at Liverpool. He was discharged on 3 March 1919.[7]

After trying his luck as a gold miner, through most of the 1920s McNeill was steadily employed as an inspector of drawn wire, used for fencing, at the Lysaght Brothers' wireworks at Abbotsford. It was work he described as semi-skilled. He became politically active and in 1926 took part in a small demonstration against unemployment.[8] During the 1920s, McNeill was thinking beyond the local interests of Balmain and was concerned about the rise of Mussolini:

> *I had always hated fascism from the advent of Mussolini, with the prosecution of progressively minded men and women, its inroads on freedom, its castor oil etc.*[9]

In 1927 the economy began to worsen. Farmers reduced their spending on fencing when the prices they received for agricultural products fell, and in August McNeill lost his job at the wireworks. The job must have meant something to him, as he kept a Lysaght Brothers' wire gauge with him for the rest of his life.[10]

Ted Dickinson

Freshly unemployed, McNeill joined the Industrial Workers of the World (IWW or Wobblies) and it was there that he met Ted Dickinson. There was nothing in Dickinson's early family life to indicate that he

---

[7] NAA: 1957897 and 1957925.
[8] *Tribune*, 15 September 1976, p. 10.
[9] Letter from McNeill, dated 22 July 1965, in the Saffin Collection, State Library of Victoria, MS SEQ Box 15.
[10] Jim McNeill – Wendy Lowenstein, Wendy Lowenstein Collection, access courtesy of Martie Lowenstein (WL interview); Personal information from Vanessa McNeill, 18 January 2023. The wire gauge is now part of the McNeill Collection in the Illawarra Museum.

would become a charismatic firebrand of Australia's radical left. Born on 21 April 1903 in Grimsby, England, Edward Alexander (Ted) Dickinson was named after his father, Edward Dickinson, and his maternal grandfather Alexander Ross. His father, a fishmonger, died at Swansea in 1906, leaving Dickinson's mother, Mary Cormack Dickinson (née Ross), a widow at the age of 29. She took in washing to care for Dickinson and his older brother, James Forsyth Dickinson, who grew up to become a Congregationalist clergyman. Some years later, Mary married Ernest James Newman, a piano repairer and dealer, and in November 1913 the family moved to Melbourne, where Dickinson attended Coburg primary school. The family moved on to Armidale in NSW, but Dickinson soon returned to Melbourne.[11]

There is no record of Dickinson accounting for the development of his political thinking. His adolescence and early adulthood coincided with the Great War, the bitter conscription debates, and the Bolshevik revolution. Lenin's revolution received an eager and enthusiastic response from the Australian left, which celebrated the Soviet Union as the first workers' state.[12]

By 1923, Dickinson was frequenting Andrade's, a radical bookshop at 201 Bourke Street, Melbourne, where he engaged in political discussions and debates with all varieties of left-wing opinion. From this he joined the Labour Propaganda Group, which met every second Saturday evening. Its aim was to consider current issues, both Australian and international, and to inspire the working class to move away from what these activists saw as apathy. As part of this effort, Dickinson addressed the Victorian Trades Hall Council asking that the Unemployed Union be allowed to affiliate. This request was declined on the grounds that

---

[11] *Hull Daily Mail*, 8 June 1906, p 3; Death certificates for Mary Newman and James Dickinson sourced from the NSW Registry of Births, Deaths and Marriages; John Playford, 'History of the Left-wing of the SA Labor Movement, 1908-36', BA thesis, University of Adelaide, 1958, p. 137; Ray Broomhill, 'Dickinson, Edward Alexander (Ted) (1903–1937)', Australian Dictionary of Biography, National Centre of Biography, Australian National University, https://adb.anu.edu.au/biography/dickinson-edward-alexander-ted-5976/text10197, published first in hardcopy 1981, accessed online 13 July 2024.

[12] Stuart Macintyre, *The Reds: The Communist Party of Australia from Origins to Illegality*, St Leonards, 1998, pp. 48-9.

members of the Unemployed Union may not be members of their union, but the Trades Hall Council did agree to use Trades Hall as a relief depot for the unemployed.[13]

Dickinson encountered the writings of Marx through his studies with the Workers' Educational Association. At 20 he joined the IWW and with his fiery street oratory became one of its leading identities. The IWW had been established by American copper miners in 1905 as a radical, militant and revolutionary working-class organisation. In Australia, the group espoused uncompromising political activity that included strikes, industrial sabotage, boycotts, provocative street meetings, and entertaining forms of propaganda (such as songs, cartoons and posters), as it campaigned for the creation of One Big Union that would unify the working class and overthrow the capitalist system.

Dickinson said that he did not join in a "sudden spasm" and that he was attracted to the IWW because of the priority it gave not to violence or mass action, but to the "educational weapon as far as the working class is concerned".[14] In Australia, the organisation attracted a following of mainly itinerant working-class men. Its leaders were typically unmarried and footloose militants. They dismissed Labor parliamentarians as timeservers interested in their own parliamentary careers rather than in advancing the cause of the working class, and existing craft union leaders as negotiators ever willing to do deals with capitalists. A contemporary observer, the labour activist and eminent archaeologist V. G. Childe, said that the IWW "displayed energy and unflinching courage. Members were entirely careless of their personal safety."[15]

---

[13] Bertha Walker, *Solidarity Forever: A part story of the life and times of Percy Laidler – the first quarter of a century*, Melbourne, 1972, p. 151, pp. 197-205.

[14] This was in Dickinson's defence statement during his trials in Adelaide and likely reflects the priority of that circumstance.

[15] V G. Childe, *How Labour Governs*, London, 1923, p. 153; Frank Cain, *Biography and Ideology in the Industrial Workers of the World in Australia 1911-1922*, Paper to the 2011 Australian Society for the Study of Labour History Conference.

Charles Reeve

Due to its forceful anti-war activities, the IWW was suppressed by the Australian government during the Great War. Dickinson was central to its revival in the 1920s. He met Charles Reeve, a short and heavily tattooed Englishman who, like Dickinson's father, had worked as a vendor of fish and oysters. A stalwart of the IWW, Reeve was older and more experienced than Dickinson. He had gained notoriety from his time in New Zealand where he served as the IWW's Auckland secretary. During the Great Strike of 1913, Reeve had made incendiary speeches including one where he proposed that the strikers should march into the countryside and "wreak their vengeance" on the wives of the farmers who were acting as strike-breaking special constables.[16]

In Australia, Reeve was gaoled as one of the Sydney Twelve, a group controversially convicted of arson and conspiracy following a set of mysterious fires in Sydney. After a long campaign by the broad labour movement, Reeve and the other prisoners were released. Reeve then travelled across Australia establishing or reviving IWW branches wherever he went. Recognised as a compelling, entertaining and effective speaker he criticised anyone and anything, including royalty, churches, trade unions and the Communist Party of Australia (CPA), which he derided as the "Comical Party" full of "tin pot Lenins". While compelling on the stump, his fellow Wobblies saw him as a "bloody madman" who would "fight the world – so long as it was looking on", while the police recognised him as one of the IWW's "most aggressive" speakers.[17]

In Melbourne, Dickinson was mentored by Reeve and established a reputation as a charismatic and magnetic political agitator, who wrote and spoke enthusiastically on behalf of the IWW. He was physically impressive, with brown hair, blue eyes and a carriage as "straight as a ramrod". McNeill described Dickinson's voice as musical, noting that he could lead crowds in singing radical songs, while another colleague

---

[16] *The Oamaru Mail*, 5 December 1913, p. 3.

[17] Verity Burgmann, *Revolutionary Industrial Unionism: The Industrial Workers of the World in Australia*, Cambridge, 1995, p. 39 and p. 263.

recalled him as "tall, well-built and strikingly handsome…one of the most likeable personalities one could meet". In later years, his widow was to remember him as speaking very much like the Australian trade union leader and Prime Minister Bob Hawke.[18]

Dickinson applied his political skills in different ways. In 1924 he chaired a meeting of the IWW that called for a boycott of Californian goods, as that state had outlawed the IWW and imprisoned more than 200 Wobblies. He explained to the press that no resolution was carried as "the IWW believed in direct action rather than in the efficiency of resolutions", but advised in a letter published in the CPA's *Workers' Weekly* that more than £10 had been raised to assist the imprisoned Wobblies. He subsequently addressed the Victorian Trades Hall Council and suggested that a boycott of the visiting American fleet should be initiated.[19]

The Californian issue illustrated the political concerns and themes that would define the rest of Dickinson's life. His speech demonstrated concern for the underdog, the persecuted and downtrodden. It illustrated his internationalist outlook, and his willingness to act for workers and the disadvantaged wherever they were. Dickinson's ideological framework was socialist internationalism, his politics were neither narrowly defined nor parochial in their outlook.

In early 1925, Dickinson used his entertaining street oratory to draw a large crowd to an intersection in Prahran, which spilled across the street and onto a tram line. Dickinson, who was working as a driver, was charged with obstructing a carriageway and received a small fine. A charge laid against another Wobbly for leading the crowd in singing *The Red Flag* and *Solidarity* was dismissed.[20]

---

[18] WL interview; James McNeill, 'Ted Dickinson', *Australian Left Review*, December 1966, p. 42; *Workers' Star*, 7 January 1938, p. 2; David Young noted that Myrtle Ankers made the Hawke comparison when he met her after directing the play *Dickinson* at the 1978 Adelaide Festival Centre, email to the author, 12 April 2023.

[19] *Argus*, 17 November 1924, p. 18; *Workers' Weekly*, 3 October 1924, p. 3; 13 March 1925, p. 4.

[20] *Argus*, 7 January 1925, p. 9; *Age*, 8 January 1925, p. 11.

Dickinson and Reeve in Adelaide

Within a couple of months Dickinson and Reeve moved from Melbourne to Adelaide where they initiated a round of political agitation. Reeve commenced the campaign provocatively, telling a crowd of 2000 people in the Botanic Park that 50,000 returned soldiers had been infected with venereal diseases and that "mothers sending their daughters with those returned soldiers were practically asking them to try and get syphilis".[21] In an Australia that honoured its returned Anzacs, such challenging remarks were certain to arouse hostility. Dickinson took a room and displayed the three stars of the IWW on a sign in its window.[22] Taking a less antagonistic approach than Reeve, he concentrated his efforts on the issue of unemployment and, as the secretary of an unemployed committee, was soon making comments in the Adelaide newspapers, organising protests and leading deputations.

In 1925, unemployment in South Australia among trade unionists stood at 4.3 per cent, the lowest incidence of any of the states and well below the national average of 8.8 per cent.[23] Untroubled by this relatively benign position, Dickinson claimed that there were between 3000 and 4000 unemployed in Adelaide. It was a claim disputed by the secretary of the South Australian Labor Party, who said that there were "only about 350 unemployed registered in the State".[24] Despite this, Dickinson was able to draw more than 1000 people to an unauthorised gathering on the steps of the Trades Hall where he put the case for the unemployed. This effort was followed by a smaller demonstration of 150 men outside the Treasury Building which resulted in a deputation, led by Dickinson, receiving a sympathetic hearing from the Labor Premier, John Gunn, who promised to look into the issues raised. Dickinson though, remained unsatisfied, saying that the unemployed were not

---

[21] *News*, 11 June 1925, p. 1.
[22] *Mail*, 8 August 1925, p. 1.
[23] The official statistics measured and reported unemployment in this way. Ray Broomhill, *Unemployed Workers: A Social History of the Great Depression in Adelaide*, St Lucia, 1978, p. 13.
[24] *News*, 11 July 1925, p. 4.

prepared to wait.²⁵

Each morning unemployed men would assemble at the Labour Exchange on Molton Street where available jobs were allocated. Dickinson and Reeve used this daily gathering as an opportunity to address the unemployed men. On one occasion, Dickinson led the unemployed on a march to Trades Hall to demand that the police not interfere with their meetings. On another, Dickinson led 300 unemployed protestors to the offices of the Adelaide Steamship Company where, in response to an advertisement seeking workers placed in the midst of an industrial dispute, they chanted "We will not scab."²⁶

Dickinson in Sydney

Within months of arriving in Adelaide, Dickinson departed for Sydney where he re-established an IWW presence. He quickly came to the attention of the authorities for selling IWW literature in the Domain without a permit. Dickinson told a large crowd that he would keep selling his books, which he said were "mental dynamite", despite the prospect of prison: "If any of you want a couple of weeks' free board and lodging come along and give us a hand."²⁷ The *Truth* newspaper, noting that Dickinson was a "hero" of many similar prosecutions, provided a detailed account of the subsequent court hearing:

> *On being informed that he was fined a 'fiver' or a month's hard labour, Dickinson said, "The only reason I can see for not getting a permit is because twelve of our men were imprisoned during the war."*
>
> *Regarding the fine, he stated that he did not intend to pay it, but would do the time instead. He then turned, with the air of a martyr, walked to his comrades, bade them adieu and marched out of court in company of a constable.*²⁸

---

25 *News*, 11 July 1925, p. 4; 14 July 1925, p. 1.
26 *Register*, 16 July 1925, p. 3; 18 July 1925, p. 13.
27 *Stratford Evening Post*, 20 August 1925, p. 2.
28 *Truth*, 6 September 1925, p. 15.

The NSW Police recorded Dickinson as being six feet tall, with a thin build and blue eyes. He was said to be generally dressed in a grey suit with a grey felt hat, and tan shoes. His occupation was listed as canvasser.[29] In fact, Dickinson worked in a variety of jobs - lift attendant, factory hand and salesman.

He maintained his political activity by speaking regularly on the IWW platform in the Domain. At a May Day celebration in 1926, he spoke in support of striking British coal miners and proposed a resolution that sent "fraternal greetings to our comrades overseas".[30] In February 1927 he participated in the Hands Off China campaign and as the representative of the IWW addressed a large public meeting held in the Sydney Town Hall to protest Britain's trade concessions in China. These concessions were expressions of Britain's imperial power and were imposed on a weakened and humiliated China through the threat of military force. They gave British subjects commercial and legal privileges and represented the curtailment of Chinese sovereignty in China itself. Dr Woo, a visiting Chinese Nationalist, spoke to loud cheers. Dickinson proposed a resolution:

> *This meeting of citizens, believing that for a foreign power to seize Sydney, call it a 'concession,' land large bodies of troops, and concentrate warships in its harbour would be a great injustice, calls upon the people of Australia to refuse to participate in any way in the perpetration of such an injustice against another country.*[31]

Dickinson claimed that the Returned Soldiers' League was gauging the views of its members about sending a force to China to support Britain's imperialistic claims. This allegation sparked a letter of rebuttal from the League's state secretary who called on Dickinson to "apologise for having made unfounded statements". No apology from Dickinson was forthcoming.[32]

---

[29] *NSW Police Gazette*, 14 March 1928, p. 165.
[30] *Workers' Weekly*, 7 May 1926, p. 1.
[31] *Sydney Morning Herald*, 15 February 1927, p. 12.
[32] *Sydney Morning Herald*, 16 February 1927, p. 19; 17 February 1927, p. 6; 18 February 1927, p. 9.

Away from public meetings in the Sydney Town Hall, Dickinson expressed his opinions in letters to newspapers. Consistent with his concern for socialist internationalism, he wrote to the *Labor Daily* condemning the coal miners at Lithgow who sought to ban foreigners from joining their union. Writing to the *Workers' Weekly*, he then attacked the *Labor Daily* for being an "abortion of third-rate journalism".[33]

In Adelaide, by the end of 1927, the IWW had almost exhausted itself through a gruelling free speech campaign that had seen many of its members imprisoned for speaking in the Botanic Park without a permit. The IWW had applied for a permit, but found that permission was never granted for its speakers. In distress, it sought support from the Sydney IWW. Reeve moved that Dickinson and any other Wobblies who were available should travel to Adelaide and provide assistance. McNeill, a new recruit, had just lost his job at the wireworks and agreed to join Dickinson on the rescue mission. The pair was given £10 for expenses and set out on a train for Adelaide.

---

[33] *Labor Daily*, 18 January 1926, p. 4; May 1926, p. 6; *Workers' Weekly*, 6 May 1927, p. 5.

Photo 1: Jim McNeill (L) and Ted Dickinson (R) in Adelaide, 1927. (Illawarra Museum)

2

Despair entered your mind!

There is a photograph of the two mates standing in front of the Scarfe drinking fountain in the Adelaide Botanic Gardens. Taken in November 1927, the image shows them immaculately dressed in suits and ties. They are two young radicals who expect to be arrested. McNeill is 27 and wears a double-breasted suit. Holding his hat by his side, he looks nervous and uncertain. Dickinson, a younger but more politically experienced man, is dapper in a three-piece suit. He stands one step higher than McNeill and appears comfortable and relaxed, even jaunty. He holds his hands behind his back. Dickinson is 24, has an open, amiable countenance and looks confident and assured.

Campaigning for free speech

The pair had just arrived in Adelaide, determined to embark on a politically motivated campaign of civil disobedience. They took a room to share in a house with two other Wobblies and immediately commenced their free speech campaign. They distributed leaflets brought with them from Sydney to promote their unauthorised speaking appearance.

The free speech campaign was centred on a tree stump in the Botanic Park where the IWW spoke each Sunday without having the required permit from the governing board of the Botanic Gardens. The campaign attracted the public's interest and on Sunday 13 November, a huge crowd, estimated by the police at 2000 to 3000, attended to watch the

Wobblies defy the authorities.[1] As the police approached, Dickinson noted that there seemed to be new officers present, a reference to a corruption scandal involving bribes from brothels which had wracked the force and seen many officers leave the service. McNeill recounted what happened next:

> *A policeman asked Ted his name and he replied in a loud voice, 'Edward Alexander Dickinson' and then he asked, sort of confidentially, 'Well, what's yours?' and the policeman, being naïve, gave his name in full too! And the crowd roared with laughter! Dickinson had the crowd right in his hand.*[2]

The charges arising from the meeting were used as a campaigning opportunity with more than 300 men marching to the Adelaide Police Court for the hearing. Dickinson told the court that the Botanic Gardens board was denying freedom of speech to individuals who happened to be working-class. This argument did not sway the judge and each of the six defendants were fined five shillings plus costs.[3] An additional charge against Dickinson for using profane language was heard separately. The police testified that Dickinson had referred to the dismissal of police officers by saying:

> *All those who gave evidence against Charlie Reeve have been sacked. They were not fit even to be members of the Police Force, and by ----- -- that is not saying much.*

Conducting his own defence, Dickinson called several witnesses who stated that they did not hear him use the words "Jesus Christ". Dickinson then declared that he had a total of 123 witnesses to call and asked that they all be admitted to the court. This announcement caused an uproar from lawyers who were waiting patiently for their own cases to come up. The magistrate ruled there was nothing to stop a defendant from calling as many witnesses as he wanted. At this point, sensing his opportunity,

---

[1] The crowd figure was given by Constable Ivey during the subsequent legal proceedings, see *News*, 25 November 1927, p. 5.

[2] WL interview.

[3] Australian pre-decimal currency involved pounds, shillings and pennies. There were 12 pennies in a shilling, and twenty shillings in a pound. Five shillings in 1927 would be worth approximately $25 in 2024.

Dickinson quietly rose to his feet and said, in view of the stress it would place on what he emphasised were rather more important cases, he would rest with the existing witnesses who were representative of hundreds of others. There were audible cries of relief from the lawyers. The magistrate, who had clearly heard enough, dismissed the charges, leaving Dickinson to be cheered by his supporters as he left the court.[4]

Members of the IWW routinely did not pay the fines imposed on them and, in default, served time in gaol before returning to the stump for the process to be repeated. McNeill was arrested several times and served time in the Yatala gaol. As a result of this organised civil disobedience, the courts quickly became congested with Wobblies conducting their own defences and being imprisoned for the innocuous offence of taking part in a public meeting without first obtaining the written permission of the board. In the face of this sustained recalcitrance, the authorities responded by progressively reducing the length of the sentences from a month, to seven days, to 24 hours. After about six weeks, the Wobblies were called to a meeting with the police and advised that if the IWW gave the names of those who wanted to speak, then they would be given permission.[5]

Campaigning for the unemployed

With that victory won, Dickinson and McNeill were able to concentrate their efforts on the issue of unemployment. The economy of South Australia had deteriorated sharply since Dickinson's previous visit. Unemployment among trade unionists reached 15 per cent in 1928, on its way to a peak of 34 per cent in 1932, and was likely even higher than the official figures recorded.[6] McNeill recounted that a sense of despair was created by the bleak economic conditions:

> *Instead of hearing of someone getting a job which would give you hope, you'd only hear of others put off. One place had put off twenty, and*

---

[4] *News*, 25 November 1927, p. 1; *Advertiser*, 26 November 1927, p. 17; McNeill, *Ted Dickinson*, p. 43.

[5] WL interview.

[6] Broomhill, *Unemployed*, p. 2.

> *another place forty, and another place a hundred.*
>
> *Despair entered your mind!*[7]

Support for the unemployed, in the years before the advent of the modern welfare state, was not accepted to be the responsibility of governments. What welfare existed was meagre and mean-spirited. Dickinson and McNeill lived a subsistence lifestyle and quickly used up the £70 of savings from the wireworks that McNeill had brought with him. The pair lived cheaply, visiting the markets to buy cabbages and lettuces, and occasionally receiving a rabbit or chicken from a Wobbly visiting from the country.[8]

To make some money, many of the unemployed went door-to-door, attempting to sell household essentials like mothballs and needles. McNeill tried his hand at selling cakes of toilet soap, which could be purchased at three shillings a dozen and then sold for a sixpence each, generating a small profit.

> *I remember having a go at that but failing dismally as a salesman. I was diffident about it. I had to brace myself, but gave up after two attempts.*

Eventually, McNeill did succeed in getting some employment out on the Mallee, where he worked at stick-picking, a job that entailed collecting thousands of partially burnt sticks after farmers had used fire to clear the bush. On another occasion he worked for several months as a rabbit trapper.[9]

With mass unemployment now a feature of Australian life, governments looked to charities to take a leading role in providing for citizens in need. Such was the official contempt for the unemployed that the government only provided rations to the destitute as it was believed that cash support would be badly spent. The rations provided small

---

[7] Wendy Lowenstein, *Weevils in the Flour: An Oral Record of the 1930s Depression in Australia*, Brunswick, 1998, p. 61.

[8] WL interview; Letter from McNeill to John Playford, 14 February 1958, McNeill Collection, Illawarra Museum.

[9] WL interview.

amounts of rice, tea, oatmeal, raisins, jam, soap and vouchers for bread and meat.[10] Collecting this support was often humiliating. To be eligible for the rations, unemployed men had to attend the Labour Exchange each morning and prove they were ready for any work that was available. But with no jobs going, McNeill regarded turning up as a futile and depressing exercise:

> *A sort of hopeless position. You went there day after day and no-one was called. And you went there again.*
>
> *Somewhere to go, that's all.*[11]

This requirement for daily attendance was depressing but did provide a strategic advantage for the IWW as it meant that the unemployed assembled each day. This provided a ready and receptive audience for Dickinson and McNeill, who would stand on a kerosene case to deliver rallying speeches. Dickinson would regularly lead demonstrations down the streets of central Adelaide, with the marchers singing Wobbly songs.

One demonstration commenced with Dickinson telling the unemployed that they would make a call on their "comrade and unemployed friend, the Lord Mayor of Adelaide". At the Town Hall the gates were closed. Dickinson gave a vehement address in which he proposed that if civic leaders would not meet with them, then the men would march to the officials' private residences and compel them to listen. The men, he said, demanded what was rightfully due and were not going to peacefully accept second-hand clothing cast to them by parsons. The demonstrators, urged by Dickinson to form up into fours so that they were not seen as "a disorganised rabble", then sang *Solidarity for Ever* and *The Red Flag* as they returned to the Labour Exchange.

On another occasion, when Premier Richard Butler (Liberal Federation) was not immediately available to meet a deputation to discuss the policy of employment preference for the allocation of jobs, 1000 marchers rushed the doors of the Treasury building. The police drew their batons. Dickinson told Police Inspector Henry Joseph Church

---

[10] Broomhill, *Unemployed*, pp. 78-9.
[11] WL interview.

and the Premier's secretary, Malcolm Pearce, that if the Premier would not see them, then they would try "other tactics". Under questioning by the police, Dickinson clarified that his "other tactics" did not mean violence, but involved winning the support of Lionel Hill, Leader of the Labor Party. After the disturbance, Premier Butler met with the Lord Mayor and Police Commissioner and issued a statement affirming the government's determination to maintain law and order.[12]

Dickinson's position on employment preference was that all unemployed men, married or single, returned soldiers and civilians, Australians, English and "our friends, the Maltese", should have an equal chance to obtain whatever work was available. It was more evidence of Dickinson's concern for the international unity of the working class. During another demonstration, the procession halted at Hindley Street where some Greeks were standing in front of the Athenian Club. After a short conversation it was reported that the Greeks, together with some Maltese and other foreigners, joined the march.[13]

Dickinson sought improved support for the unemployed and led a deputation to Premier Butler seeking the payment of some Christmas cheer. Dickinson asked for between £20,000 and £30,000 to be distributed and, in what has become a stock tactic of Australian politics, challenged the Premier to live on the rations being issued to the unemployed. The Premier replied that if he was destitute, he would willingly live on the rations and subsequently announced that £1000 would be distributed as Christmas cheer. Dickinson responded that considering there were more than 2800 unemployed men registered with the Labour Exchange, this "was a most inadequate sum".[14]

On another occasion Dickinson was at a spontaneous demonstration against an eviction and, in discussion with a police inspector, suggested that to defuse a potentially violent situation, a collection be made to enable the payment of the outstanding rent. According to McNeill, Dickinson told the inspector:

---

[12] *Advertiser*, 29 November 1927, p. 13.

[13] *News*, 17 November 1927, p. 4.

[14] *Chronicle*, 17 December 1927, p. 58; *Observer*, 24 December 1927, p. 51.

> *If the eviction is persisted in, there'll be a lot of unemployed injured, but also some police. I might be able to restrain the men, but I've got no control over the women!*
>
> *I suggest we take up a collection. There's very little amongst the unemployed. The only ones present who are working are the police. You, for instance!*

Presented with a hat, the inspector obliged, gave four bob and the eviction did not proceed.[15]

Dickinson's energetic leadership of the unemployed came to a halt in January 1928 with the announcement of his resignation from the unemployed committee. He blamed uncomplimentary comments that were being made about him for his decision to withdraw. He also noted his disapproval of those who wanted the unemployed's activism to focus on charity and "old clothes". Dickinson said he "was not prepared to participate in anything that tended to convert workers into beggars".[16] It seems likely that the resignation was prompted by his success in obtaining some work clearing land and grubbing out stumps on a property at Mallala, some 58 kilometres north of Adelaide.[17]

Reviving *Direct Action*

By May though, having survived unscathed a car crash on the Main North Road at Gepps Cross, Dickinson was ready to resume his political activity.[18] With funding obtained from miners at Broken Hill, Dickinson and McNeill relaunched *Direct Action*, the IWW newspaper that had, in its first incarnation, been suppressed by the Australian government during the Great War.

The paper's motto, emblazoned across the top of its front page, was "Education, Organisation, Emancipation", and in its opening editorial

---

[15] Lowenstein, *Weevils*, p. 61.
[16] *Advertiser*, 13 January 1928, p. 14.
[17] WL interview.
[18] *Saturday Journal*, 10 March 1928, p. 1.

the paper explained its purpose:

> *Direct Action breathes the revolutionary air, it expresses revolutionary thoughts, it is a living vital healthy protest against a rotten system of exploitation. Its aim and object is to show the workers the way out, it is not destructive, rather is it gloriously constructive; we come to build up, to create a new ideology that will express itself in a new system. On the horizon, we see a lone light burning, the light of knowledge, which, when formed will arouse the working class to a new understanding, which will usher in a new world.*
>
> *We want your support— let every worker be a veritable dynamo of energy, let this paper be distributed far and wide. Knowledge is power, fellow workers, by your help we will succeed, and by our united strength on the industrial field we shall usher in the new society in our time. On with the Revolutionary Education!*[19]

As editor, Dickinson produced a strident and witty publication that did not hesitate to publish vituperative articles that criticised employers, trade unions, parliamentarians and almost everyone and everything else. Stories raised the plight of the local unemployed, with one highlighting the degrading housing conditions in the fetid camps where they were expected to live. Other articles examined international developments with one, "Fiendish Fascism", tallying the number of workers killed by Mussolini and other "capitalist thugs".[20]

McNeill and Dickinson wrote many of the articles, with McNeill, who was the assistant secretary of the Adelaide IWW, providing regular reports on the branch's activities which included economics and debating classes, lectures, and dances on Saturday nights. One of his articles addressed the issue of unemployment, which he found to be the "putrid cankerous outgrowth of a vile, corrupt and faulty economic system". McNeill urged readers to pass on their copy of the paper and to become "active fighters in the class war".[21]

---

[19] *Direct Action*, 13 May 1928, p. 2.
[20] *Direct Action*, 17 November 1928, p. 3.
[21] *Direct Action*, 7 July 1928, p. 1; 13 May 1928, p. 1 and p. 3.

The paper came, almost immediately, to the attention of the authorities. A parliamentary question by Thomas Thompson MP (Protestant Labor Party) asked about an article that encouraged workers to forget Anzac Day and celebrate May Day instead.[22] In the chamber, Thompson waved a copy of *Direct Action*, which he described as a "rag".[23]

Within minutes of the question being asked a group of 30-40 unemployed men created a disturbance in the public gallery leading to parliamentary proceedings being suspended. The Hansard recorded the event:

> HOUSE INTERRUPTED – UPROAR IN STRANGERS' GALLERY
>
> *A Voice in the Strangers' Gallery – What are you going to do about the starving unemployed of Adelaide? We demand the right to live. It is up to the government to do something. What are you going to do about the men sleeping on the banks of the Torrens?*
>
> *Mr Treasurer – I call your attention, Mr Speaker, to a noise in the Strangers' Gallery.*
>
> *(Uproar in the gallery)*

The media did not name the "young man" who triggered the "unprecedented scene", but did record the following exchange:

> *"What about you, Thompson – asking questions about proceedings being taken against the workers' paper?*
>
> *Mr Thompson sat still and smiled.*
>
> *"You are a traitor, Thompson!" another man yelled.*[24]

In the next edition of *Direct Action*, Thompson was mockingly described as the paper's parliamentary correspondent and thanked for the publicity he had generated. Thompson was promised that he would be provided with future issues for free and, as a change from parliament, was invited

---

[22] Hansard of the South Australian Parliament's House of Assembly, 8 May 1928, p. 30.
[23] *Chronicle*, 12 May 1928, p. 51.
[24] *News*, 8 May 1928, p. 1.

to debate in front of an "intelligent audience" at the IWW's meeting rooms.[25]

The newspaper was printed in a run of 2000 and distributed across Australia through the IWW's networks. A friend of Dickinson's handled distribution in Brisbane; Reeve did the same in Sydney. In Adelaide, the paper was sold at the Labour Exchange, workplaces and at public meetings held by the IWW in the Botanic Park.[26] Selling the paper resulted in more legal troubles, with Dickinson and other Wobblies fined for selling it in the Botanic Park without the written permission of the board.[27]

More demonstrations, marches and protests were organised. The experience of unemployment and the way relief was provided created deep feelings of degradation and humiliation for men whose self-esteem and social status was shattered by the loss of work.[28] As a consequence, there was a strong reaction to a newspaper interview given by Miss Annie Green of the Adelaide City Mission in which she claimed that of the 5000 unemployed men in Adelaide, only 4000 were honest men. The others, she said, were "unscrupulous men who are old hands at begging" and "scoundrels" who were taking money that should be used to assist "the deserving".[29] In response, Dickinson led 500 "highly incensed" unemployed men in a protest march to the charity's premises. During a meeting, Dickinson asked Green if she would name the 1000 imposters, which she declined to do.[30]

Dickinson's attention returned to the parliament. A petition of 485 citizens was presented by the Labor Party asking that permission be given to a delegation, led by Dickinson, to address the House. The government defeated the proposal, with Premier Butler stating that he was "surprised" that the "names submitted included that of Mr Dickinson", who was a

---

[25] *Direct Action*, 20 May 1928, p.1 and p. 4.
[26] Wilfred Prest (ed), *The Wakefield Companion to South Australian History*, Kent Town, 2001, p. 280.
[27] *News*, 17 July 1928, p. 13.
[28] Broomhill, *Unemployed*, pp. 41-2.
[29] *News*, 30 June 1928, p. 4.
[30] *Advertiser*, 3 July 1928, p. 16.

leader of a "Communistic party in South Australia". Dickinson, he said, had come to South Australia not to alleviate suffering but to "preach the pernicious doctrine of the overthrow of the British Empire". Butler said he had already met Dickinson in his office, but the "overthrow of the capitalistic system was about the only thing he talked about. He can talk of nothing else". The Premier said that the inclusion of Dickinson's name in the petition was enough to condemn it:

> *Unfortunately, Mr Dickinson, as he is a man possessing a certain amount of ability, has a tremendous power as far as the unemployed are concerned and he is today recognised as a leader by a section on account of his force of character and his doctrines, which, I regret to say, bear fruit with some of the unemployed, and not only the unemployed, but with some of the workers.*[31]

As the Premier's remarks indicated, Dickinson's political activism ensured that he enjoyed a growing personal reputation. His efforts were noticed by the IWW's rivals in the CPA who, in the pages of the *Workers' Weekly*, noted that Adelaide was home to the only local of the once powerful IWW and, moreover, that Dickinson was "the 'I' in this particular IWW".[32]

Dickinson continued to use the pages of *Direct Action* to advocate socialist internationalism. He had no patience with trade unions that embraced nationalism ahead of a concern with class. He returned to this theme with a broadside against the waterside workers of Port Adelaide who were reported to have restricted membership of their union to only British subjects.

> *Could there be anything more reactionary than the idea that only true British stock, in future, have the right to offer their carcasses to be exploited on the waterfront. Surely the papers lie. It is inconceivable that even slaves would sink so low as to demand the sole right to be exploited; just fancy, a monopoly of slavery, reserved wholly and solely for 'men of the bulldog breed,' 'with hearts of oak and brains of reinforced concrete.' What stupidity! What boneheadedness! Furthermore, what a*

---

[31] *Parliamentary Debates*, 1928, Third Session of the Twenty-sixth Parliament, pp. 548-54.
[32] *Workers' Weekly*, 24 August 1928, p. 3.

> *wonderful weapon in the hands of the boss.*
>
> *We have seen in the past how the working class have been kept apart by racial misunderstanding, how, in Ireland, the north has been played against the south, to the edification of the land owners and capitalists; how in India the Mohammedan and the Hindu have been used against each other. Thus, while the workers are fighting each other they cannot find time to fight the powers that exploit them and live on the surplus values that they create.*[33]

In contrast to this sort of "stupid national and sectarian outlook", Dickinson proclaimed the internationalism of the IWW.

> *There is no prejudice in the ranks of this fighting organisation: we stand for the organisation of the working class irrespective of class, colour or creed, for the purpose of overthrowing capitalism.*[34]

In September 1928, Dickinson took up the plight of restaurant and café workers who could not speak English. He criticised "stupid and reactionary trade union officials" who neglected these workers, leaving them to the "tender mercies of their greedy exploiters". Dickinson pledged to use the pages of *Direct Action* to publish a "damning exposure of Hindley Street Hells, Crook Cafes and Sweated Slaves".[35]

Events, however, were about to escalate dramatically and the promised exposé never eventuated.

---

[33] *Direct Action*, May 1928, p. 3.
[34] *Direct Action*, 3 September 1928, p. 2.
[35] Ibid., p. 1.

3

Get into it

During the later months of 1928 the industrial situation on Australia's wharves reached a crisis point. Relations between employers, the Australian government and the Waterside Workers' Federation had been difficult for years. They deteriorated sharply when a new industrial award was introduced. It was promptly rejected by the union and waterfront strikes commenced across Australia.

Waterfront strike at Port Adelaide

At Port Adelaide, employers were determined to break the strike and recruited volunteers to undertake the work. In response, on 27 September, thousands of waterside workers stormed the docks and drove the volunteers from the ships. Some of the volunteers jumped overboard and swam to safety on the opposing river bank. A further melee erupted when another crowd, of about 2000 men, marched from Adelaide to meet up with the waterside workers. Shots were fired, stones were thrown and a general sense of disorder prevailed. The police drew their batons and eventually the crowds dispersed.[1]

Such scenes were unprecedented in Adelaide. The Butler government responded with an emergency midnight cabinet meeting and a statement:

> The issue is mob rule or constitutional government. The government will, with all the forces at their command, see that rights of citizens

---

[1] R.N. Wait, 'Reactions to Demonstrations and Riots in Adelaide 1928 to 1932', MA thesis, University of Adelaide, 1973, pp. 32-6.

are upheld. There is no excuse whatsoever for the action of the strikers, who have openly defied the law, and so forfeited all sympathy, and the government feel that the public will stand firmly behind them in their efforts to maintain the reputation of this country for strict adherence to the law. The government have every confidence in the capacity of the Commissioner of Police to control the situation.[2]

Hotels were ordered to close. A Citizens' Defence Brigade was established to protect the strikebreaking volunteers with 1000 special constables being sworn in and issued with armbands, rifles and bayonets.[3] Premier Butler justified his response to the riot by claiming that extremists aimed to cut off the supply of electricity to Adelaide, pull up railway lines, and blow up a powder magazine at Port Adelaide. Several weeks later, when mocked in Parliament by the Labor Party for this "political scare-mongering", the government contended that the extremists were no longer at large and prosecutions had already been launched.[4]

Arrest and trial

This was a reference to another of the Commissioner of Police's actions to control the situation. Early on the morning of 1 October Dickinson, described as a "well-known agitator", was arrested at his home and charged with seditious libel and unlawfully taking part in a riot.[5] The charge of seditious libel related to articles published in a strike edition of *Direct Action*. The police had purchased copies while listening to Dickinson speak in the Botanic Park. As editor, Dickinson was held responsible for all the articles in the publication, regardless of whether he had personally authored them or not. Nonetheless, the prosecution highlighted the opening editorial written by Dickinson:

As we go to press the fight still rages. If correctly led by fearless, class-conscious leaders, the men cannot lose. Let our motto be: 'No compromise;

---

[2] *Advertiser*, 28 September 1928, p. 15.
[3] Wait, 'Reactions', p. 38.
[4] *Advertiser*, 18 October 1928, p. 12; *House of Assembly Hansard*, 23 October 1928, p. 1428.
[5] 'Report of the Commissioner of Police for the year ended June 30th, 1929', pp. 10-11, in *Proceedings of the Parliament of South Australia, 1929, Volume 2*.

we are many; they are few,' and let us understand the fundamental truth of that great quotation: 'We have nothing to lose but our chains and a world to gain.'

GET INTO IT.

E. A. DICKINSON, *Adelaide*.

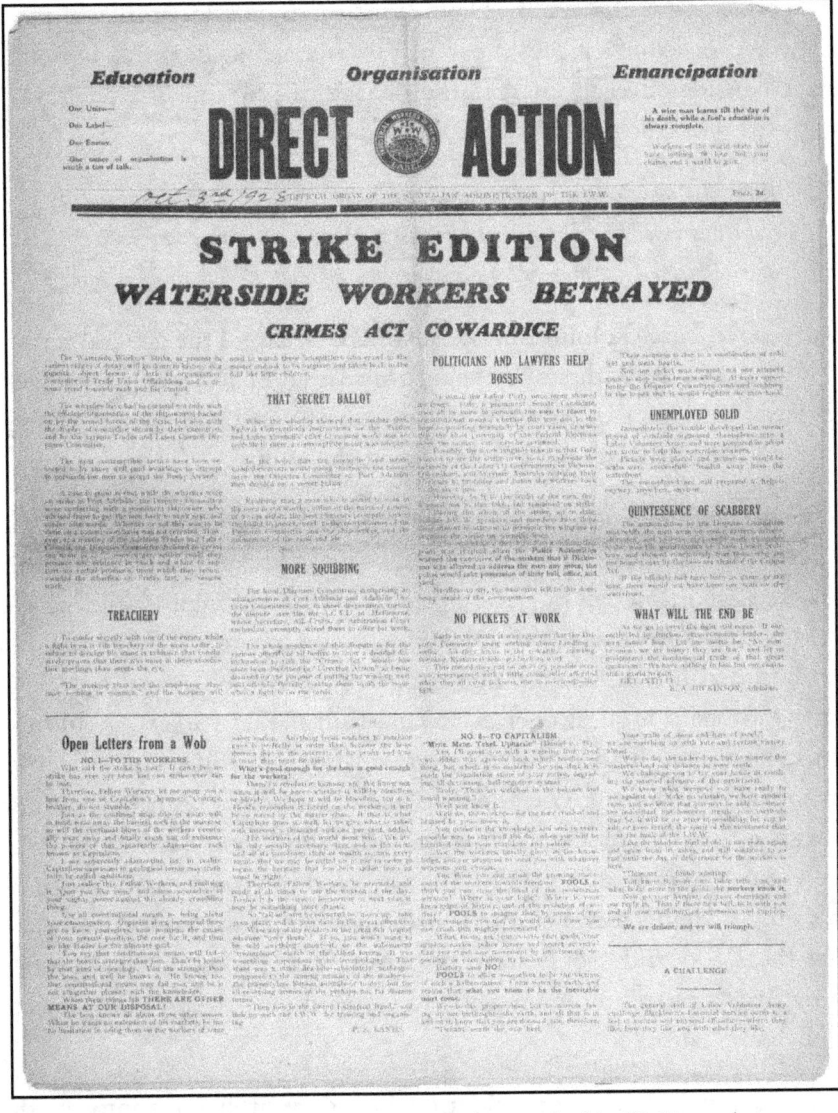

Photo 2: The front page of *Direct Action* that resulted in Dickinson being gaoled for sedition. (State Library of NSW)

Dickinson was eventually released on bail, but his efforts to raise funds for his own defence were hampered by again being refused permission to speak at the Botanic Park. Instead, he took to giving lectures at the IWW's premises.

Dickinson's trials on the two charges took place in December 1928 before the Chief Justice, Sir George Murray, a pillar of Adelaide's conservative establishment. Dickinson's high public profile ensured that the proceedings received extensive coverage in the press. Different juries considered each charge. The charge of sedition was dealt with first, with Dickinson, a labourer, accused of being a:

> *Wicked, malicious, seditious and ill-disposed person, he committed seditious libel by writing and publishing and causing to be written and published a 'statement' in a pamphlet headed, Direct Action.*[6]

A detective, Percival John Bourke, testified that amid the general tumult at Port Adelaide, with stones being thrown and batons being wielded, he saw Dickinson in front of the procession call out: "Let us break through the lines and pull every scab off the boats."

Several Wobblies appeared as witnesses for Dickinson's defence. McNeill declared his occupation as a wireworker and said that he did not see Dickinson call out or behave in an excited manner during the incident. Acknowledged as Dickinson's roommate, McNeill further testified that he had been selling copies of *Direct Action* at the Botanic Park and heard a questioner ask Dickinson if the workers should use arms. Dickinson had replied "I don't advise the workers to use rifles or bayonets, I don't advise them to arm themselves with bayonets or pickets – they can please themselves." William Francis, a fitter and the literature secretary of the IWW, then assured the court that, though he was only a young member and didn't know what direct action meant, that the IWW did "not believe in bomb outrages and all that sort of thing. It is a peaceful organisation to bring about a new society and to abolish capitalism."

In his defence, Dickinson said that he not written or approved the

---

[6] Transcripts of Dickinson's trials are available from Courts SA.

article which had appeared without his permission. Dickinson admitted to writing only the "insignificant bit at the end, which quoted from Karl Marx's book, *Capital*, which could be found in every library and school of note in Australia". He further rejected the charge that he was a "malicious or ill-disposed person" and said he had "taken great interest in church work and studied whenever he had the opportunity. He had never advocated violent action."

Giving a detailed account of his movements at Port Adelaide, Dickinson outlined giving a cigarette to Detective Burke with the two taking a moment to enjoy a smoke together. Dickinson said he paid careful attention to McNeill, who had just been discharged from the Adelaide Hospital having spent a month there as a patient. He asked the jury to "please remember and centre your minds" on his assurance that he had "never at any time advocated violence". The jury, described by the *Workers' Weekly* as being class-based and composed of "shopkeepers and farmers who are thoroughly imbued with a capitalist outlook", took less than an hour to find Dickinson guilty.[7]

In the riot matter, six police officers gave evidence. Detective Burke testified that Dickinson was in the leading file of the men in the procession and had called on the men to "pull off every scab" from the boats. Under cross-examination he testified that he saw no violence committed by Dickinson, nor did he see him throw anything - "at no time did the accused show any hostility to the police". Even so, he emphasised that the attitude of the men was "to create terror" in the minds of the "volunteer workers" on the ships.

A clerk employed in the Adelaide Police Commander's office, Edward Lucas Halifax, testified that he had attended the Botanic Park meeting and had taken down Dickinson's speech in shorthand. He recounted to the court Dickinson's address to the crowd:

> *A certain police officer issued instructions that if you get a chance baton Dickinson first and arrest him afterwards. I just missed it by inches.*
>
> *There is one thing that the IWW has shown when it comes to a pinch*

---

[7] *Workers' Weekly*, 21 December 1928, p. 4.

> *that we have the courage of our convictions and the guts to do what we talk about. I was down at the outer harbour. It's no good me denying it. I was down there and proud of it.*
>
> *If the workers all over Australia gave a 24 hours demonstration like the wharfies did on Thursday you would not have to worry about scabs. There would be no more strikes because the moment the working class, over the whole of Australia, showed for 24 hours on end the same solidarity as the wharfies did, the moment the whole of the workers do that there will be no more strikes because there will be no more capitalists.*

Dickinson's defence submitted that there was no case to answer. Chief Justice Murray ruled against this submission. Dickinson then gave a sworn statement in his own defence and restated his protestations of innocence. He denied taking a leading position in the procession, pointing out that it was led by 200 cyclists. He contended that he was only present as a journalist to gather material for *Direct Action* and that McNeill could account for his movements. Dickinson denied telling the Botanic Park crowd there would be "no more capitalists", although he may have said "no more capitalism". He said that the IWW was an entirely peaceful organisation: "Its objects are lawful and peaceful. It does not advocate the use of force."

Cross-examined by the prosecution about the cause of the violence, Dickinson put the blame on the police:

> Mr. Chamberlain— Did you see anything that was likely to cause casualties?
>
> *The Witness*— Yes. The troopers galloping between the men.

The jury retired shortly after noon and returned at 2.30pm with a guilty verdict, qualified by a strong recommendation of mercy given Dickinson's youth.

To charge someone with sedition over articles published in a newspaper appears to have been an unprecedented occurrence in South Australia. Chief Justice Murray was unmoved by this and had no hesitation in administering a severe punishment. Dickinson, he said, had travelled from state to state and had been "generally indulging his taste for public speech". Murray said that he was not convinced that the accused was not prepared to make use of violence to achieve his object. Dismissing the jury's call for leniency, he noted that Dickinson was 25 and "not so young that he deserved special consideration on that ground".[8] Even so, Murray contended that he had been as lenient as possible, given that:

> *Revolution was spoken of as looming up. The right of freedom of speech, and the liberty of the press, as recognised by the law, did not permit the enunciation of doctrines of that sort.*

For the charge of seditious libel, Murray sentenced Dickinson to six months imprisonment and a fine of £40. On the riot charge, Dickinson received three months without hard labour and a fine of £10. The sentences were to be served cumulatively and Dickinson was to remain in gaol until the fines were paid.

Reaction to the conviction

The IWW saw the prosecution as a "warning to workers" orchestrated by the employing class. It decried the charges against Dickinson as a "vicious persecution" that put the IWW as an organisation on trial. A Dickinson Defence and Release League was established to raise money to pay for both the legal defence and the fines. Donations were forthcoming from miners at Broken Hill, numerous trade unions including the Meat Industry Employees' Union, Builders' Labourers' Federation, the Liquor Trade Employees' Union, and from among the unemployed themselves, who contributed from the "pitiable allowances" the government disbursed at Christmas.[9]

The secretary of the Liquor Trades Employees' Union, Fred Standish, gave a detailed explanation of his support for Dickinson. In an argument that had apparently eluded the Cambridge-educated Chief Justice,

---

[8] The trial was extensively covered by the Adelaide newspapers. The account here draws on that published in the *Register* on 5,6,7,8 and 12 December 1928.

[9] *Direct Action*, 20 October 1928, p. 1 and p. 4; *Register*, 28 December 1928, p. 11.

Standish referenced the work of John Stuart Mill that no government had the right to prevent a man from speaking freely given that, if he was right, then suppression would be a crime; if he was wrong, the public would realise it and his utterances would be futile. Standish contended that many measures advocated by "so-called extremists" in past years were now accepted. He said that the working conditions of brewery workers, who had a 44-hour week, annual leave and sick pay, were thanks to the efforts of men like Dickinson.[10]

Other trade union leaders were not as sympathetic. In anonymous comments they suggested that Dickinson frequently attacked union officials, yet expected their help when in trouble. Dickinson, they said, "was a hard man to help, for he declined to listen to advice from those who wished him well and seemed to desire classification as an industrial martyr".[11]

Whatever private misgivings some union leaders may have had, publicly the campaign to free Dickinson enjoyed their blessing. The United Trades and Labor Council resolved that Dickinson should be treated as "a political offender rather than a criminal". Handbills were circulated, funds were collected, the fines paid, resolutions were passed, and a petition to the Governor seeking Dickinson's release was signed by 3700 people. Beyond South Australia, a call for his release was presented to a national Peace-in-Industry Conference convened in the Sydney Town Hall in an effort to resolve the long running troubles on the waterfront.[12]

Members of the public wrote to the newspapers expressing their concerns about Dickinson's gaoling. "Hackney", of Walkerville, thought that "our much-extolled British justice" was indicted by the case, and that Dickinson was a conscientious man without malice. Another correspondent compared Dickinson to Christ who "suffered death on account of what was, to the age in which he lived, his extremist

---

[10] *Advertiser*, 28 December 1928, p. 14.
[11] *Register*, 28 December 1928, p. 11.
[12] *Advertiser*, 26 December 1928, p. 13; *Advertiser*, 20 February 1929, p. 13; *Advertiser*, 9 April 1929, p. 15.

teachings". A "Justice" of Wayville held that the "the case is not generally in line with British justice" and sought an explanation for the whole affair, while a H. G. Coker of Goodwood believed that the sentence was "undoubtedly excessive" and hoped it would receive early reconsideration. In contrast to the prevailing sentiment, Gawler's "Cit" believed that Dickinson had been a "stirrer up of trouble" and should be shipped off to Russia.[13]

The IWW held that Dickinson was a working-class fighter who had become a prisoner in the class war. *Direct Action* told its readers that Dickinson was gaoled because he had dared to fight for the working class and that he "had a principle to uphold and did so unflinchingly". It also detailed the "vindictiveness" of the treatment that Dickinson was receiving in custody. Being sentenced without hard labour meant, the paper explained, he was not eligible for remission due to good conduct. He was also being held in the Adelaide Gaol instead of the Yatala Labour Prison, where the food was better. The Defence and Release League wrote to the authorities seeking permission to supplement Dickinson's diet; this was refused.[14] Almost fifty years later, McNeill would look back and reflect on the Adelaide establishment's victimisation of Dickinson: "They knew him, they wanted him. He was recognised as the leader."[15]

Free again

Dickinson served his full sentence and was released on Saturday 3 August 1929. He immediately resumed his political agitation and was welcomed back by a crowd of 2000 in the Botanic Park. Dickinson took the time to write to the *Workers' Weekly* providing a report "On the South Australian Battle Front." He decried the poverty afflicting the unemployed and the apathy he saw among the working class:

> *The rich get richer and the poor get poorer. On every hand the parasites flaunt their booty and treat their erstwhile slaves with the contempt*

---

[13] There were numerous letters to the editor published. For these and others see *Advertiser*, 1, 3, 5 & 8 January 1929, and the *Bunyip*, 11 January 1929, p. 9.

[14] *Direct Action*, 20 April 1929, p. 4; *Direct Action*, 22 May 1929, p. 1.

[15] WL interview.

that they deserve while they are content to tolerate such a topsy turvy state of society.[16]

The note of disenchantment about the slaves receiving the contempt they deserve suggests that, after sustaining almost two years of energetic and creative activism, Dickinson was disappointed with what had been achieved. No one could fault his drive and enthusiasm, he had lived meagrely and been imprisoned, yet the IWW remained only a small sect within the South Australian labour movement. He was recognised as providing leadership for the destitute, but far from abandoning what Dickinson saw as "Labor's fakirs", the working class cleaved, as the economy worsened, more strongly to the Labor Party.

Labor governments were elected in Canberra in October 1929 and in Adelaide in April 1930; in contrast, the IWW was soon to disappear. Perhaps recognising this reality, Dickinson's letter to the *Workers' Weekly* also contained a plea for unity among militants. He was, at the time, working on proposals to put to a unity conference to be attended by the CPA, IWW and Socialist Labor Party.[17]

With unemployment increasing, Dickinson resumed his leading role in organising demonstrations through the streets of Adelaide. This soon led to a bitter clash with the Labor Leader, Lionel Hill. On 4 September 1929, a deputation of Labor MPs and union officials met with the government to put the case for the provision of additional relief to the unemployed. The conservative Butler government made it known that it would not meet with any deputation that included Dickinson. Excluded, he led a march of 1000 people to Victoria Square where he addressed the assembled unemployed.

The United Trades and Labour Council then condemned Hill for not participating in the demonstration. This was enough provocation for Hill who, having seen the Labor Party provide support for Dickinson's petition and deputations, said he was "sick and tired of the machinations of these spurious 'Reds.'" He told the Adelaide newspapers:

---

[16] *Workers' Weekly*, 6 September 1929, p. 6.
[17] Letter from Jim McNeill to John Playford, 14 February 1958, McNeill Collection, Illawarra Museum.

> *The Communists have never gained a foothold in South Australia and never will, but there are a few disturbers posing as 'reds' — counterfeit Communists whose real colour is yellow... Their leadership is like that of Mr. E. A. Dickinson during the waterside dispute. He and his satellites persuaded the watersiders to disregard their executive and the Trades Hall Disputes Committee, but when the real fight came Mr. Dickinson and his co-workers were conspicuous by their absence.*

Dickinson rejected Hill's comments as a "hysterical outburst". He defended his record and then challenged Hill to a public debate, with any funds raised donated to the relief of the unemployed.

> *I take strong exception to his imputation that I played a coward's part in the waterside dispute. He has purposely distorted the facts, and has not disclosed, although it is well known to him, that I was sentenced to a term of imprisonment for my efforts on behalf of the workers in that fight. I suggest that if Mr. Hill is sincere in his outburst he meet me in a public debate. I am willing to take the side of Communism or to affirm that the Labor Party as represented by Mr. Hill is an enemy of working- class organisations.*[18]

This appears to have been Dickinson's last political action in Australia, as other matters took his attention. On 19 October, Dickinson married Myrtle Ankers, a seamstress, in the Anglican Trinity Church on North Terrace, Adelaide. The service was conducted by the Rector, Reg Pulford, who was noted for his "moderate practicality", a quality he may have drawn on in marrying one of South Australia's most prominent radical agitators in South Australia's pioneer church.[19] Myrtle was one of four sisters and her attendance at occasions such as surprise birthday parties had been noted in the social pages throughout the 1920s.[20]

Dickinson also became involved in two businesses, the Russian Oil Company Ltd and Russian Imports, which had been formed with the

---

[18] The dispute between Hill and Dickinson was extensively covered in the Adelaide newspapers including the *Mail*, 7 September 1929, p. 1.
[19] Brian Dickey, *Holy Trinity Adelaide 1836-2012: The History of a City Church*, Adelaide, 2013, p. 108.
[20] *News*, 17 September 1926, p. 6.

idea that it would be possible to import cheap oil from the Soviet Union. According to McNeill, a couple of Adelaide "go-getters" thought that having a "well-known Red" as part of the enterprise would help them realise their ambitions and so made Dickinson their representative. The scheme was the subject of a later exposé in *Smith's Weekly*, which sneeringly described Dickinson as a "martyr" and "hero" of the Port Adelaide riots. It contended that he had received £1000 for his appointment to the putative oil companies and had travelled to Sydney in September 1929 to pay £50 to Jock Garden, the secretary of the Sydney Trades Hall and ally of the NSW Premier Jack Lang (Labor), for his assistance. The report also included Dickinson's appraisal of several members of the Scullin Labor government, and correspondence from Arthur Rae, a veteran Labor senator, which expressed the hope that Dickinson was "on a bit better wicket than in the near past".[21]

The details of this oil play remain unclear. Within days of their wedding Dickinson and his new bride left Adelaide for England, probably on a honeymoon and possibly with the intention of travelling on to Russia to try to progress the oil deal. With his friend Dickinson having departed there was no reason for McNeill to stay in Adelaide and he returned to Sydney at the end of 1929. The IWW could not overcome the loss of its leading South Australian activists and began to decline. It was defunct across Australia by early 1931.

Beef Riot and Bill Morcom

The protests by the unemployed did not cease, with the CPA assuming the leadership role vacated by the IWW. A series of demonstrations was organised through the course of 1930, climaxing in a violent demonstration, known as the Beef Riot, in January 1931. The cause of the strife was a decision by the government to replace beef with mutton in the relief rations. For the unemployed, losing their beef was a humiliation that could not be ignored and it became a flashpoint for all the other degradations that mass unemployment had inflicted. A protest was organised with one group marching from Port Adelaide

---

[21] *Smith's Weekly*, 26 December 1931, pp 1-2; WL interview; Playford, 'History', p. 72.

and another from the Labour Exchange. Chanting "We want beef" the crowd of 2000 marched past Parliament House, taunted some parliamentarians, and then proceeded to the Treasury Building where an interview with Premier Hill was sought.

Photo 3: The unemployed march for beef, King William Street, Adelaide, 1931. The march turned into a riot. (State Library of South Australia, B 60882)

A violent riot erupted while officials looked on. Police grappled with the unemployed who armed themselves with wooden spikes, banner poles, metal pipes and half-bricks. A running battle was fought across several city locations. Newspaper reports confirmed "within a very short while a fierce struggle was in progress and blood was flowing freely on both sides". At its conclusion, seventeen people were in hospital, including ten police officers. A dozen men were in custody charged with riot, offensive behaviour and stone throwing.[22] Trouble also broke out that night at Port Adelaide. A meeting of 500 people protesting at

---

[22] *Advertiser*, 10 January 1931, p. 10; Broomhill, *Unemployed*, pp. 176-7.

the conduct of the police erupted with more injuries and arrests.[23]

Premier Hill placed the blame on the CPA. It was a claim not denied; the *Workers' Weekly* stated that the Young Communist League had "played a most active part, both in the demonstration and in the riots that followed". The paper gleefully reported that a lesson from the riots was that all the conditions in South Australia were in place for "the most terrific struggles".[24]

One of the CPA's South Australian leaders was William Arthur (Bill) Morcom, secretary of the Adelaide District Committee. He also served on the Unemployed Prisoners Relief Committee, formed to raise funds for the rioters' legal defence, and to provide reports to the *Workers' Weekly* on the poor conditions that the prisoners were enduring in the Adelaide gaol.[25]

Born on 11 August 1901 in Plymouth, England, Morcom had left school at 14 and taken a position as a clerk in a munition works. After obtaining a wireless certificate, he joined the merchant navy and travelled the world as a radio operator, before becoming a radio salesman in Devonshire and Cornwall. He migrated to Australia in 1927. He obtained work in Melbourne manufacturing and selling radios, but by the time the Depression hit, he was an itinerant farm labourer working across Victoria and South Australia.

He joined the CPA in 1930 and devoted his time to working among the unemployed in Adelaide. After the Beef Riot, he returned to Melbourne and became a leader of the Metropolitan Council of the Unemployed and an executive member of the Unemployed Workers' Movement, a CPA auxiliary organisation. By then it was clear that his organisational skills had marked him as a future leader of the CPA. He studied dutifully and could say he had read most of the works of Lenin, Stalin, Marx and Engels.

He was sent to Sydney and became the secretary of the CPA's City and

---

[23] Playford, 'History', p. 140.
[24] *Workers' Weekly*, 23 January 1931, p. 1 and p. 5.
[25] *Workers' Weekly*, 20 February 1931, p. 2.

Waterfront Section, where he worked closely with waterfront workers and seamen. He was then posted to Lithgow to gain experience of a mining district, as the coalfields were becoming strongholds for the CPA. Early in 1937 he returned to Sydney and became the treasurer of the NSW CPA, working as a full-time functionary for the party.[26]

Morcom was highly regarded by his comrades, and despite only being in his thirties, earned the nickname "Pop" because of his paternal and collegial manner. Earnest, dedicated and sincere, he was a steady, measured and reliable man, who didn't drink. As a fervent believer in the historic and manifest inevitability of communism, he gave up smoking so that he might live to "see as much of socialism as possible".[27]

---

[26] RGASPI 545/6/68/175/19-25.
[27] Inglis, *Australians*, pp. 16-17.

4

I believe in it enough to fight for it

In London, Dickinson's Russian oil venture quickly soured. In the short term, the marriage was more successful and in 1931 the couple welcomed the arrival of a daughter, Mary. Longer term though, the marriage failed with Myrtle returning to Australia to live in Melbourne with her daughter.

In Adelaide, Dickinson was gone but not forgotten. In the final days of the 1931 federal election campaign, the Labor candidate for the seat of Boothby, Cecil Skitch, was attacked by the *Advertiser* for his past association with Dickinson, described by the newspaper as "one of the most notorious revolutionaries in Australia". Skitch, although never a member of the IWW, had worked with Dickinson in the free speech fights and had been a member of the committee that campaigned for the unemployed. The newspaper's attacks did not assist his campaign and he was heavily defeated in the election.[1]

International Freedom League

In England, Dickinson's political commitment remained resolute. Soon after his arrival he was addressing the public in Hyde Park and at other speaking locations around London. As in Australia, this led to difficulties with the authorities, providing Dickinson with additional opportunities for political agitation.

In September 1931 he was summonsed for distributing literature, in

---

[1] *Advertiser*, 17 December 1931, p. 18.

contravention of by-laws, in Finsbury Park. The Highgate Police Court was told that Dickinson had been speaking on behalf of the International Freedom League. On hearing that Dickinson would be fined £8, men and women stood on their seats in the court and shouted. The uproar led to the court being cleared, but the disturbances continued in the corridor and outside the courthouse. Speakers climbed on top of a car to address the crowd. One of the speakers, a tobacconist Thomas Raymond, was remanded in custody charged with using insulting words having proclaimed: "This is a free country. I will show the _____ justices."[2]

Earlier, in March 1930, Dickinson spoke at Clapham Common on the Meerut conspiracy case, a controversial prosecution launched by the British Raj against trade unionists and communists in the Indian city of Meerut.[3] Dickinson's interest was consistent with his anti-imperialism and internationalist support for workers subject to persecution.

Without the IWW, Dickinson formed the International Freedom League as a broadly based organisation that could enable his activism. This new organisation was initially met with hostility from the Communist Party of Great Britain and other established sections of the British left. This did not prevent Dickinson's leadership attracting thousands of members with many students, particularly foreign students, joining the organisation.[4]

Dickinson's anti-imperialism was again displayed during the visit of Gandhi to London in 1931. The independence leader had travelled to England to participate in the Second Round Table Conference with the aim of advancing constitutional reform for India. The visit aroused great interest among the British public who seemed in Gandhi's thrall as he toured the country in his dhoti and sandals. Eschewing the more fashionable parts of London, Gandhi opted to stay in a communal boarding house in the working-class East End.

---

[2] *The Times*, 1 October 1931, p. 6; *Daily Telegraph*, 1 October 1931, p. 5.
[3] *Daily Worker*, 29 March 1930, p. 3.
[4] Letter from Jim McNeill to John Playford, 14 February 1958, McNeill Collection, Illawarra Museum.

To provide a suitable welcome for Gandhi, Dickinson organised a procession to march from the Friends Meeting House in Euston Road (where an official reception was being held) to Kingsley Hall in Bromley-by-Bow, where Gandhi was to stay. Dickinson told the newspapers that the procession, which was to feature bands, banners and "native students in Indian costume", was being organised because:

> We are dissatisfied with the arrangements made by the official reception committee.
>
> Under the proposed arrangements, only a select few will be able to meet Gandhi and thousands of his admirers will be denied the opportunity.[5]

Despite pouring London rain, the welcome procession was a success. Gandhi greeted more than 1000 Londoners from the balcony of Kingsley Hall. Newsreel footage recorded the procession's marching band, flags and banners.[6]

In August 1931, Dickinson travelled to Scotland to represent the International Freedom League at a meeting attended by 7000 at the Nelson Monument on the Glasgow Green. Convened by the Council of Action for Free Speech, at stake was the right of speakers to address audiences in Glasgow without complying with a permit system, an issue nearly identical to the free speech fight that Dickinson and McNeill had successfully fought in Adelaide. Dickinson delivered what a critic described as a "brief but violent" address.[7]

The Glasgow Green free speech campaign grew to attract huge crowds, estimated at 50,000. In October 1931 a demonstration erupted into serious rioting. A central figure in the campaign was Guy Aldred, a veteran anarcho-communist, who claimed in his own newspaper, *The Council*, that Dickinson was "suspected of being a police agent and his conduct warranted that suspicion". He contended Dickinson's speech had been repudiated by the Council of Action, and that the International Freedom League had repudiated Dickinson and disbanded on 23

---

[5] *North Mail and Newcastle Daily Chronicle*, 12 September 1931, p. 1.
[6] https://www.youtube.com/watch?v=Se0kpkJIhH8
[7] *The Council*, Vol. 1, No. 4, May 1932, pp. 40-2.

October 1931. His denunciation of Dickinson rehashed material from the *Smith's Weekly* expose on the Russian oil deal, including the flourish that Dickinson had proclaimed himself to be "classed A1 in Moscow".[8]

Aldred's attack on Dickinson came as a comprehensive falling out between Dickinson and his former allies in the Australian left was underway. In mid-April 1932 several Australian newspapers published Dickinson's attack on his former business associate Jock Garden, with claims of "irregularities" in the affairs of the Sydney Trades Hall. Dickinson said that Garden controlled the government of Premier Jack Lang and claimed to have documentary evidence that industrial leaders and Labor parliamentarians "had deliberately misused their positions for their own ends". Dickinson declared that he was glad to have realised the dangerous path he was travelling before it was too late to turn back:

> *Personally, I now regret that most of my life has been spent on deliberately fooling the workers of Australia… After years of agitation I have decided, to use the Americanism, 'to quit the racket,' for a 'racket' it is, and explain to the workers just some of the byplay that takes place behind the scenes of the extreme left section of the Labor movement. I have addressed hundreds of meetings, pulled strings, and bribed and organised basher gangs — so I know.*[9]

Dickinson's attack on Garden came at a moment when NSW politics was in crisis. The economy was in the depths of the Depression, the Labor Party had split and Premier Lang was about to be dismissed by the Governor, Sir Philip Game. Dickinson's attack seems to have been calculated to inflict maximum political damage. Despite the febrile atmosphere, Dickinson's allegations did not prompt further attention from any authority or cause Garden additional political difficulties.

In the week before this article appeared, the *Sydney Morning Herald* carried a report on the London conference of the Independent Labour Party which included the thoughts of an unnamed "notorious Australian agitator". It is not known if there was anyone, apart from Dickinson,

---

[8] Ibid.

[9] The article appeared in several newspapers including the *Uralla Times*, 11 April 1932, p. 2, and the *Kyogle Examiner*, 15 April 1932, p. 7.

fitting that description in London at the time. The unnamed source said it was hopeless to expect the British people to support Russian teachings. It is a comment that certainly echoes the IWW's mockery of the CPA's "tin pot Lenins", but whether it was Dickinson briefing the journalist cannot be established.[10]

Challenging a fascist to a duel

Across Europe, fascism seemed ascendant. In Germany, Hitler came to power in January 1933 and immediately began persecuting Jews and outlawing political opponents, including communists, socialists and trade unionists. Hitler withdrew Germany from the League of Nations, commenced rearmament and introduced military conscription. In Italy, the fascist dictator Mussolini, in power since 1922, pursued an aggressive policy against Abyssinia (as Ethiopia was then known), that culminated in a war beginning in October 1935.

In June 1935, as the situation in Abyssinia deteriorated, the Labour Party's Deputy Leader, Clement Attlee, addressed the House of Commons. He said that Italy had imperialist designs on Abyssinia, was the aggressor in the dispute, and in the event of conflict, should be denied access to the Suez Canal.[11] This prompted Captain Fanelli, the editor of the fascist newspaper *Secolo Fascista*, to challenge Attlee to a duel "with any weapons in any neutral country". The challenge was promptly dismissed by Attlee who decried duelling as "barbarous and obsolete".

Unfazed by this, Dickinson stepped forward and challenged Fanelli to allow him to take Attlee's place, telling the newspapers he held the same views about fascism as Attlee.

> *I sent this Capt. Fanelli a registered letter on the 8th [of July], in which I said that I would consider it an honour if he would allow me to take Major Attlee's place. If this fire-eating Italian fellow wants to eat fire,*

---

10   *Sydney Morning Herald*, 1 April 1932, p. 9.
11   *Hansard*, House of Commons, 7 June 1935.

I will give it to him to eat.[12]

The papers noted that Dickinson was six feet tall, well-built, had lived in Australia for 17 years, and was prepared to leave the choice of weapons to Fanelli. A photograph of Dickinson, a cigarette dangling from his lips, accompanied an article noting that he had undergone military training in Australia and was used to handling firearms.[13] One paper described Dickinson as "sturdily built" and stated he had been in Australia where he had "taken part in more than one rough house". Dickinson said he held strong views and was prepared to back them up:

All my life I have believed in free speech, and I believe in it enough to fight for it.

I have had many conflicts in political and other spheres and feel quite capable of looking after myself in a challenge of this kind. I would enjoy a rifle duel – with Fanelli and myself stalking each other through the Abyssinian jungle.[14]

The story was picked up by the Reuters news agency and published in newspapers around the world. In Adelaide, the papers reported on Fanelli's gracious refusal: "Your letter confirms my conviction regarding English subjects whom Labor principles have not made rotten."[15]

Soon after Dickinson, who described himself as "an ordinary individual occupied in the fish trade at Billingsgate Market", was courted by members of the left wing of the Labour Party who offered him preselection for a safe London seat in the House of Commons if he was prepared to join them. Dickinson considered the proposal for several days but declined the invitation.[16]

---

[12] *Nottingham Evening Post*, 12 July 1935, p. 10.

[13] This is likely a reference to the basic military training provided through the Universal Service Scheme. There is no military personnel file for Dickinson in the National Archives of Australia.

[14] *The Irish Weekly and Ulster Examiner*, 20 July 1935, p. 5; *Daily Mirror*, 12 July 1935, p. 1; *News Chronicle*, 13 July 1935, p. 13.

[15] *News*, 18 July 1935, p. 19.

[16] Letter from Jim McNeill to John Playford, 14 February 1958, McNeill Collection, Illawarra Museum.

The reference to Dickinson being engaged in the fish trade at Billingsgate Market is interesting and not only because it represented a return to the calling shared by his father and Reeve. George Orwell, writing in his 1932 essay *Clink*, claimed to have worked as a porter at the market.[17] It is not clear if he actually did or if this was only a cover story he adopted while seeking to be imprisoned, posing as a drunkard, as part of his undercover research into British social conditions.

Legion of Blue and White Shirts

Fascism continued to advance. In March 1936, Hitler ordered the *Wehrmacht* into the Rhineland, an act which violated the demilitarised status of the region as established by the Treaty of Versailles. Neither France nor Britain took action to challenge the remilitarisation. In May 1936, Mussolini completed his conquest of Abyssinia. In England, members of Oswald Mosley's British Union of Fascists, known as the Blackshirts, were staging rallies and marches. Resistance to the Blackshirts culminated in a major riot in the East End's Cable Street during which anti-fascist protestors violently battled the police.[18]

By this time Dickinson had already established himself as a prominent anti-fascist. As well as the challenge to fight a duel, Dickinson was actively involved with two anti-fascist associations - the Ex-Servicemen's Movement Against Fascism and the Legion of Blue and White Shirts. These were organisations that had emerged in response to concerns from some in the community that the official positions of both the Labour Party and the Board of Deputies of British Jews were inadequate to the threat presented by Mosley. These new bodies did not accept that relying on traditional reforming strengths, such as education, persuasion and a general sense of fair play, were sufficient.[19]

---

[17] *Clink* appears in *The Collected Essays, Journalism and Letters of George Orwell: Volume 1 - An Age Like This 1920-1940*, Edited by Sonia Orwell and Ian Angus, London, 1968.

[18] The Metropolitan Police Commissioner was Sir Philip Game, who as the Governor of NSW had dismissed NSW Premier Jack Lang.

[19] Nigel Copsey, *Anti-Fascism in Britain*, New York, 2000, pp. 52-7.

The Ex-Servicemen's Movement Against Fascism, closely aligned to the Communist Party, had a large Jewish membership. It organised an anti-fascist procession from the East End to Victoria Park which was marred by brawls with fascists.[20] The Legion of Blue and White Shirts was formed in the middle of 1936 and, as its name indicates, wore the colours of Zionism as its uniform with each shirt also patriotically adorned with the Union Jack. It took a physical approach to confronting the British Union of Fascists with the authorities estimating that at least 60 per cent of the meetings that Mosley's fascists held in August 1936 were disrupted by anti-fascists.[21]

Mosley's followers had been parading in their black outfits for years. Emergence of the Legion of Blue and White Shirts, which the Blackshirts sarcastically referred to as "the storm troops of Jewry" who looked "like lovely little forget-me-nots", brought concerns about paramilitary organisations to a head. In response, the government passed the *Public Order Act 1936* which banned the wearing of political uniforms.[22] For the Legion of Blue and White Shirts, the banning of their uniform represented a success of sorts. In announcing its formation, the *Jewish Chronicle* noted that its organisers didn't believe in political uniforms but hoped that if a proliferation of organisations adopted them, then the government would ban the lot.[23]

The Legion of Blue and White Shirts organised large public meetings which Dickinson addressed. At an outdoor meeting held in Duckett Street, Stepney, a stronghold of the British Union of Fascists, Dickinson received what the *Jewish Chronicle* reported was a "good hearing" from hundreds of residents as he analysed fascism "logically and devastatingly". This prompted the fascists present to interject, chanting the name "Mosley". The next speaker, Mr Lebovich, the secretary of the Legion of Blue and White Shirts, was subjected to a "hysterical outburst

---

[20] Daniel Tilles, 'Jewish Decay against British Revolution: The British Union of Fascists' Antisemitism and Jewish Responses to it', PhD thesis, Royal Holloway, University of London, 2011, p. 124.

[21] Copsey, *Anti-Fascism*, p. 52.

[22] Ibid; *Blackshirt*, 5 September 1936, p. 8; *Blackshirt*, 9 October 1936, p. 8; *Aberdeen Press and Journal*, 9 November 1936, p. 7.

[23] *Jewish Chronicle*, 28 August 1936, p. 15.

of anti-Jewish sneers" while the third speaker, Mr Angel, a winner of the Military Medal in the Great War, was "openly insulted". Dickinson proceeded to close the meeting by singing the national anthem, "God Save the King", a tactic that baited the fascists into resuming their chanting of Mosley's name while they gave the fascist salute. Dickinson then challenged their patriotism: "Choose whom you serve – the King or Mosley!"[24]

The fascists sought to disrupt the activities of the Legion of Blue and White Shirts by wrecking its meetings and throwing stink bombs. At a meeting of 500 people in Stafford Road, Dickinson's address was subject to "puerile questions and interjections" from the Blackshirts. At a meeting at Stepney Green, attended by a similarly large crowd, an attempt was made to educate the fascists. The president of the Legion of Blue and White Shirts, Mr Bateman, said there was a distinction between fascism, which he hated, and the fascist, which he pitied as an "ignorant zealot". Dickinson congratulated the young fascists in attendance, who were looking "ill at ease", for conducting themselves in a "quiet and orderly manner". Despite this apparent progress, in December the premises of the Legion were attacked twice by fascist gangs. Members of the Legion defended their premises and there were wild scenes with a door broken down and six plate-glass windows smashed amid shouts of "Kill the Jews."[25]

Although he devoted his time and energy to these organisations, Dickinson was not a Jew. He married in an Anglican church, his brother was a pastor in the Congregationalist church, and his mother's funeral service was to be conducted by another Congregationalist pastor. Consistent with his established world view of socialist internationalism, Dickinson understood the threat that fascism posed to the Jews and was determined to resist it.

Immediately upon coming to power in 1933, Hitler began passing laws

---

[24] *Jewish Chronicle*, 11 September 1936, p 13; Daniel Tilles notes the LBWS's concern with its British credentials in 'Jewish Decay', p. 124.

[25] Reports on the activities of the LBWS can be found in the *Jewish Chronicle*, 6 November 1936, p. 31; *Jewish Chronicle*, 27 November 1936, p. 19; *Jewish Chronicle*, 15 December 1936, p. 14; *Jewish Chronicle*, 1 January 1937, p. 15; *Daily Herald*, 12 December 1936, p. 11.

that persecuted Germany's Jews. With the authority of the German state, fascists organised and enforced boycotts of Jewish businesses. Jews were progressively excluded from many aspects of normal life including the universities, armed forces and the civil service. New laws revoked citizenship and voting rights. The Nuremburg Laws of 1935 prohibited marriages between Jews and Germans. Fascist publications like *Der Sturmer* kept up a near continuous barrage of anti-Jewish propaganda.

From late 1935, there was a temporary easing of the persecution as the Nazis strove to present a respectable face to the world ahead of the Berlin Olympics of 1936. They were largely successful with this effort. Observers like William L. Shirer, an American journalist, noted "They have put up a very good front for the general visitors, especially the big businessmen" who were said to be "favourably impressed by the Nazi set-up".[26] In October 1936, Rabbi Stephen Wise, a leader of the World Jewish Congress, met the American President Franklin D. Roosevelt. The president said that he had received reports from two recent visitors to Germany who had told him: "The synagogues were crowded and apparently there is nothing very wrong in the situation at present."[27]

Warning of the Holocaust

Dickinson was not so easily deceived. In the summer of 1936 he wrote a pamphlet, *The Black Plague: An Exposure of Fascism*, which was published by the Legion of Blue and White Shirts. It appeared in September 1936, just weeks before the Cable Street riot, and drew a comparison between fascism and the bubonic plague that struck London in the 1660s – a blight that was only cleansed by the Great Fire of London in 1666. The pamphlet set out Dickinson's political thinking and illustrates his thoroughgoing hostility to the fascism that had established itself in Europe and spread to Britain:

It is, indeed, hard to find words adequate enough to describe this

---

[26] Richard J. Evans, *The Third Reich in Power*, London, 2005, pp. 570 – 2.
[27] Saul Friedlander, *Nazi Germany and the Jews: The Years of Persecution 1933-1939*, New York, 1997, p. 180.

foul, slimy, blood-spattered product of diseased minds, this cancerous, cowardly, maniacal, peace-destroying, blood-sucking monstrosity – Fascism.

Fascism means war; Fascism worships war; Fascism is war – a war waged on everything decent, everything human. Fascism is devoid of all feeling. Fascism is a merciless machine, leaving in its tracks only horror, suffering, death, and imprisonment.

Crucially, at a time when the political leaderships of Britain and Australia were committed to the policy of appeasement, Dickinson was presciently aware of the genocidal intent of Nazism. Written five years before the German army received its orders to take "ruthless and energetic action" against the Jews as part of its invasion of the USSR, Dickinson's pamphlet warned of the looming genocide:

We see these power-lusting maniacs reintroducing that terrible blot on world history – pogroms of members of the Jewish faith.

It is nauseating to an Englishman to read of, or witness, men, women and children slaughtered, tortured and imprisoned just because they have committed the awful crime to be born, and, being born, demand the right to think, to study, to express themselves in their unions, guilds, or societies.

*It is even more nauseating for us, in England, to witness the unpardonable attempt to wipe out of existence a **whole race of people**, their only alleged crime that of being of the Jewish race.*[28]

By the time Dickinson published his pamphlet warning of the desperate threat posed by fascism, the Spanish Civil War had begun.

---

[28] E.A. Dickinson, *The Black Plague: An Exposure of Fascism*, Fulham, 1936, p. 3. Emphasis in the original.

5

All into action now

The Spanish Civil War began on 17-18 July 1936 when right-wing military officers rose in insurrection against the democratically elected government of the Second Spanish Republic.[1]

Reform and reaction

The background to the conflict was the struggle to modernise and reform the country. At the end of the 1920s Spain was a deeply divided society. Less economically developed than other countries in Western Europe, many of its people lived in dire rural poverty on estates owned by large, and often absent, landholders. Illiteracy rates across the regions ranged from a quarter to over half of the population.[2] There were unresolved conflicts about the roles of the church and army, and tensions between regional ambitions and the central government.

The Catholic church's place in Spanish society was contentious. It was strongly associated with the landowners, who kept the poor in distressing conditions often bordering on starvation, while amassing phenomenal wealth for itself. In the early years of the twentieth century, it was claimed the church owned one-third of the wealth of

---

[1] There are thousands of books and academic articles on the Spanish Civil War. This chapter provides only a brief overview to provide context for the volunteers' decisions to go to Spain. Much more detail (in English) is available in books by historians such as Paul Preston and Helen Graham.

[2] Antony Beevor, *The Spanish Civil War*, London, 1999, p. 38.

Spain. Orwell described it as a "huge, parasitic church".[3] Accumulating wealth and consorting with the landowners, while preaching that the poor should meekly accept their poverty as evidence of God's will and await salvation in the next life, caused resentment of the church gliding into hatred. Superstitious and backward, the church denounced science, with priests even accusing doctors of sorcery. In some areas, church schools stopped teaching children to read as a way of preventing them from reading socialist books. Education was reduced to memorising catechisms.[4]

Despite these efforts, Spain was no longer the solidly Catholic nation it had been in previous centuries. One estimate was that by the 1930s, two-thirds of the population were not practising Catholics, and in some areas the church's unpopularity meant that the priest conducted Mass alone.[5]

The military also no longer enjoyed widespread popular support. Its prestige had been shattered by humiliating defeats in the Spanish-American War and in disasters such as the Battle of Annual in North Africa, where thousands of mainly conscript troops were massacred during the Rif War. The officer class was corrupt, evinced by officers who sold their soldiers' food and arms to the enemy. Many ex-officers and soldiers served in the Civil Guard, a widely hated paramilitary force meant to maintain law and order in the countryside. It acquired a reputation for only ever acting viciously against the poor.

This was the Spain that established itself as a republic after support for the monarchy, discredited by its facilitation of an erratic and corrupt dictatorship, finally collapsed. An election in 1931 gave a clear mandate for change. Victory went to a left-centre coalition of parties. Of the 473 seats in the *Cortes*, (parliament), the right won only 60 members.[6] A new constitution was adopted and the government embarked on a

---

[3] George Orwell, 'Spilling the Spanish Beans', (1937), in *The Collected Essays, Journalism, and Letters of George Orwell* (Edited by Sonia Orwell & Ian Angus), Volume 1, *An Age Like This*, London, 1968.

[4] Beevor, *Spanish Civil War*, p. 22 and p. 38.

[5] Hugh Thomas, *The Spanish Civil War*, London, 1962, p. 31.

[6] Thomas, *Spanish Civil War*, p. 1 and p. 45.

sweeping reform program designed to modernise Spain and address the profound inequalities that marred Spanish society. The Catholic church was disestablished, a regional government established in Catalonia, the privileges of the army's bloated officer class were reined in, women were given the vote, there was significant spending on secular education, noble titles were abolished, and the first steps of a land reform program were taken.

The reform program aroused intense hostility from traditional, conservative Spaniards, yet did not satisfy the rising expectations of the country's poor. The difficult economic conditions of the early 1930s compounded the challenges inherent in implementing a comprehensive reform program. Tensions within the governing coalition, combined with a reorganisation of the re-energised right-wing parties, saw the government defeated in elections held in November 1933. The new right-wing government set about reversing the reforms wherever it could. The situation became increasingly unstable with strikes, lethal acts of sabotage and assassination attempts on leading politicians. In 1934 there were left-wing revolts in Madrid, Barcelona and, most seriously and violently, in the mining centre of Asturias, which was ruthlessly suppressed by General Francisco Franco, an anti-Semitic officer who had made his reputation during brutal colonial campaigns in North Africa.

Spain was a country without a traditional attachment to parliamentary democracy and the extremes were strengthening on both the left and the right. The fascist Falange was formed in 1933. The Spanish Communist Party, entirely loyal to Stalin's Soviet Union, started to grow, although it was small compared to the Socialists and Anarchists, the mainstays of the Spanish left, which commanded mass memberships through their union affiliates, the UGT with 1.44 million members, and the CNT with 1.58 million members.[7]

Despite the political clashes that had been occurring, the elections held in February 1936 were conducted fairly and without widespread violence. The result was a narrow victory for the parties of the left, which

---

[7] Beevor, *Spanish Civil War*, p. 27.

had patched up their differences sufficiently to form the Popular Front. The new government was headed by Manuel Azana, a liberal of the Republican Left. Its composition was moderate, with the Socialists not taking any cabinet positions. The Communists were a minor part of the coalition, with only 17 seats out of the 278 won by the Popular Front.

The American Ambassador to Spain, Claude G. Bowers, described the new Government in his memoirs:

> *There was not one communist in the government.*
>
> *There was not even one socialist of the mild type of Besteiro.*
>
> *There was not one who could be described as an extremist; not one who was not a republican and democrat in the French and American sense.*[8]

This responsible moderation did not allay the fears of the right, which saw its electoral defeat as conclusive evidence that parliamentary democracy could not work in Spain.[9] The Falange, which had not been able to win a single seat, began to grow and established a national presence.[10]

The new government appealed for calm, but the country was soon in a state of uproar. There were strikes, a flight of capital, sporadic street fighting and rumours of impending right-wing coups. Politically suspect generals, like Franco, were transferred to remote postings in an attempt to prevent them from causing trouble. Political shootings took place regularly. There were lethal confrontations between peasants and the Civil Guard, and tit-for-tat assassinations.

The war begins

These intense divisions culminated in right-wing military officers attempting their coup d'état. From the outset it was planned to use

---

[8] Claude G. Bowers, *My Mission to Spain: Watching the Rehearsal for World War II*, London, 1954, p. 194.

[9] Beevor, *Spanish Civil War*, p. 56.

[10] Judith Keene, *The Last Mile to Huesca: An Australian Nurse in the Spanish Civil War*, (Revised Edition), London, 2023, p. 69.

extreme violence to achieve political ends. One of the coup's leaders, General Emilio Mola, gave instructions:

> We have to terrorise, we have to show we are in control by rapidly and ruthlessly eliminating all those who do not think as we do.[11]

But what was intended to be a quick and deliberately violent seizure of power stalled in the face of popular resistance. With the formal law and order entities of the Spanish state paralysed by the officers' uprising, with many Republican leaders murdered in the first days of the rebellion, and confusion about who among the military, police and authorities remained loyal to the Republic, there was a vacuum of control. Hastily armed militias, drawn from trade unions and political parties, formed and assumed control of towns and cities. In some regions, the impromptu collectivisation of factories, businesses and landholdings was undertaken. In response to the calculated terror of the uprising, which included massacres of those who served or supported the Republic, there were explosive spasms of revolutionary violence. Churches and convents were attacked and desecrated, priests and nuns were murdered, as were those people deemed to have assisted or been sympathetic to the rebel officers.

As the military's uprising faltered in the face of popular resistance, Hitler and Mussolini made a crucial intervention and airlifted Franco's African army across the sea and into Spain. Hitler, Mussolini and Portugal's Salazar were to provide substantial amounts of military support for the rebels, which, after a fortuitous plane crash eliminated Mola, came to be led by Franco. Mussolini sent a total of 80,000 men, while Hitler's Condor Legion totalled 19,000, being mainly aviators and technical staff. Salazar provided somewhere between 2000 and 20,000 troops.

Britain and France reacted with a policy of non-intervention, ostensibly in the hope of avoiding a wider war in Europe. In reality, non-intervention meant denying the legitimate government of Spain the ability to purchase weapons to defend itself. The scale of the assistance that Franco was receiving from Hitler, Mussolini and Salazar meant that

---

[11] Helen Graham, *The Spanish Republic at War 1936-1939*, Cambridge, 2002, p. 117.

non-intervention was, from the outset, a ridiculous sham. In practice, Britain's conservative National government favoured a victory for Franco,[12] with Churchill observing that a majority of the Conservative Party admired Franco.[13]

Photo 4 - Hitler and Franco inspect a guard of honour at the Irun railway station, Spain, October 1940. (National Digital Archive, Poland)

Stalin had been seeking to advance the idea of collective security with Britain and France against Germany, and initially signed-up to the policy of non-intervention to demonstrate his willingness to work cooperatively with the democracies. As the amount of support provided to Franco by Hitler and Mussolini became evident, and threatened to quickly overwhelm the Republic, Stalin changed his position and, hoping to see Hitler tied up in a Spanish quagmire that would prevent

---

[12] Judith Keene, *Fighting for Franco*, New York, 2001, p. 47.
[13] *Sydney Morning Herald*, 12 January 1939, p. 10.

him from looking east, began supplying military aid to the Republic. The Soviet Union sold arms and sent 2000 men, mainly pilots and senior officers, to provide support.[14] Mexico also provided military materiel.

Formation of the International Brigades

As the leading democracies blocked the properly elected government from acquiring arms, aiding the Spanish Republic in its struggle against a fascist revolt became a cause for the broad left around the world. To harness this spontaneous popular support, the Communist International (Comintern) established the International Brigades. From their formation in October 1936 to their withdrawal in September 1938, some 35,000 volunteers travelled from around the globe to fight for the Spanish Republic.

Many were communists or socialists from Italy or Germany. They saw the Spanish conflict as an opportunity to resist the same forces that had persecuted them in their own countries. Thousands more came from France, Poland, the Balkans, North America, Britain, and dozens of other countries, including Australia and New Zealand. They represented a broad spectrum of political beliefs, being communists, socialists, anarchists, republicans, liberal democrats, trade unionists, adventurers and idealists of all types. The Comintern coordinated the response and brought it all together.[15]

One volunteer, Jason Gurney, an English sculptor who served alongside Dickinson in the British Battalion, expressed his motivations:

> *The Spanish Civil War seemed to provide the chance for a single individual to take a positive and effective stand on an issue which appeared to be absolutely clear. Either you were opposed to the growth of Fascism and went out to fight against it, or you acquiesced in its crimes and were guilty of permitting its growth.*[16]

---

[14] Keene, *Fighting for Franco*, p. 19; Thomas, *Spanish Civil War*, p. 637.
[15] Giles Tremlett, *The International Brigades: Fascism, Freedom and the Spanish Civil War*, London, 2020, p. 65.
[16] Jason Gurney, *Crusade in Spain*, Great Britain, 1976, p. 36.

Orwell understood the conflict and summarised the reasons for going to Spain in similar terms:

> *When the fighting broke out on 18 July it is probable that every anti-Fascist in Europe felt a thrill of hope. For years past the so-called democratic countries had been surrendering to Fascism at every turn... But when Franco tried to overthrow a mildly Left-wing Government the Spanish people, against all expectation, had risen against him. It seemed – possibly it was – the turning of the tide.*[17]

Communist parties around the world took a leading role in encouraging volunteers. It made a useful, and noble, distraction from the Great Terror that Stalin had initiated in the USSR. The British communist leader Harry Pollitt set out the position in unequivocal terms.

> *ALL INTO ACTION NOW!*
> *DEFEND THE SPANISH REPUBLIC!*
> *THE HAND OF BERLIN*
>
> *Let there be no mistake, therefore, that the Spanish people are fighting a battle for the people of all countries that are, at present, based on a democratic regime. The British working class have especially a great responsibility. They can make their weight felt. They can demonstrate their international solidarity.*
>
> *In this solemn hour, when the people's future is being shaped in heroic sacrifice and valour, we cannot, we dare not, fail our Spanish comrades.*[18]

By November 1936, the Communist Party in Britain was openly recruiting and sending volunteers to Spain. Dickinson, with his proven and public anti-fascism and willingness to stand with the international working class, found the pull of the Spanish Civil War irresistible and was soon on his way to Spain. Indeed, before he departed, he may have even been involved in some recruitment activities himself. In February 1937, the *Daily Mail*, a right-wing newspaper strident in its support

---

[17] George Orwell, *Homage to Catalonia*, 1938, p. 34.
[18] *Daily Worker*, 25 July 1936, p. 1.

for the fascist rebellion, interviewed some British prisoners of war. One man, named as "E" from Hackney who, given his predicament, may have wanted to be seen as an innocent dupe in the hope of being released, said that a man named Dickinson had promised him work as a carpenter if he went to Spain. Instead, he ended up in the front lines at the Battle of Jarama:

> *Time and again they assured me I should be there as a civilian, and on that understanding I went. I had been in the line for two days and had never even been shown how to use my rifle when I saw the anti-Red troops on every side of us.*[19]

By the time "E" made these comments Dickinson was dead and made a convenient scapegoat.

---

[19] *Daily Mail*, 22 February 1937, p. 13.

6

How much they hated us

McNeill's return to Sydney at the end of 1929 came as the economy was worsening, signalled to the world by the Wall Street crash. Economic circumstances became increasingly desperate, with unemployment among trade unionists in NSW reaching 21.7 per cent in 1930, on its way to a peak of 32.5 per cent in 1932.[1]

With few prospects, McNeill's stay in Sydney was short. In the absence of any better opportunities, he spent most of 1930 living in Sussex Inlet, on the South Coast of NSW, working as a fisherman with his brother Frank. The brothers did well catching fish and would have made a reasonable living in normal circumstances, but not in 1930. The price of fish collapsed, with the two men scarcely making a pound a week between them.[2]

From Sussex Inlet, McNeill wrote as "Mack" to *Direct Action* despairing at the "sorry spectacle" and "utter incompetence" of the Scullin Labor government as it was overwhelmed by the scale of the Depression. He concluded that under capitalism, no government could legislate in the interests of the working class and true democracy could only be fought for on the industrial field. By this time the IWW was almost finished. His letter was published in what was to be the last issue of the paper.[3]

---

[1] Broomhill, *Unemployed*, p. 13.
[2] WL interview.
[3] *Direct Action*, 29 November 1930, p. 2.

Joining the CPA

After a year as a fisherman, McNeill returned to Sydney, living first in Glebe, then Drummoyne. With the IWW defunct, McNeill and some other Wobblies joined the CPA. In a letter to the *Workers' Weekly*, he explained his reasons. He cited the narrowness of the IWW during the capitalist crisis and saw the organisation's refusal to run parliamentary candidates at elections, when the masses were in a particularly receptive mood, as evidence of this limited outlook. In contrast, McNeill considered that the Communist Party had "roots in the masses and by virtue of its job committees, factory meetings, activity amongst the unemployed, is doing practical revolutionary work".[4]

The CPA welcomed its new recruits, seeing their decision to join as evidence that all revolutionary proletarians were "uniting for the purpose of building the Party of Lenin, the workers' party in this country, and of a real preparation for the revolutionary struggle".[5] Less ideologically, the party simply needed the new members. With a membership of just 486 the CPA was, in 1930, a tiny party with meagre resources.[6]

The only irritation for McNeill was the decision of Reeve not to join him in the ranks of the CPA. Instead, he continued with his orations in Sydney's Domain, which McNeill now dismissed as nothing but "Sunday afternoon propaganda". Reeve later opened a small bookshop that functioned as a drop-in centre for Sydney radicals. He joined the New Theatre and acted in politically-themed plays. He died in 1942. Although his differences with the CPA were not resolved, the party paid him tribute, noting that "despite his political limitations, in his prime 'Charlie' Reeve did much to arouse a militant feeling among the workers".[7]

The CPA had been formed in Sydney in October 1920 by a small band of enthusiasts inspired by the revolutionary success of Lenin's Bolsheviks. Its first years were characterised by splits, schisms and personality disputes. Soon two rival communist parties were in operation. These

---

[4] *Workers' Weekly*, 10 April 1931, p. 2.
[5] *Workers' Weekly*, 13 February 1931, p. 2.
[6] Macintyre, *The Reds*, p. 179.
[7] *Tribune*, 17 June 1942, p. 4.

difficulties were eventually overcome and by the early 1930s, the CPA was formally recognised by the Comintern. Like all communist parties around the world, it was subordinate to the authority of Stalin's dictatorship, an authority that was consolidated by the training that selected Australian cadres received at the International Lenin School in Moscow.[8]

McNeill joined the CPA as it was entering its ultra-left Class Against Class period. This phase saw the party adopt a purist approach that employed absolute hostility to the Labor Party and reforming trade unions. Labor was dismissed as "social fascist" while the unions were led by "bureaucrats" who were bogged down in "legalism". Throughout the 1930s the party would demonstrate a dogged and uncompromising fidelity to Stalin's policies: collectivisation, purges, terror, show trials and the Nazi-Soviet Non-Aggression Pact.[9] Every action that the Kremlin took would be justified and supported by the CPA.

For many working people like McNeill, who were suffering so badly during the Depression, the Soviet Union symbolised the hope that a better world was a possibility. Orwell described this adulation as the "stupid cult of Russia",[10] but in desperate times, when all else had failed, believing in the possibility of a workers' paradise provided a powerful sense of optimism. It was a hope that helped combat the futility and despair that many felt during the Depression's grim years. What was remarkable about this attachment to the Soviet Union was not that it arose, but that it persisted for so long. Endlessly contorting itself to the twists of Soviet policy would discredit the CPA in the eyes of many Australians, but the faithful, having set their hearts to the task, would remain loyal for decades to come.

McNeill's activism in the Communist Party involved him joining the Sydney District Committee in 1931 and working in the Propaganda Department from 1932 until his departure for Spain in 1938. He commenced a reading program that took him through the classics of

---

[8] Macintyre, *The Reds*, pp. 132-3.
[9] Ibid., p. 164 and pp. 183-8.
[10] George Orwell, *The Road to Wigan Pier*, 1937, Hammondsworth, p. 190.

the communist canon including Marx's *Wage Labour and Capital* and *Value, Price and Profit*; Lenin's *The State and Revolution* and *What is to be Done?*; and Stalin's *Leninism*.[11] His other reading included *Soviets To-Day*, the official organ of the Australian Friends of the Soviet Union, a front organisation for the CPA. Alongside typically banal propaganda articles such as "Painless Childbirth for Soviet Mothers" and "Synthetic Rubber Plants Double Output", the magazine included pieces like "The Terrorists' Trials" and "The Generals Die But Socialism Remains" that defended Stalin's purges, show trials and executions.[12]

Although McNeill was a loyal party member, he didn't always support the CPA's strictures or agree with its policy approaches. A relief committee organised soup kitchens on Drummoyne Oval and collected donations of second-hand clothes and leftover fruit and vegetables for distribution to the unemployed. At a meeting of the committee a couple of CPA members, described by McNeill as "left as can be, as sectarian as can be", moved that the relief committee affiliate to the party's own Unemployed Workers' Movement, a militant organisation which led street protests and fought evictions. When the proposal was defeated a split ensued, the different groupings no longer working together. Most of the unemployed shifted to the relief committee. Recalling the episode, McNeill considered the CPA's sectarianism to be a serious strategic error as "the opportunity to unite with people that never thought the same as you was lost by antagonising them. I think it was a terrific mistake."[13]

Confronting the New Guard

As the Depression worsened, there were intense upheavals across the political spectrum. The Labor Party split and the main conservative party, the Nationalists, was reborn as the United Australia Party. A far-right paramilitary organisation, the New Guard, emerged to challenge the demagogic Premier Jack Lang (ALP) and to physically confront the

---

[11] RGASPI 545/6/68.

[12] *Soviets To-day*, January 1936, p.14; December 1936, p. 7; March 1937, p. 4; July 1937, p. 7.

[13] WL interview.

CPA on the streets of Sydney.

The New Guard was formed in the early months of 1931 and grew quickly under the leadership of Eric Campbell, a lawyer and company director who had served as a major in the Australian Imperial Force. With ex-servicemen strongly represented in its ranks, within months it had 36,000 members in Sydney and 3000 in country districts.[14] The New Guard was the Australian version of the fascism that was flourishing across Europe and Campbell was open in his admiration of Mussolini's regime, stating in 1932:

> *Democracy cannot cure the existing state of affairs. Only discipline, patriotic and spiritual belief can do this ... Inspired by the example of Italy, the New Guard will create in Australia a new spirit in the people.*[15]

Photo 5: Eric Campbell, Leader of the New Guard, Sydney, 1931. (Fairfax Photographic Archive)

---

[14] Andrew Moore, *The Secret Army and the Premier: Conservative Paramilitary Organisations in New South Wales 1930-32*, Kensington, 1989, p. 147; Keith Amos, *The New Guard Movement 1931-1935*, Carlton, 1976, p. 22.

[15] Moore, *The Secret Army*, p. 137.

Campbell travelled to Europe and in 1933 met Sir Oswald Mosley, who he found to be "a fine cut of a man". Mosley provided him with letters of introduction for his visits to Berlin and Rome, where he unsuccessfully tried to meet both Hitler and Mussolini. Returning to Australia he published a book, *The New Road*, which explained that his belief in fascism was grounded in "a close study of the affairs of both Italy and Germany, with information gained at first-hand, and a background of historical and political reading".[16] In his later memoir, *The Rallying Point: My Story of the New Guard*, published in 1965, Campbell admitted to being "deeply impressed with the regimes in both Germany and Italy".[17]

Much of the New Guard's activity involved flying squads of members who drove across Sydney to disrupt political meetings of its opponents. Resisting this brought McNeill into physical conflict with the New Guard. In Drummoyne, McNeill described the members of the New Guard as "just above the ordinary workers, respectable types", who owned cars, including a local doctor and chemist.[18] The CPA in Drummoyne held regular Friday night street meetings. Prominent speakers such as Stan Moran of the Unemployed Workers' Movement and Tom Payne of the CPA addressed large crowds.

On one occasion in late November 1931, when a council election candidate, Bart Thompson, was holding a street meeting at the corner of Brent Street and Lyons Road, Drummoyne, the New Guard assembled on the opposite corner and descended on the communists' meeting. To defend their speaker, McNeill and others formed a ring around Thompson, who was addressing the crowd while standing on a wooden soap-box. Scuffles broke out and a shot was fired.[19] The *Daily Telegraph* reported that it was a "miracle no one was hit". McNeill's photo was featured on the front page, and although he declined to give his name, he told the reporter:

> *The revolver was levelled at me while I was standing alongside the*

---

[16] Eric Campbell, *The New Road*, Sydney, 1934, p. 50.
[17] Eric Campbell, *The Rallying Point: My Story of the New Guard*, Carlton, 1965, p. 136.
[18] Lowenstein, *Weevils*, p. 103.
[19] Ibid., p. 102.

soap-box. I cannot understand yet how it was that I was not hit.[20]

McNeill would later recall the incident:

I felt it whistle just past my ear. I was hit twice in Spain but I never felt one go closer than what this bullet did. It was a real bloody bullet alright.[21]

The incident was raised in the NSW Parliament by Labor's Bob Heffron who asked the Colonial Secretary, Mark Gosling, if he was aware of the "organised interruption of public meetings by members of the New Guard?" and what steps would be taken to "preserve the right of free speech and freedom of thought?" Gosling responded by ridiculing press reports of the shooting as "exaggerating, distorting, and inventing disturbances" and that the "shot was fired by a lad about 16 or 17 years of age with a toy pistol". He took the charge about the organised disruption of public meetings more seriously, and said it was "unfortunately only too true and freedom of speech is seriously threatened". He assured the chamber that the police would act to protect freedom of discussion.[22]

The following week, the *Workers' Weekly* reported that a neatly typed anonymous threat against CPA members had been circulated around Drummoyne:

I am directed to advise you that any further effort on your part to repeat last Friday night's performance at Drummoyne will not meet with the approval of my organisation, whose intention it is to deal with the offenders in no uncertain manner. It is well to remember that the river is close by, and it is said to be very cold and infested with sharks.

THIS NOTICE is given you on behalf of an organised body of citizens, SO BEWARE: BEWARE!

---

[20] *Daily Telegraph*, 25 November 1931, p. 1.
[21] WL interview.
[22] *Hansard*, NSW Legislative Assembly, 1 Dec 1931, p. 7293.

Many braver men than you lie asleep in the deep, so beware!

In the event, the next CPA meeting at Drummoyne passed without incident, with the *Workers' Weekly* claiming that the job of cleaning up fascism had begun and deriding the New Guard as the "White-Livered Guard".[23] The conflict with the New Guard was not always defensive, with gangs of CPA members and Unemployed Workers' Movement supporters using knives to slash the tyres of cars parked outside halls where the New Guard was holding its rallies. When the New Guard ventured from the relatively well-to-do Drummoyne, to the more working-class suburb of Rozelle, they received rough handling from the locals and were soon, as McNeill put it, "running like hares off the streets".[24]

The sense of political crisis eased after Lang was dismissed by Governor Game in May 1932. An election followed which resulted in Lang's Labor Party being heavily defeated. With its nemesis out of power the New Guard faded away. For McNeill, the lessons of the New Guard's emergence were to stay with him and informed his later decision to travel to Spain and join the International Brigades:

> *One of the things that animated me [to go to Spain] was the experience with the New Guard, seeing what vicious types they were and how much they hated us, and what they would do if they were in power.*
>
> *I saw they had to be beat in Spain. I realised that Spain was the first place to organise against the fascists or Nazis, Mussolini or Hitler, or in Portugal.*[25]

Unemployment remained high and the government provided relief work, such as digging drainage ditches or laying footpaths. A quota system shared the work around, but single men like McNeill were only eligible for one week's work in every five. The work available was never enough and people continued to struggle. Eventually, McNeill picked up intermittent work back at the Abbotsford wireworks. He'd be engaged

---

[23] *Workers' Weekly*, 4 December 1931, p. 1.
[24] WL interview.
[25] WL interview.

for several months and then be put off again. Frustrated by being unable to find permanent full-time employment, in 1935 McNeill moved with his mother to Corrimal, a suburb north of Wollongong in the Illawarra region of NSW. He found a job in the Port Kembla steelworks and embraced the region's political culture.

7

The slaughter yards

Wollongong was rapidly developing as a centre of heavy industry. Coal mines had opened along the verdant Illawarra escarpment in the last decades of the nineteenth century and the Great War provided the stimulus for the development of a metals industry around Port Kembla. Attracted by the coal and the port, the Hoskins family relocated its steelworks from Lithgow to Port Kembla in the 1920s. In a deeply unfortunate piece of timing, the works commenced production just prior to the full impact of the Depression being felt. Demand for its products sank and mass retrenchments followed. The firm, which was probably under-capitalised given the scale of its ambitions, struggled. There were rumours that the steelworks was to close and in 1935 the Hoskins' Australian Iron & Steel was acquired by its larger competitor, the Broken Hill Pty Co Ltd (BHP). Astute at deploying capital, BHP sustained the flow of investment that the steelworks required.[1]

A steelworker

The working conditions McNeill encountered at Port Kembla were primitive, demeaning and dangerous. The company did not provide lockers, washing facilities or dining rooms for the workers, and there were no footpaths or formalised roads around the mills.[2] Safety precautions

---

[1] Cecil Hoskins, *The Hoskins Saga*, Sydney [?], 1969, pp. 93-102.
[2] Len Richardson, *The Bitter Years: Wollongong During the Great Depression*, Sydney, 1984, p. 175.

were a low priority for BHP and the situation was excoriated in the federal parliament by the local MP, Labor's Bert Lazzarini:

> *At the 36-inch mill at Port Kembla the men work under conditions of white heat and become exhausted. Their vigilance soon ceases to be 100 per cent and accidents of various kinds frequently occur. The works are known in the district and on the railways on the South Coast as "The Butcher's Shop", or "The Slaughter Yards".*
>
> *I say definitely that those in charge of the works to which I have referred are acting indecently. They have reached the stage at which they regard a workman as a chattel. They show an arrogance born of the success of which they boast. They have their powerful machinery, and they seem to have an idea that they have almost the same power to crush the men in their employment - to pound the men as their machines pound the metal used in the industry.*[3]

Faced with this brutal working environment, McNeill became active in the Port Kembla Branch of the Federated Ironworkers' Association. As a job delegate and then as a member of the Committee of Management, he helped resuscitate the union as a viable industrial force. The Depression had hit the union hard. For several years through the height of the economic crisis, the Port Kembla Branch had only a nominal existence. The New Guard was active throughout the Illawarra and at Port Kembla ironworkers were attacked by New Guardsmen whose ranks were said to include managers from the steelworks.[4]

As the economy began to recover, employment in the steelworks rose. Membership of the union recovered, from just 28 in 1934 to 2212 in 1938. Even as the economic recovery strengthened, it was clear that the misery of the Depression years had left its mark on Wollongong and had fostered the development of a distinctive industrial culture. At the national level, the two largest unions in the Illawarra were led by communists. Ernie Thornton, a member of the CPA, became the Ironworkers' national secretary in 1936. The CPA's success in the steel

---

[3] *Commonwealth Parliamentary Debates*, 19 March 1936.
[4] J.A. Merritt, 'The Federated Ironworkers' Association in the Depression', *Labour History*, 1971, No. 21, p. 57.

industry matched what it had achieved in the mining sector. The miners had elected a communist, Bill Orr, as their general president in 1934.

These national CPA advances were matched by local industrial and political developments. There was a strong communist influence in many of the local mining lodges and members of the CPA assumed the leadership of the Port Kembla Ironworkers' in 1937.[5] The new secretary, Pat McHenry, known as the "Grey Ghost", was a gaunt, doctrinaire, hard-bitten man, who had spent most of the Depression living with his family in a tent. His was not a unique experience, with hundreds of Port Kembla families still living in humpies made from kerosene tins and hessian bags in 1938.[6] McHenry and his fellow communist leaders were successful in building the union's effectiveness in the face of BHP's virulent anti-unionism.[7] After respectable showings by communist candidates in NSW elections, the CPA proclaimed the Illawarra region to be the "red belt of the blue pacific".[8]

The united front in Wollongong

In 1935, the CPA abandoned the revolutionary isolationism of its Class Against Class phase in favour of the collaborative politics of the united front. As always, this was in accord with the priorities of the USSR. By the mid-1930s, the Soviet leadership was increasingly concerned with the escalating threat of international fascism. Hitler's consolidation of absolute power in Germany had been followed by coups that brought right-wing regimes to power in Austria, Latvia and Bulgaria. In Asia, the USSR faced an increasingly aggressive Japan and clashes along the border with Japanese-occupied Manchuria intensified.

In response to these menacing international developments, Stalin embraced the idea of collective security and joined the League of Nations.

The Comintern formalised its adoption of the united front in August

---

[5] Richardson, *The Bitter Years*, pp. 173-7.
[6] *Sun*, 11 September 1938, p. 2.
[7] J.A. Merritt, 'A History of the Federated Ironworkers' Association of Australia 1909-1952', PhD thesis, Australian National University, 1967, p. 222 and p. 251.
[8] *Tribune*, 21 March 1940, p. 1.

1935, the CPA dutifully followed in December. Labor Party members were no longer to be derided as social fascists. Australian communists were expected to work with all progressive elements of society who would oppose fascism, including workers, farmers, civil servants, and middle-class intellectuals.[9]

In response to the war in Spain, the CPA pursued the united front strategy and convened meetings that succeeded in engaging the broad left. In August 1936 a progressive alliance, which included representatives from the Labor Party, trade unions and churches, established the Spanish Relief Committee. Its initial aim was to raise funds to send a Red Cross unit to Spain.[10] Over the next three years, the Spanish Relief Committee was the main organisation for raising money and awareness of the Republican cause. Relief committees were established in major towns. They distributed publications, held public meetings, hosted film nights, organised petitions, lobbied parliamentarians, collected funds and provided their perspective to newspapers around Australia. The CPA's Central Committee energetically supported this with a stream of detailed instructions to its districts urging ever more activity in support of the Spanish Republic.

In Wollongong, Paddy McDonald, a militant and non-communist leader of the Port Kembla steelworkers, wrote an article in *Steel & Metal Worker*, the union's newsletter, in which he stated that the Spanish Civil War was a "workers fight". The Illawarra Trades and Labour Council also established its position: a resolution was carried which congratulated the Spanish people on their "heroic fight against Fascist reaction" and "condemned the intervention of the German and Italian Fascists".[11]

McHenry, in his role as the secretary of the South Coast CPA, was committed to the united front. He issued a public statement seeking a joint campaign with the local Labor Party to support the Spanish government.[12] By the end of 1936, meetings were held in Wollongong

---

[9] Macintyre, *The Reds*, p. 249.
[10] Inglis, *Australians*, p. 58.
[11] Richardson, *The Bitter Years*, p. 201; *Illawarra Mercury*, 28 August 1936, p. 11.
[12] *South Coast Times*, 11 September 1936, p. 16.

to explain the "grave danger of world war if the Fascist forces in Spain, supported by Hitler and Mussolini, are victorious". To sustain the effort, a South Coast Spanish Relief Committee was formally established in June 1937.[13]

The Port Kembla Ironworkers' cooperated closely with the Spanish Relief Committee. The union was the ticketing agent for an evening of community singing held in the Wollongong Town Hall Annex to raise money for the people of Spain. A film star and popular radio announcer, Claude Holland, was the main attraction of the night. In the pages of its newsletter the union gave a glowing review of the film *Blockade*, which was playing at the Princess Theatre in Corrimal. Henry Fonda starred in a screenplay written by John Howard Lawson (who was to be gaoled as one of the Hollywood Ten). *Blockade* was set in Spain in 1936 and released in 1938, while the war continued. The film closed with Fonda's character, Marco, looking directly into the camera and asking, "Where's the conscience of the world?" The *Steel & Metal Worker* found it stirring, and recommended the movie "should be seen by every man, woman and child in the district, because we feel sure that its story will be of far more value than a thousand speeches".[14]

Wollongong's May Day processions travelled down Crown Street, the town's main street, and were watched by thousands of people. The marches in 1937 and 1938 included several large placards in support of the Spanish Republic. One banner carried an image of the communist politician, Dolores Ibárruri, better known as La Pasionaria. Her cry of "It is better to die on your feet than live on your knees! *No pasaran!*" (They shall not pass) had emerged as the inspirational slogan of the Republican cause. Other placards bore different messages:

> *Barry and Dickinson – Two Australian Sons – Died in Spain for Freedom*
>
> *Every sixpence is a nail in the coffin of Hitler and Mussolini*
>
> *Spanish People Ask for Ambulances – Send One from the Coast*[15]

---

[13] *Illawarra Mercury*, 11 December 1936, p. 3; 5 June 1937, p. 9.

[14] *Sheet & Metal Worker*, 6 May 1938, p. 4; 2 December 1938, p. 2; Website of Turner Classic Movies, https://www.tcm.com/tcmdb/title/69050/blockade#notes

[15] University of Wollongong Archives, D22/12/02/01; D22/12/04/01; and D22/12/04/06.

Photo 6: - Wollongong's 1938 May Day march with a banner of La Pasionaria. (University of Wollongong Archives, collection D22/12/04/01)

Photo 7: Wollongong's 1938 May Day march. Placards read: "Barry and Dickinson – Two Australian Sons – Died in Spain for Freedom". (University of Wollongong Archives, collection D22/12/04/06)

At the 1937 celebrations a speech was given by a local member of the NSW Parliament, Bill Davies MP (ALP), who had represented the district since 1917. He reflected the strong isolationist current in Australia that had its origins in the reaction to the carnage of the First World War. He cautioned that Europe's conflicts were not Australia's quarrels, but went on:

> If people met in Germany, like the workers of Australia, they would be cast into prison. The same thing was happening in Italy. In Spain there was a tragic set of circumstances because the working class were trying to assert their rights. Men, women and children were being mowed down mercilessly by bombs from the air.[16]

Australian responses to the Spanish Civil War

In contrast to Attlee, the Leader of the British Labour Party, who was firm and clear in his support for the International Brigades and the Spanish Republic, John Curtin, the leader of the Australian Labor Party, was strictly silent on the Spanish Civil War. He is not known to have ever specifically commented on it, apart from dismissing as "childish" a conservative parliamentarian who sought to make political capital out of the departure for Spain of a group of Australian nurses.[17] Curtin campaigned against conscription in the Great War and his basic philosophy was pacifist. How could he justify his pacifism in a world becoming so dangerous? When it came to Spain he resorted to a studied, deliberate silence. Curtin found temporary relief in isolationism: "If war cannot be averted in some parts of the world, then at least the people of Australia will be spared it." He may also have been concerned that any comment about Spain could threaten the unity of his party, which had a strong Catholic presence in its ranks.[18]

Others in the Labor Party and trade unions were less reticent. Party

---

[16] *Illawarra Mercury*, 7 May 1937, p. 9.
[17] *West Australian*, 24 October 1937, p. 21.
[18] John Edwards, *John Curtin's War*, Melbourne, 2017, p. 134: Inglis, *Australians*, p. 38; Jim Moss, *Sound of Trumpets: History of the Labour Movement in South Australia*, Cowandilla, 1985, p. 326.

branches agitated and individuals like Maurice Blackburn MP spoke out in support of the Republic. The Australian Council of Trade Unions launched an appeal for funds to aid the Republic and the state labour councils were vociferous in championing the cause.

The Catholic church, in contrast to Curtin's isolationism and the unions' support for the Republic, emerged as a proud and unapologetic supporter of the fascist rebels. The church was appalled by the Republic's reforms and the revolutionary violence directed towards nuns and priests. In Bathurst, Reverend Dr Norton told a meeting of the Hibernian Society that the Spanish reds were "dupes of the denationalised Jewish Communists".[19] In Brisbane, Archbishop Dr James Duhig gave unqualified support to the generals and said the rebellion was "a thing that was very much needed". He understood the conflict to be a contest between the Catholic church and communism:

> *I ask for your prayers for the Catholics of Spain against this diabolical, un-Christian force of Communism.*[20]

In Melbourne, a young Catholic activist, B.A. Santamaria, participated in a passionate debate with supporters of the Republic that considered the proposition: "That the Spanish government is the ruin of Spain". Santamaria's view was that should the Republic win the war, the result would not be the restoration of a liberal parliamentary democracy, but the establishment of a Soviet Spain.[21] The debate ended in chaos with hundreds of young Catholics crying out 'Long Live Christ the King' and giving three cheers for General Franco.[22] It was a muscular display of Catholic anti-communism that foretold the central role that Santamaria would play in the Labor Party's split of 1955.

The Catholic church's enthusiastic support for the fascists was maintained throughout the war. The Archbishop of Sydney, Dr N.T. Gilroy, said that the part played by the Catholic church in the "'rebel conspiracy' was a glorious one – a part of which Catholics throughout the world

---

[19] Inglis, *Australians*, p. 44; *Catholic Freeman's Journal*, 29 October 1936, p. 22.
[20] *Morning Bulletin*, 27 July 1936, p. 7.
[21] B.A. Santamaria, *Against the Tide*, Melbourne, 1981, p. 34.
[22] Inglis, *Australians*, pp. 97-99.

might justly be proud".[23] The Australian Catholic Truth Society was the driving force of the campaign. In 1936 alone, it produced more than 300,000 pamphlets supporting Franco that were distributed from churches. A Catholic Spanish Relief Fund was established and raised thousands of pounds to assist with the rebuilding of churches that had been desecrated.[24]

All of this activity, whether in support of the Republican government or the fascist rebels, was contrary to the official policy of the Australian government. Following Britain, Australia was supporting non-intervention. On 11 September 1936, Sir George Pearce, Minister for External Affairs, stated that the conflict in Spain had developed into "a desperate conflict between fascism and communism" and that Australia was following a policy of "strict neutrality". The Attorney-General, R.G. Menzies, a future Prime Minister and the CPA's bête noire, was alive to the concerns of businessmen and financiers like Clive Baillieu who wrote to him advising that:

> *Our English mining friends, who have big interests at Rio Tinto, also state that everything is normal [in Spain], and with the exception of a few extremists who have been shot out of hand by the anti-Reds, everything is working normally.*

Menzies replied, telling Baillieu that in the antipodes, the "Spanish radicals seem almost to have achieved sanctity".[25] More discreetly, Joe Lyons, the Prime Minister, "appealed to the Australian public to refrain directly or indirectly from taking any partisan measures".[26]

As the war continued, the global situation became ever more threatening. Germany, Italy and Japan formed an Anti-Comintern Pact. Japan's war in China was intensifying and clashes along the Soviet border continued. In Spain, by the end of 1937, prospects for the Republic were deteriorating, with the rebels having destroyed Guernica and taken Bilbao and Santander. This solidified Franco's hold on Spain's north

---

[23] *Catholic Freeman's Journal*, 11 November 1937, p. 21.
[24] Inglis, *Australians*, pp. 45-8.
[25] NAA: CP 450/7, 217.
[26] *Commonwealth Parliamentary Debates*, 11 September 1936 and 9 October 1936.

and deprived the Republic of the region's Atlantic ports and industrial output. In the face of fascist successes on the battlefield and after the first flush of enthusiasm, the flow of international volunteers supporting the Republic was drying up.

Responding to this darkening situation, in a circular dated 8 January 1938, the CPA's Central Committee switched from its usual exhortations for public meetings and the sale of pamphlets, to an appeal for volunteers to go to Spain to fight:

> *To: All District Committees*
>
> *Comrades,*
>
> *Recent advice favours the sending of several comrades from Australia and New Zealand to reinforce the International Brigade in Spain.*
>
> *The difficulty of getting away and into Spain make open recruiting and the raising of funds difficult, even impossible. It is necessary therefore to proceed carefully but boldly for this and other reasons. The total suggested is 25 – more or less according to development.*

This represented a significant change in attitude. The CPA's original stance on volunteers was that they were to be "considered 'adventurers' and were not encouraged".[27] But the course of the war had driven a change of position and the circular set out the qualifications needed of recruits. They were to be aged between 20 and 40, be physically fit with the "moral stamina to stand up to hardship and danger". The volunteers needed to understand they were to serve in the infantry, not in the hospitals or the air force. They should not have any dependents and membership of the CPA was preferred. The Central Committee understood there was an "important moral and political influence" to be gained by having Australians in the International Brigades. The CPA wanted to proceed "carefully but boldly" and aimed to find about 25 suitable recruits who would be able to "uphold the best Australian traditions".[28]

---

[27] RGASPI 545/6/68/175/19-25.
[28] Mitchell Library, MLMSS 5201 ADD-ON 1936/Box 5 Series 01-23: Communist Party of Australia - further records, 1920-1991.

Joe Carter

In Wollongong, the word was put out that an Australian unit of the International Brigades was to be formed. Two volunteers, McNeill and Joe Carter, both ironworkers and both communists, came forward.

Photo 8: Joe Carter, 1938. (Australian National University Archives Centre)

Carter was "a tough fighter, well-built and a good boxer, very game".[29] Born as Harry Summers at Miranda in 1907, he led a hard life with only three or four years of schooling at Marrangaroo, near Lithgow. He did not know who his father was and as a young teenager had left an abusive step-father ("he'd belt the ears off me"), and gone "nippering" (providing assistance) for workers in railway camps. He never saw his mother again. After leaving home he adopted the name Joe Carter and also used other names as a variety of identities was useful for the sort of marginal, itinerant life that Carter lived. Through the 1920s he carried a swag in regional NSW and Queensland. He found work in shearing sheds and survived by doing whatever labouring or bush work was

---

[29] Nettie Palmer and Len Fox, with the help of Jim McNeill and Ron Hurd, *Australians in Spain: Our Pioneers Against Fascism*, Sydney, 1948, p. 46.

available.³⁰ There were regular brushes with the law.

The Depression was a tough experience for single working-class men like Carter. Intense and desperate poverty, combined with harsh law enforcement, left him with a resentment towards the existing economic and social system that endured for the rest of his life. In 1930 he was involved in a shearing strike at Mungindi, on the NSW-Queensland border, where, after he pulled scabs out of a shearing shed, a station owner pointed a gun at him. Disappointed with the Australian Workers' Union's conduct of the strike, he left the Labor Party although remaining a committed trade unionist. He joined the CPA at Lithgow, where he ran a boxing gymnasium. Carter was a guard with the Workers' Defence Corps, an organisation the CPA created to protect pickets, speakers and demonstrators.³¹ At Lithgow the threat to communist advocacy came not from the New Guard but from those workers who Carter felt were "confused".

His involvement with the CPA came to an abrupt end when he was expelled after being gaoled for theft. Carter and a friend had been pilfering goods from trains that stopped at Lithgow and fencing them through a shop at Glen Davis.

> *I thought I should have a little bit of property. I had none. It is pretty hard when you're hungry - and I've been hungry.*

He served his sentence in the Goulburn and Long Bay prisons. While in Long Bay he met Bill Young, another who was to join the International Brigades. On his release from prison Carter moved to Wollongong where he obtained a job at Port Kembla. He was engaged in building

---

[30] This account of Carter's life is drawn from five oral history interviews he recorded that can be found: Joe Carter – Jon Clements, Imperial War Museum IWM 3812; Joe Carter – Amirah Inglis, Australian National University Open Research Repository N171-61; Joe Carter – Glen Mitchell, Illawarra Stories, Wollongong City Library; Joe Carter – John Shipp, Wollongong University Archives B-16; and Joe Carter – Laurie Aarons, the Mitchell Library, State Library of New South Wales, MLOH 628/5.

[31] Mcintyre, *The Reds*, p. 210.

the coke ovens at the steelworks and re-joined the CPA in 1937.[32]

Carter felt that he'd been born a left-winger and described himself as a revolutionary. He gave different reasons for his decision to go to Spain. In one account he decided to volunteer after reading newspaper articles about children being attacked by aircraft at a school outside Barcelona. On another occasion he located his motivation in the scarring effect of the Depression:

> *The reason I went to Spain is because they forced me to become a hobo. Forced me to humiliate myself, knocking on doors asking for a bit of bread, a bit of bread and fat.*
>
> *It gets me very riled. It hurts me deeply.*
>
> *And you ask me why did I go to Spain?*[33]

The departure of McNeill and Carter was delayed by Gordon King, the CPA's Illawarra organiser, who wanted them to join the Labor Party before they left. In line with the united front strategy, this ploy was meant to demonstrate the broadest possible political support for the Republican cause. Frustrated by the delay, the pair approached the CPA's general secretary, J.B. Miles, during one of his visits to Wollongong. Over drinks in a pub, they explained the situation and Miles pooh-poohed the idea of them joining the Labor Party, observing that it would be "false pretences - everyone knows you're communists".[34]

With that issue settled final arrangements could be made. Accepting the possibility that he might not return, McNeill made out a will and left one third of his estate, which included the cottage in Corrimal, to the Spanish Relief Committee.[35] Neither McNeill nor Carter had previously left Australia, but with permission and credentials from Miles the pair, travelling in cahoots, caught the train from Wollongong to Sydney and commenced their long journeys to Spain.

---

[32] Palmer and Fox, *Australians in Spain*, p 46; Inglis, *Australians,* p. 126; Joe Carter – Jon Clements, Imperial War Museum IWM 3812; Joe Carter – Amirah Inglis, Australian National University Open Research Repository N171-61.

[33] Joe Carter – Glen Mitchell, Illawarra Stories, Wollongong City Libraries.

[34] WL interview.

[35] Letter from Phil Thorne to Nettie Palmer, 19 August 1938, Aileen Palmer collection, 6759, Box 1, National Library of Australia.

8

What a man!

For Dickinson and hundreds of other volunteers, travelling from Britain to Spain in 1936 was a relatively easy matter. The British authorities were certainly not supportive but did not attempt to interfere. Volunteers were vetted by the Communist Party of Great Britain in London and then simply boarded the boat train from Victoria Station to Paris. Passports were not required as they posed as weekend tourists. The passengers crossed the channel aboard a ferry and on landing in France resumed their trip to Paris.

In Spain

On arrival, the volunteers received a medical screening to ensure they were fit for service. Another train took them to the French border town of Perpignan. From there the volunteers crossed the frontier on buses that delivered them to barracks in a castle at Figueras, near Girona in Catalonia. Dickinson, one of a group of 58, was registered as arriving in Spain on 22 December 1936. His entry lists him as British, not Australian, and recorded his occupation as a salesman. His political history with the IWW and as an organiser with the anti-fascist Legion of Blue and White Shirts was noted.[1]

Arriving in the same group was Harry Fry, a Scottish cobbler who was to be Dickinson's commanding officer in the British Battalion's No. 2 Machine Gun Company. Fry was younger than Dickinson and had joined the Communist Party in 1934. He was described as tall, very

---
1   RGASPI 545/6/91/58 and 59.

good-looking, with a natural genius for organization while also being an "exceedingly pleasant man to talk to".² Fry had served in the British Army's Coldstream Guards with his service taking him to India and China. After leaving the army he had become politically active and had participated in a violent anti-Fascist demonstration held when Mosley spoke at Edinburgh's Usher Hall. He was injured while fighting Blackshirts and required seven stitches to a head wound.³

Jason Gurney, the sculptor, arrived in Spain shortly after and described how the volunteers travelled on to Barcelona, where they received an enthusiastic welcome from an enormous crowd. Orwell also arrived in Barcelona in December 1936, and joined not the International Brigades but the militia of the *Partido Obrero de Unifacion Marxista* (POUM), an anti-Stalinist Marxist party. He described the city's revolutionary atmosphere as "startling and overwhelming".

> *It was the first time that I had ever been in a town where the working class was in the saddle. Practically every building of any size had been seized by the workers and was draped with red flags or the red and black flag of the anarchists; ... All this was queer and moving. There was much in it that I did not understand, in some ways I did not even like it, but I recognised it immediately as a state of affairs worth fighting for.*⁴

The volunteers stayed in Barcelona for several days, exalting in the revolutionary fervour of the city and enjoying wild times in the heaving bars, brothels and honky-tonk shows. Leaving Barcelona, the volunteers made a short stop at Albacete, base of the International Brigades, where they were harangued in French (a language most of the volunteers did not understand) by Andre Marty, the Political Commissar of the International Brigades.⁵

---

2   Gurney, *Crusade*, p. 72.
3   James Rutherford, 'Captain Harold Fry', in *The Book of the XV Brigade: records of British, American, Canadian, and Irish volunteers in the XV International Brigade in Spain, 1936-1938*, Newcastle, 1975, p. 298.
4   Orwell, *Homage*, p. 2.
5   Gurney, *Crusade*, p. 52.

With his trademark black beret, Marty was a squat, moustachioed and jowly man, who struck one officer as "an incredibly expansive old sea-lion". During the Russian Civil War, he had led a mutiny in the French navy against an order to assist the Whites. This action earned Stalin's favour and helped him rise to a powerful position in the Comintern. In Spain, he was known for his lack of both ability and humanity. One Australian volunteer remembered him as "almost a mental case".[6] Marty developed a paranoia that drove him to seek out and exterminate anyone he considered to be a Fascist-Trotskyist spy.[7]

The International Brigades had a dual military and political command structure, modelled on the USSR's Red Army. Each unit had political commissars who exercised almost as much power as the commanding officers. The commissars attended to the soldiers' welfare and ensured that the ranks were not subjected to any capricious mistreatment by their officers. They were responsible for keeping morale high and, as part of a people's army, for ensuring the soldiers understood the political cause for which they were fighting. But at their worst they could be like Marty - little more than sinister secret police on the hunt for imagined Trotskyite conspiracies.[8]

The British Battalion's commissar was Dave Springhall, a London builder and experienced communist who had studied at the Comintern's Lenin School in Moscow. Gurney found his speeches to be "exceedingly boring homilies", but other volunteers were more positively impressed.[9] The Reverend Robert Hilliard, who had been a pastor before becoming a Marxist (and entertaining his comrades with the benediction – "In the name of Marx, Engels and Lenin"), thought that the work by both the Communist and Labour parties "worked wonders". He wrote home to a friend giving an account of Springhall's speech to the volunteers explaining how they should see themselves:

> Comrade Springhall, political commissar to the battalion, started with

---

6   Lloyd Edmonds – Wendy Lowenstein, Wendy Lowenstein Collection, access courtesy of Martie Lowenstein.
7   Beevor, *Spanish Civil War*, p. 184; Thomas, *Spanish Civil War*, pp. 300-1.
8   Tremlett, *International Brigades*, p. 77.
9   Gurney, *Crusade*, p. 61.

> *a lecture which summed up the nature of our struggle against fascism, to the effect that fascism could not be fought by individuals – that only collective effort of all democrats could ensure victory; that as a democratic army we could command the best brains in the world, brains which as sectarians would be denied us; that in contra-distinction to the imperialist army, political thought and activity were encouraged… the army believed that the greater the political activity the stronger and more effective would be the fight against fascism.*[10]

At Albacete, the men were issued with their military uniforms – a cotton corduroy jacket, trousers of various shades of brown, boots, khaki beret and a tin-helmet. Gurney was unimpressed by the thinness of the helmet which he felt made it useless in providing protection against anything other than kids throwing stones. They were also given two thin cotton blankets and a groundsheet cape.[11] As officers, Fry and Dickinson wore Sam Brownes (a leather belt worn diagonally across the chest) and pistols.

Training

A short truck ride brought the volunteers to Madrigueras, a poor village where the newly formed British Battalion established its training camp. One Brigader reported the local people to be "fervently republican" and "absolutely marvellous" in their support for the volunteers, but Gurney found them to be "silent and taciturn people" who had given up hope. In the centre of the town was a desecrated church, and this was where the British made their mess-hall.

Perhaps used to the benign social role played by the churches in Britain, many of the volunteers were puzzled by the anti-clericalism. Gurney saw the desecration of the churches as a response to religious hypocrisy, "of deceiving the poor for the benefit of the rich". Another volunteer, David Crook, a Londoner who had graduated from Columbia University

---

[10] John Corcoran, 'Fighting the Good Fight: The Rev Robert Martin Hilliard', *Saothar*, Vol. 3 (2006), p. 60.

[11] Gurney, *Crusade*, p. 55.

in New York, was told that with "the connivance of the priest, local landlords had hidden machine guns in the church". The machine guns had then been used on local people in the first days of the attempted coup.[12]

The British Battalion's billets were primitive, with no provision for baths and laundry. The few toilets were inadequate for the number of men who had to use them and became "unspeakably disgusting". Despite these miserable conditions, Fry's company, Gurney observed, "worked hard and were full of enthusiasm". In contrast to the other companies, the men kept their billet reasonably clean.[13] The local Popular Front Committee provided Dickinson's company with wooden beds and palliasses to sleep on. The men felt they were in luxury compared to the other companies that slept on the floor of their billets.[14]

The British had expected Spain to be sunny, but the weather at Madrigueras was poor, with a constant drizzle of rain. The British also had to come to terms with food that was very different to what they were used to. The result was that many suffered from diarrhoea. A typical breakfast was coffee with hard bread and marmalade. The evening meal could be a watery stew of vegetables and canned meat, or beans, lentils and mule meat. A treat was an invitation to eat in the homes of villagers, where they could enjoy eggs, chips and occasionally meat. For a sweet treat, *churros* could be bought from a street-vendor. Tobacco was scarce and of poor quality, but alcohol, in the form of red wine, grappa and anis, was readily available.[15]

Fry insisted on a strict no-alcohol rule for his company, but elsewhere the excessive consumption of alcohol gave rise to discipline problems. A drunken brawl broke out between English and Irish volunteers. Tensions existed between the national groups, with a number of the Irish having fought with the Irish Republican Army, and a number of

---

[12] Gurney, *Crusade*, p. 60; Ben Hughes, *They Shall Not Pass! The British Battalion at Jarama*, Oxford, 2011, p. 56.

[13] Gurney, *Crusade*, p. 60; p. 65 and p. 72.

[14] Leeson, IWM 803, Reel 2.

[15] Gurney, *Crusade* p. 65 and p. 76; Hughes, *They Shall Not Pass*, pp. 57-8; Leeson, IWM 803, Reel 2.

the English believed to have undertaken covert actions in Ireland for the British Army. Such difficult relations culminated in a group of Irish volunteers deciding to leave the British Battalion and join instead the American Abraham Lincoln Battalion.[16]

The British Battalion and the Abraham Lincoln Battalion were two of four that constituted the XVth International Brigade, the others being the Dimitrov and 6th of February, made up of, respectively, mainly Balkan and French/Belgian volunteers.[17] The XVth International Brigade was headed by Colonel Gal, a Red Army officer of Hungarian birth who served, at least notionally, as a volunteer. His real name was Janos Galicz and he was seen as tough, ruthless, bad-tempered and incompetent.[18]

The Battalion's stay in Madrigueras was ostensibly for the training needed to transform it from a group of randomly assorted civilians into an organised and disciplined fighting force. But as the men had not been issued with rifles Gurney thought their training seemed "a little absurd" relying, as it did, on a few antique firearms, sticks in lieu of rifles, and rattles to imitate the sound of a machine gun. They received instruction on how to use a Mills hand grenade, but they had no such grenades and never received any.[19]

One of the men, George Leeson, whose political awakening had come with the realisation, while serving in China with the Royal Navy, that Britain was doing the wrong thing in imposing its trade concessions on that country, recalled the training as ineffective.[20] Long marches through the countryside kept the men fit, but apart from teaching them how to take cover from aircraft, there was no tactical training at all. Crook recorded in his diary that he learnt how to advance in formation under artillery fire. He regarded Dickinson as "a typical bluff profane

---

[16] Gurney, *Crusade*, pp. 76-7; Richard Baxell, 'The British Battalion of the International Brigades in the Spanish Civil War 1936-39', PhD thesis, London School of Economics and Political Science, 2001, pp. 147-8.
[17] Thomas, *Spanish Civil War*, p. 377.
[18] Tremlett, *International Brigades*, p. 214; Thomas, *Spanish Civil War*, p. 376.
[19] Gurney, *Crusade*, p. 76.
[20] Leeson, IWM 803, Reel 1.

humorous regular army officer".[21] This was a sound character reference to receive, as Crook was soon recruited as an informer for Stalin's menacing secret police, the NKVD.[22]

As a machine gun company, No. 2 Company received eight old Maxims, reliable weapons that dated from the Great War.[23] In early February the British Battalion's rifles finally arrived, with each man issued a Russian-made Mosin-Nagant rifle, a fixed bayonet and 150 bullets. The rifle had an effective range of 500 metres, but there was only a single day before the British Battalion was moved to the front. For three quarters of the men, that single day was the first time they held a weapon.[24]

More disruption to the British Battalion's preparations came with the recall, in controversial circumstances, of their commander, Wilfred Macartney. Macartney had been imprisoned in Britain for spying for the USSR and a condition of his release was regular reporting to the authorities. Preparing to return to fulfil this obligation, he was shot while exchanging pistols with Peter Kerrigan, a political commissar. Rumours spread that he had deserted or suicided. The almost comical circumstance of a battalion commander sustaining such an injury led many to believe that it was the result of a communist conspiracy to have Macartney removed from his command.[25]

Macartney survived the shooting and stayed in Britain to recover. He was replaced in early February 1937 by Tom Wintringham, a veteran of the Great War who wrote articles on the military for the Communist Party's *Daily Worker*. Wintringham had four companies reporting to him: No. 1 headed by Kit Conway; No. 2 by Fry with Dickinson as second-in-command and Donald Renton as political commissar; No.

---

[21] Transcript of Crook's diary for 10 January 1937, Marx Memorial Library, SC/VOL/DCR/1.
[22] Leeson, IWM 803, Reels 1 and 2; David Crook, *Hampstead Heath to Tian An Men - The Autobiography of David Crook*, 1999, at davidcrook.net, pp. 3-18.
[23] Gurney, *Crusade*, pp. 76-79.
[24] Hughes, *They Shall Not Pass*, p. 65; Judith Cook, (ed), *Apprentices of Freedom*, London, 1979, p. 65.
[25] Hughes, *They Shall Not Pass*, p. 63; Vincent Brome, *The International Brigades: Spain 1936-1939*, Great Britain, 1965, pp. 125-6; Leeson, IWM 803, Reel 2.

3 by Bill Briskey; No. 4 by Bert Overton. Fred Copeman, who had led a mutiny in the Royal Navy, was the battalion's "spare officer".[26] Wintringham had a high regard for Dickinson, who he saw as "one of my most promising officers" with a voice "that made him a first-rate open-air speaker".[27] Dickinson was put in charge of advance parties as he had the ability to engage the local population and quickly win their cooperation for whatever the objective was.[28]

The Battle of Jarama

British volunteers had fought in earlier battles, but the British Battalion first saw action in the Battle of Jarama. The rebellious generals had tried to seize Madrid, Spain's capital, in the first days of the rising. Their attempt was resisted and defeated by a popular militia. In November 1936 the fascists tried to take the capital by direct assault, and were again defeated in desperate fighting on the city's outskirts. Franco then planned to take the city by severing its links to Valencia. To achieve this he needed to cross the Jarama River and drive northeast with the aim of taking control of the Madrid-Valencia road. This would deny the Republic the ability to supply Madrid. The Republican government, which by November had largely re-asserted control of its zone and put a stop to the revolutionary violence that marked the first weeks of the war, had to fight to maintain the lifeline to Madrid. If the city fell to the fascists, it would be a grievous and probably terminal blow.

To fight the Battle of Jarama the fascists assembled thirty battalions into five brigades totalling 25,000 men, six 155mm artillery batteries and a Condor Legion artillery unit of 88 mm guns. This was the first time the 88 mm gun, a cornerstone of the arsenal of the German *Wehrmacht* in the Second World War, was used in battle. There were also two Panzer companies and air support from both the Condor Legion and the Italian air force. The experienced fascist troops were considered

---

[26] Hughes, *They Shall Not Pass*, p. 68.
[27] Tom Wintringham, *English Captain*, London, 1939, p. 226.
[28] Letter from McNeill to John Playford, 14 February 1958, McNeill Collection, Illawarra Museum.

elite and included the loosely described Foreign Legion - which was actually largely Spanish - and Moors, toughened colonial mercenaries recruited from Spanish Morocco. Franco's Catholic crusade for Spain actually relied heavily on Islamic troops from Africa. They were widely feared by the British on account of their reputation for cruelty, savagery and penchant for inflicting execution by the severing of genitals.[29]

The fascists launched their attack on 6 February with four columns advancing across an 18-kilometre front. The column that would fight the British Battalion was under the command of Asensio Cabanillas, a Franco loyalist who had secured the Moroccan city of Tetouan in the first days of the rebellion. His forces made progress and on the night of 11-12 February his Moors used their curved *koummya* knives to stealthily slit the throats of the sentries guarding the San Martin de la Vega Bridge. Having fought their way across the Jarama River, Asensio's forces began their advance towards the town of Morata de Tajuna.

With the fascists across the river and advancing, the situation was fast becoming critical and early on the morning of 12 February, the raw British Battalion, with about 600 men, was sent into battle against 1600 hardened fascist soldiers - about 600 Moors and 1000 legionnaires.[30]

The British had left Madrigueras on 7 February. One of the commissars, George Aitken, marked the occasion with a rousing speech to the men that reinforced their ideological motivations:

> *In the past, many battalions of British soldiers had left the shores of Britain to fight in foreign lands. But ours was the first Battalion of British workers which had left Britain to fight for freedom and democracy. The eyes of the workers of Britain and of the whole world are on us.*[31]

They had been put on a train that took them from Madrigueras to Albacete, and then on trucks that conveyed them to Chinchon. From

---

[29] Thomas, *Spanish Civil War*, p. 374; Hughes, *They Shall Not Pass*, pp. 76-7.
[30] Hughes, *They Shall Not Pass*, p. 77.
[31] James K. Hopkins, *Into the Heart of the Fire: The British in the Spanish Civil War*, Stanford, California, 1998, p. 185.

there, on 12 February, with only coffee and a poor night's sleep to sustain them, the troops were transported to the Battalion's field headquarters arriving at 5.30 am. They were ordered to advance to positions on a ridge overlooking the Jarama River, but had to do so without proper maps and without knowing where their enemy was located.

The march up to the ridge in the crisp early morning was hard going for the machine gunners. Each gun, with wrought iron wheels and a thick steel shield, weighed 140 pounds and had to be hauled up a steep gully to the top of the ridge. It was exhausting work and as the day warmed up the men started discarding their blankets and overcoats to reduce what they had to carry up the hill. This left Dickinson furious, as he knew that while the day was warming up, the night would be cold. The work was so strenuous and the ground so hard going that the men had to take breaks to rest. While they did so, they watched a dogfight as the Condor Legion's Heinkels fought the Republic's Russian Polikarpovs. They cheered as three of the German aircraft were shot out of the sky.[32]

At the top of the ridge there was a plateau covered in groves of olive trees. Moving beyond the trees the British Battalion took up their positions on the ground that fell away into the river valley on the other side of the ridge. The ground was stony and sparsely covered in scrubby aromatic plants that provided no real cover. Conway's No. 1 Company moved up to an advanced position on what the British called Conical Hill. Overton had his No. 4 Company on a double-headed hill that was soon to be named Suicide Hill, with Briskey's No. 3 Company to his left. Fry's No. 2 Company set up along the ridge overlooking the action, with steep ground falling away in front of them.

Without proper entrenching equipment, the men on the hills did not have time to prepare their defensive positions. So inexperienced were some of them that when they first heard gunfire they mistook it for the chirping of insects or the twittering of birds. They were soon under intense artillery and machine gun fire that lasted for hours. The Battalion was being slaughtered as raw recruits, who only weeks before had been coal miners, dock workers and clerks, were attacked by a

---

[32] Tremlett, *International Brigades*, p. 215; Hughes, *They Shall Not Pass*, p. 69.

professional army. The artillery fire blew some of them to bits, as one survivor described it:

> If there is anything worse than seeing a dead or horribly wounded man it is seeing just an arm or leg ripped off and flung aside by the explosion of a shell.[33]

The Moors were skilful at moving across the landscape without being detected. They were pouring fire onto the British, who were now retreating from Suicide Hill. Another volunteer, Charles Morgan, recalled:

> Some of those poor bloody lads never even had a chance to fire a shot on the Jarama – they went over the top without training or experience of any kind and were just slaughtered.[34]

Incredibly, in an indication of how unprepared the British were, the machine gunners had been supplied with the wrong ammunition for their Maxims, which were the most powerful weapons in the battalion. The men could fire some shots from their rifles, but their fearsome machine guns sat silent while appalling scenes stretched out beneath them. Eventually, Copeman reached the No. 2 Company and confronted Fry about his passivity.

> I said, 'What the bloody hell has happened to you?'
>
> He said, 'We've got the wrong ammunition.'
>
> I said, 'Well, why haven't you gone and got the other ammunition?' He looked a bit dumb. I drew him off a bloody strip and called him all the names in bloody hell.[35]

Copeman, who was said to treat bullets like a buffalo treats mosquitoes, set out to find the correct ammunition and get the machine guns ready for action.[36] When the ammunition was eventually located, the

---

[33] Walter Gregory, *The Shallow Grave: A Memoir of the Spanish Civil War*, London, 1986, p. 47.
[34] Cook, *Apprentices of Freedom*, p. 66.
[35] Copeman, IWM 794, Reel 2.
[36] Wintringham, *English Captain*, p. 185.

explanation for its absence was that a drunken sergeant had crashed the truck transporting it to the front.[37] A second ammunition truck appeared with the correct ammunition, but the bullets still had to be manually loaded into the belts and hauled back up to the machine gunners, a task made hard as the battlefield was chaotic with dead and injured men strewn about, no food or water available, and the British being attacked by dive-bombing planes. Tony Hyndman, a former Welsh Guardsman who had been in a relationship with the poet Stephen Spender before coming to Spain, was one of the men lugging the ammunition:

> *The planes whirled, ready for another dive. I curled up, convinced they would get me this time. Some instinct concerning my manhood made me put the two metal cases [containing the ammunition] across my middle parts. It was ridiculous. One bullet into either of those cans and away I'd go, balls and all.*[38]

Late in the afternoon the machine guns were finally ready for action. Unaware that they were there, the fascists advanced thinking that all that stood between them and the Madrid-Valencia road was what remained of the savagely mauled and retreating British. Mounted officers, in dashing red and blue cloaks with glinting sabres drawn, led the Moors and legionnaires forward. Copeman made sure the gunners held their fire until it could be most devastating:

> *Not a bloody round has got to be fired [until my command]… And when I say 'Fire', you fire from the right to the left all together and keep going backwards and forwards until there isn't a bloody thing left alive.*
>
> *You're going to get the show of your life. You'll never see how many men you can kill in a short time.*[39]

The British waited on the ridge until the fascists were well within easy range and then commenced shooting, catching their enemies in the

---

[37] Baxell, *British Battalion*, p. 163.
[38] T. A. R. Hyndman, 'Volunteer in Trouble', in Valentine Cunningham, (ed) *Spanish Front: Writers on the Civil War*, Oxfordshire, 1986, p. 35.
[39] Copeman, IWM 794, Reel 2.

open. The result was a massacre. John Tunnah, the battalion's postmaster, described the scene:

> You might think to see men mown down as if a scythe was going through them wouldn't be possible, but this is literally what happened. It just stopped them like a stone wall.[40]

Wintringham, positioned behind the lines, could see what was happening:

> As I stood up, I saw what every machine-gunner longs for, and seldom sees – enemy infantry in the open, with a skyline behind them and no good cover available.[41]

Copeman could see that some of the fascists, caught in the open, were playing dead. He gave the order: "Keep on bloody well firing, there's a lot of live bodies in that lot".[42] The machine guns became so hot that to keep them operational, the men resorted to urinating into a helmet and pouring the contents over the barrels, which then sizzled.[43] It was an exercise not easily completed, as one volunteer explained:

> You try peeing under fire…but they had to be water-cooled, and that was the only way we could do it. All hell would be breaking over your head and you'd be afraid to pull it out in case it got shot off.[44]

Eventually the guns ceased firing. Surveying the obliteration, the British gave vent to their elation by cheering and shouting abuse at their fallen enemies. Hyndman recalled his feelings at the end of the day's fighting:

> Suddenly there was silence. I sat, leaning against the wall, carefully lighting a cigarette. What I dreaded most was not happening. There were no tears yet.[45]

The British Battalion's first day of action had been a horrendous

---

[40] Hughes, *They Shall Not Pass*, p. 111.
[41] Wintringham, *English Captain*, p. 193.
[42] Copeman, IWM 794, Reel 2.
[43] Hughes, *They Shall Not Pass*, p. 112.
[44] Cook, *Apprentices of Freedom*, p. 75.
[45] Hyndman, 'Volunteer in Trouble', p. 35.

experience with 100 killed, 145 wounded, and shattered survivors scattered across a wide area of the front. Two company commanders, Conway and Briskey, were among the dead and 75 men were unaccounted for. Fry and Dickinson's No. 2 Company had, eventually, saved the day and was essentially intact. From the Battalion's original strength of 600, Wintringham now had less than 300 exhausted and hungry men. During the night, he gathered up the remnants and prepared them to face the next day's fighting.

The machine gunners spent the night entrenching their commanding position with a gun pit that ran along the ridgeline. They made sure that each gun had ample supplies of the correct ammunition. Their work was disrupted by the calling of a wounded Englishman, lying somewhere out in the darkness of no man's land. Wintringham refused to let the men mount a risky rescue operation, but for the men in No. 2 Company: "It [was] horrible to hear a man's voice, calling hour on hour…dying…slowly." Eventually, defying Wintringham's direct order, three of the men went out on a rescue mission, but the calling ceased, and without it to guide them they did not succeed in finding the dying man.[46]

Early the next day, Wintringham reorganised his forces. He left No. 2 Company in its now forward position on the ridge with Overton's No. 4 Company to the right, No. 3 Company further right and No. 1 Company to the left. The day's fighting opened shortly after dawn with another assault by the Moors, but the No. 2 Company's machine guns were again effective, and the advance faltered and broke-up in a rout. Copeman described the devastation:

> *In the morning they came towards us and we opened up – God, you should see what Maxims can do, they dig a trench you know. It mowed them down. Some of them had the sense to fall down as if they'd been hit, but I said to keep firing into the mob, don't stop. They lost nearly a whole battalion.*[47]

A lull settled over the battlefield and the troops could enjoy the sunshine while watching another bout of aerial combat. The Republic's

---

[46] Ibid., p. 124.
[47] Cook, *Apprentices of Freedom*, p. 71.

aircraft shot down two more of their opponents' planes. By midday the fighting resumed with the British attempting to relieve the pressure that the front to the north of them was under. The rebels then launched an artillery barrage. The No. 2 Company had dug in well and was able to endure the bombardment without suffering a great deal of damage. One shell landed just in front of Fry, leaving him covered in dirt but otherwise uninjured. He drew on his pipe, laughed, and asked "Did I hear something?"[48]

The men of Overton's No. 4 Company, who were protecting the machine gunners' flank, were not faring so well. These men were not properly dug in and the bombardment caught them with only scant cover. Struck by panic, Overton led his company on a wild retreat through the olive groves which left the machine gunners, in their forward position, hopelessly exposed.[49] The result was an immediate catastrophe.

Captured and executed

Unaware of what Overton had done, the machine gunners were initially confused by the fascists' swift advance from an unexpected direction. Some thought the advancing soldiers were Republican Spaniards coming to relieve them. The ruse was aided by the legionnaires donning clothing taken from dead International Brigaders. In this attire the fascists waved their rifles in greeting and gave the clenched fist salute of the Republic. The deceptions created just enough momentary confusion to allow the rebels to swarm over the trenches and take the men of No. 2 Machine Gun Company prisoner.

In the first moments of capture, Dickinson was battered with rifle butts, while others were beaten. Dickinson attended to Fry, whose arm had been smashed by a bullet, and ripped off the insignia that would identify Fry as an officer. Bill Meredith, a labourer and member of the Northumberland Labour Party, was returning to the company having run a message from Fry to Wintringham. Seeing what was happening

---

[48] *The Book of the XV Brigade*, Newcastle, 1975, p. 53.
[49] Hughes, *They Shall Not Pass*, p. 144.

and under fire, he turned and fled:

> *Fry and Dickinson, his second-in-command, stood together and although I hardly noticed Fry, I well remember Dickinson, his attitude and dress.*
>
> *Overcoat, top boots and smartly clipped moustache, legs apart and back as straight as a poker, he still looked every inch a soldier, despite being surrounded by fascists. He looked at them with contempt written all over his face and it was obvious that his capture would never shake his calm courage.*
>
> *These two, Fry and Dickinson, were two of the finest leaders under whom men could wish to go into battle.*[50]

The British attempted a rescue but it was doomed to fail as the legionnaires now occupied a commanding position. The situation was desperate and Gurney felt "a kind of madness" descend on the surviving British. Soldiers were "running around shouting and behaving in all manner of peculiar ways". Wintringham was shot in the leg almost immediately, but forty others went forward. Only six returned. It was a futile waste.[51]

The legionnaires handed their prisoners over to the Moors who marched them, with their hands above their heads, from the front and down the valley. At a pause, one of the captives, Phil Elias, motioned for permission to smoke. This was granted, but as he reached into his pocket a Moor fired a machine gun killing him and another captive, John Stevens, who was standing alongside him. Dickinson looked at the Moors and snarled his disgust and contempt.[52] There are several eyewitness accounts of what happened next. While they vary in detail, all confirm that Dickinson performed a last act of defiance and died a hero's death. The official report of the action states:

> *The men were ordered to march down the valley to a spot 400 metres*

---

[50] *Tribune*, 6 July 1966, p. 7.

[51] Gurney, *Crusade*, p. 121; Hughes, *They Shall Not Pass*, p. 150.

[52] William Rust, *Britons in Spain: The History of the British Battalion of the XVth International Brigade*, London, 1939, p. 63.

off. The Spanish officer, mad with delight, ordered Ted Dickinson, second-in-command of the Machine Gun Company, out of their ranks. Dickinson, knowing what was coming, displayed marvellous courage. He stepped smartly out of the ranks, marched towards the tree indicated by the fascist officer, turned about, and with the words "Salud Comrades" fell with fascist bullets in him.[53]

A Scottish communist, Tommy Bloomfield, was said to be Dickinson's greatest mate in the British Battalion and believed him to be an Australian lawyer. He emphasised that Dickinson was given a choice between joining the fascists or death.

He was given the choice of dying or soldiering for Franco. He chose death. He marched up to a tree like a soldier on parade, did a military about turn saying 'Salud comrades' the second he died.

What a man!

When he was shot, I felt my hair stand on end, my scalp prickle, then my life flashed through my mind, things that happened to me in my early youth, then a cold sweat and my senses went completely blank.

I felt like fainting. But when I saw that man die he put the backbone right back in my body, and I said to myself: "Tam, if you get out of this ye're coming back to have another go."[54]

Donald Renton, another Scot and the company's commissar, saw Dickinson's death as a heroic example to be followed:

At the end of this valley there was a sharp turn and here Ted Dickinson was executed. Now Ted was an Australian by origin. He had been very, very active in the Jewish Ex-Servicemen's Movement for Peace in East London. He was a comrade of outstanding ability in military terms and in being able to lift and rouse people in the most difficult conditions.

---

[53] Baxell, *British Battalion*, p. 234.
[54] Daniel Gray, *Homage to Caledonia: Scotland and the Spanish Civil War*, Edinburgh, 2009, p. 59; MacDougall, *Voices from the Spanish Civil War*, p. 48. The reference to the friendship between Dickinson and Bloomfield is from *Tribune*, 6 July 1966, p. 7.

> *Well, the Fascists sorted this man out as a very, very obvious leader of men. A Fascist officer pointed at Ted and pointed at a tree. They carried through a form of execution with rifles lined up only a few inches from the head of the person so that the whole effect is to blow the complete top of the head off.*
>
> *Ted before dying gave us all the Republican salute. "Salud, comrades", said Ted, and we responded in like manner. Inspired by his example, frightened though we were, expecting the same thing to happen to us, at least we felt it was absolutely necessary to carry forward the splendid example, if necessity arose, that Ted had displayed in his last few minutes.*[55]

James Maley, a Glasgow communist, recalled that all the captives thought they would be shot:

> *Mr Dickinson was placed three yards away from two soldiers, and when he had given the Spanish salute, his brains were blown out. We all thought that we would share the same fate, but the officer in charge of the soldiers marched us away from the spot.*[56]

Dickinson has no known grave.

Maley's view was that the Moors believed their prisoners to be Russian and were going to execute all of them.[57] It was only when a German officer recognised them as British that they were spared, perhaps to be used as fodder for propaganda or out of concern that an outrage, like the mass execution of British prisoners of war, might threaten the sustainability of Britain's policy of non-intervention.

The killing of prisoners, especially officers, was a feature of the Spanish Civil War. The savagery had been established with the massacres and atrocities that occurred in the very first days of the uprising. The British may have been shocked by the killing of Dickinson and other prisoners at Jarama, but became accustomed to the convention and practiced it themselves. The English communist poet and writer Miles Tomalin

---

[55] MacDougall, *Voices from the Spanish Civil War*, pp. 26-7.
[56] Gray, *Homage to Caledonia*, p. 59.
[57] Willy Maley (ed), *Our Fathers Fought Franco*, Edinburgh, 2023, p. 36.

served from May 1937 to December 1938. In August 1937, after taking Quinto as part of the assault on Belchite, he wrote in his diary:

> A bunch of Fascists held out in the church long after the village was ours... Thirteen men surrendered; five officers remained, knowing that they would not save their lives by giving in. Officers are shot. What else can you do? Every convinced Fascist alive adds to the danger in which their kind has placed the world.[58]

The No. 2 Company prisoners were menaced by Moors who gestured with their knives that they were, as Maley put it, "going to cut the privates off us".[59] The men were tied together by their thumbs with field telephone wire that cut into their flesh and marched off to a brutal captivity. Kept in crowded, filthy cells, the men were soon infested with lice. Their heads were shaved, they were interrogated and regularly beaten. Many became ill. Maley recalled the experience:

> Well, we were nine to a cell. And eh, it was one big dish of food. And we all ate out of it with our hands. And there was a wee toilet in the corner that you couldn't flush. And you couldn't wash your hands. And there was no toilet paper. And the nine of us ate with our hands out of that dish all the time it came in. There was nothing to drink, it was a thick, a sort of mass of whatever it was, but we all ate off our hands. Hands were ... which proves you can do a lot of things when you're hungry.[60]

There was also psychological torment, with the prisoners taunted by Italian fascists who would bring their senoritas with them to watch the Moroccan guards beat the captives.[61] The men were put to work digging pits for mass graves for those prisoners who were executed. Each afternoon they were told *"manana todos muertos* – tomorrow morning you all die".[62]

The *Daily Mail* obtained a photograph of the men standing on the back

---

[58] Brome, *International Brigades*, p. 220.
[59] Transcript of Maley, IWM 11947, Reel 2, available at: https://willymaley.scot/2020/11/07/james-maleys-memories-of-spain-in-1937/
[60] Maley, *Our Fathers*, pp. 36-7.
[61] Ibid., pp. 70-1.
[62] Gray, *Homage to Caledonia*, p. 60.

of a truck. The paper ran a patronising article claiming the men, who were staunchly ideological in their commitment to the Republic, were "misguided and hapless". The article did though provide comfort to the prisoners' families who now knew they were alive.[63] A propaganda newsreel was made showing the men lined up and being given food and cigarettes. When the camera stopped filming, the guards took the cigarettes back.[64]

In May, the prisoners were subjected to a show trial. Most were sentenced to long terms of imprisonment, but a number, including Fry and James Rutherford, a 19-year-old Scottish miller, received capital sentences – they were condemned to die in Spain. Renton said of Fry: "His shrug of the shoulders was an eloquent testimony to the fact that he could die as Dickinson had died."[65] Shortly after the trial, a prisoner swap for a group of Italian fascists held by the Republic was arranged. The British prisoners were fingerprinted and signed statements pledging not to return to Spain. In another flurry of fascist propaganda, they were issued with new suits, shoes and a "pretty senorita" handed them 500 francs as they were transported to the French border and released.[66]

Reaction to Dickinson's death

News of Dickinson's death came with the arrival of the prisoners in Britain. Hailing Dickinson as a hero in the fight against fascism, the men gave interviews to the press recounting their brutal experiences as prisoners of war. Rutherford, from Edinburgh, said that the prisoners had been punched and bitten, and gave another account of Dickinson's death:

> *A man called Dickinson, who was in command of the company, was put up against a tree and his head blown off.*

---

[63] Ibid., p. 61.
[64] https://www.youtube.com/watch?v=ctcA_PJQ_Ls; Maley, *Our Fathers*, p. 118.
[65] *Daily Worker*, 9 November 1937, p. 2.
[66] *Liverpool Echo*, 1 June 1937, p. 4.

*It was sheer brutal murder.*⁶⁷

In London, Harry Pollitt, in an editorial in the *Daily Worker*, hailed Dickinson as one of the bravest fighters the British Battalion had ever produced. He drew a sharp contrast between Dickinson's heroism and the perfidy and weakness of Sir Anthony Eden, Britain's Foreign Secretary:

> *Eden and Dickinson. It is a sin to mention them in the same breath. Only to show the difference between the supporters of Fascism and those whose hatred of Fascism is only smothered when they are murdered in cold blood.*

The *Daily Worker* returned repeatedly to Dickinson's death over the following months. He was a "heroic leader", "one of the best and bravest fighters in the International Brigades" and a "magnificent leader" whose death was "cold-blooded murder".⁶⁸ In mid-1937, when the outcome of the war was yet to be decided, articles such as these usually included appeals for funds to support the Republic's war effort.

As none of the initial British reports mentioned Dickinson's Australian connection, it took a further two months for news of his death to reach Australia. The news came from Ron Hurd, a Melbourne seaman and International Brigader, in a cabled news report. Hurd had been injured but not captured at Jarama and had received an eyewitness description of Dickinson's execution from a Liverpool docker, James Pugh, who told him that 40 British volunteers were captured with Dickinson with twelve being shot at random. According to Hurd:

> *[Dickinson] muttered "If we'd 10,000 Australian bushmen here, we'd wipe up these _____ in three weeks." Either this remark or Dickinson's formidable physique attracted the attention of the rebels, who ordered him to step out of the ranks. He strode forward 12 paces to the nearest tree, and turned around and shook his fist at the rebels, shouting: "So long, boys! Keep your chins up!" Three rebels then advanced*

---

⁶⁷ *Evening Telegraph and Post*, 1 June 1937, p. 1.
⁶⁸ *Daily Worker*, 5 June 1937, p. 1; 8 June 1937, p. 3; 16 August 1937, p. 1; 24 August 1937, p. 2; 8 September 1937, p. 11.

*and blew off the top of his head.*⁶⁹

The additional flourish about the military worth of Australians was new and had not featured in the reports published in the British newspapers. In Australia, Dickinson's death made headlines around the country. He was described as being a former member of the IWW who had been closely associated with the trade unions in Sydney. Many reports emphasised Dickinson's bravery as a particularly Australian characteristic. In Sydney, the *Sun* said "Defiant to Last: Australian Knew How to Die"; the *Newcastle Sun* stated "Australian Shot in Spain – Defiant Shout When Taken Prisoner"; the *West Australian* proclaimed it as "An Australian's Bravery". ⁷⁰ The reports noted Dickinson's impressive physique and speculated that his height and strength may have been a factor in the fascists' decision to kill him.

In Adelaide, the *News* reported his death under the headline "Spanish Rebel Troops Shoot Former Adelaide Radical". The article provided a heroic account of his execution, but contained the incorrect statement that Dickinson had been the Adelaide secretary of the Communist Party. Unnamed union sources said that Dickinson was a "man of revolutionary outlook but possessing intellectual attainments". They said that, while they might have disagreed with his tactics, they "admired his courage and ability". He was an "upstanding man, who commanded attention wherever he went".⁷¹

The *Workers' Weekly* immediately proclaimed Dickinson as a "hero of the Australian labour movement" and noted that he was "a brilliant and energetic speaker", "a great personality" and "a steadfast defender of liberty and peace". The paper's front page featured an illustration titled "Farewell, Comrade!" that depicted Dickinson's defiance as he was executed by helmeted gunmen tagged as hate, murder, fascist butchery and terror. The report said he was shot while fighting for democracy and peace.⁷²

---

⁶⁹ *West Australian*, 21 August 1937, p. 19.
⁷⁰ *The Sun*, 20 August 1937, p. 1; *Newcastle Sun*, 20 August 1937, p. 7; *West Australian*, 21 August 1937, p. 19.
⁷¹ *News*, 23 August 1937, p. 10.
⁷² *The Workers' Weekly*, 24 August 1937, p. 4; 27 August 1937, p. 1.

Photo 9: "Farewell, Comrade!" The *Workers' Weekly* illustrates the news of Dickinson's execution. (SEARCH Foundation/State Library of NSW)

In Melbourne, Dickinson's widow Myrtle, unaware that he had travelled to Spain, read of his death in the newspapers. She wrote to the commandant at the headquarters of the International Brigades:

98 Lewisham Rd
Prahran S1
Melbourne, Victoria
Australia

Commandant
Headquarters International Brigade

Dear Sir

I am writing re an article I saw in the paper, of the death of Edward Alexander Dickinson. I am Mr Dickinson's wife.

I was wondering if you could give me any particulars in regards to his death, also whether he left any message or provision for myself & child.

If you could let me know I would be very much obliged.

Wishing you the best of luck in your great fight.

Yours truly
M. Dickinson. [73]

There is no record of her receiving a reply.

There is also no record of the reactions of Dickinson's old IWW comrades Reeve and McNeill to the news of his death, but McNeill would soon follow Dickinson's example and leave for Spain.

As in Britain, Dickinson's story became a staple of Australian fundraising and publicity campaigns in support of the Republic. In 1938, the Spanish Relief Committee published a booklet, *Australians in Spain* by Nettie Palmer. The booklet said that Spain's fight was the world's fight, and that the people who had answered the call were "Internationalist" Australians who were "followers of the finest traditions of a liberty-loving people". Dickinson had acted with the "courage and enthusiasm" typical of members of the IWW. The booklet also recorded the death of Jack Newman, a seaman from Port Adelaide, killed in the Battle of

---

[73] RGASPI 545/6/546/53.

Jarama. Newman was, according to Hurd, "the most popular man in the battalion".[74] His death occurred, according to one eye witness, when he was shot "plum through the centre of his helmet".[75]

A foreword to the publication was provided by Ricardo Baeza, the Consul General for Spain, who bitterly criticised the policy of non-intervention. He said that it was denying the Spanish government the ability to defend itself by blocking the purchase of arms and ammunition. He warned that the logical outcome of the policy being followed by the democracies was that "when they at last feel in the mood to fight they may find it is already too late".[76]

Despite his war wounds, Hurd undertook a national speaking tour that involved addressing 500 meetings, including some held in remote mining towns. Hurd, in his gravelly voice, was known to call "a spade a spade and a Fascist a Fascist".[77] He spoke about the war, fascism, praised the service of the Australian nurses and sought financial support for the cause. Dickinson's fate formed a key part of Hurd's narrative.

> *"Ted" Dickinson, to those of us who knew him, was one of the most likeable personalities one could meet. Tall, well-built and strikingly handsome. With unlimited courage and endurance, he proved the ideal leader in any emergency.*
>
> *Ted's diabolical murder at the hands of Franco's butchers has been avenged a hundred-fold, but we Australians, members of our mighty trade unions, should thrill with pride in the knowledge that he was a product of them.*
>
> *He was second-in-command of No.2 Company of our Battalion, approximately 40 of whom were captured late in the afternoon of February 13, having been trapped in a flanking movement by a battalion of Moors. Fourteen of these lads were immediately murdered,*

---

[74] Palmer, *Australians in Spain*, [Sydney, 1938?], pp.18-20 and 30.
[75] Letter from Rex Morgan to Amirah Inglis, 3 October 1992, Amirah Inglis Collection, Noel Butlin Archives, Australian National University.
[76] Palmer, *Australians in Spain*, p. 2.
[77] *Workers' Star*, 3 December 1937, p. 1.

> *Ted being the first. They were first lined up and this brave man was told to fall out back to a tree. Three riflemen stood ten feet from him.*
>
> *Ted, great man that he was, conscious he was about to die, showed the fascist blackguards how a son of the people could meet death. He defiantly gave the "Red Front" salute and calmly cried, "Salud Comrades, keep your chins up."*
>
> *With that the top of his head was blown off.*[78]

Hurd's tour was effective and may even have convinced some who were less than sympathetic to the cause. The newsletter of the Western Australia Branch of the Returned Soldiers' League, *Listening Post*, noted Hurd's powers as a public speaker and found the fighting spirit of the Australians in Spain to be in the revered Anzac tradition:

> *Whatever one may think of the merits of the cause they are serving, it is gratifying to learn that the old strain of Gallipoli and Pozieres is running true to form.*[79]

Not everyone was as impressed. An editorial in the *Southern Cross*, the official organ of the Catholic church in South Australia, berated the Australian Broadcasting Commission and questioned its competence for giving Hurd time in its programming.

> *Just why the ABC considered it advisable to invite Mr. Hurd (or did Mr. Hurd invite himself?) to enlighten on the iniquities of Fascists in Spain is not clear. We think that we are entitled to know.*[80]

While Hurd used Dickinson's tragic fate as the cornerstone of his address, he was careful to maintain the orthodox CPA line and included a denunciation of Trotskyists and the POUM in his commentary. He blamed Trotskyists for creating divisions between the socialist and communist soldiers, for abandoning their posts and allowing towns to fall to the fascists.[81]

---

[78] *Workers' Star*, 7 January 1938, p. 2.
[79] *Listening Post*, 17 December 1937, p. 15.
[80] *Southern Cross*, 17 December 1937, p. 10.
[81] *Workers' Voice*, 29 January 1938, p. 2.

Back in Spain, after more ferocious fighting at Jarama, the Republic's defences held. The fascists did not take control of the road between Madrid and Valencia and a stalemate settled upon the front. While the fascists looked to some territory won as a marker of success, their strategic objective had been to encircle and isolate Madrid and in this they were thwarted. Jarama was a victory for the Republic and Madrid remained in its hands until the war's end. The battle had been fought at great cost, with casualties estimated at 20,000 for the fascists and up to 25,000 for the Republicans.[82] Though most of the dead and injured were Spanish, the International Brigades made a crucial contribution to the Republic's success. Casualties had been correspondingly high.

Wintringham blamed Overton for the losses taken by the British Battalion. In his 1939 memoir, *English Captain*, he lambasted Overton as thoroughly unfit to be a soldier:

> *A fool, a romantic, a bluffer who wanted to be courageous but had lived too easily, too softly.... I cannot be angry now; though I can grieve still for the lives wasted by his cowardice.*[83]

Even those, like Gurney, who were more charitable, conceded that Overton was "hopelessly inadequate" to the task of leadership and "had failed in a position of responsibility".[84] Aitken, the commissar, said that Overton feared being shot by his own side because of what he had done:

> *He was scared, he said to me, he was scared that if he went back into the line someone would shoot him because of what he had done in the first days.*[85]

It may not have been a baseless fear. Overton went missing during the Battle of Brunete and was never seen again.

A number of the men who had been captured with Dickinson disregarded the pledges they had signed on their release and returned to Spain. Bloomfield kept the promise he had made to himself and

---

[82] Thomas, *Spanish Civil War*, p. 380.
[83] Wintringham, *English Captain*, p. 229.
[84] Gurney, *Crusade*, p. 82.
[85] Aitken, IWM 10357, Reel 2.

returned in early 1938, fought in the Battle of the Ebro on Hill 481 and survived the war. Rutherford and Fry, the two Scots who had been condemned to die, were not so fortunate. Rutherford was captured again at Calaceite, near Teruel. He used the pseudonym "Jimmy Smalls" in an attempt to conceal his identity, but after being identified in the San Pedro de Cardena concentration camp as a returned prisoner of war he was executed.[86] The commander of No. 2 Company, Fry, was back in Spain within two months of his release from captivity. He left Edinburgh the day before his son was born. Appointed the commander of the British Battalion, he was killed in action at Fuentes de Ebro on 13 October 1937. The *Daily Worker* reported that "he died at the head of the battalion he was leading".[87] Copeman believed it was suicide:

> *Fry, in his first action, as soon as got to the line went straight over the bloody top, kept walking and he got killed. They just shot him down, - he committed suicide.*[88]

---

[86] Baxell, *British Battalion*, pp. 240-1.
[87] *Daily Worker*, 9 November 1937, p. 1.
[88] Copeman, IWM 794 Reel 2.

9

From Corrimal to Catalonia

Travelling from Australia to Spain in 1938 was not a straightforward matter as the Australian government had suspended the issue of passports for Spain. Further, anyone who made it to Britain had to contend with the British government's enforcement of the *Foreign Enlistment Act*, which applied to Australians, which made volunteering to fight for another power a criminal offence.[1] McNeill and Carter would have been fully aware they could not openly declare their intentions and that subterfuges would be necessary to get to Spain.

The first step in their journey was to take the train to Sydney and visit the CPA's Sydney office.[2] They left Wollongong on 9 March, just as Hitler was annexing Austria, an act that met without any serious response from the other nations of Europe. At the CPA's office they met Bill Young, who had first encountered Carter when they were both doing time in Long Bay prison. Young said that he too was there because he was interested in going to Spain. After a wait of several hours Bob McWilliams, the New South Wales secretary of the CPA, returned to the office.

McWilliams told them he had contacts among a group of visiting

---

[1] *Sydney Morning Herald*, 8 May 1937, p 17; Baxell, *British Battalion*, p. 32.
[2] Unless otherwise noted, this account of the journeys to Spain is drawn from oral history interviews. McNeill with WL; Joe Carter – Amirah Inglis, Amirah Inglis Collection, Noel Butlin Archives, Australian National University; Joe Carter – John Clements, Imperial War Museum, IWM 3812. The dates of shipping movements have been determined from the shipping news columns of newspapers.

British seamen who had just delivered a new ship, the *Iron Chieftain*, from Glasgow to Newcastle for BHP. They were to return to Britain as passengers on another ship, the *Orontes*, of the Orient Line.[3] Some of these seamen wanted to stay in Australia. They had made it known that their tickets and eligibility for the wages they'd be entitled to for the return trip (known as a brief or a book) were for sale at a price much lower than the standard fare to anyone who wanted to take on the task of impersonating them. But McNeill, Carter and Young were too late. The *Orontes* had departed at noon for Tasmania, with two other Australian volunteers having already taken the opportunity of buying the briefs. However, McWilliams told them that after visiting Tasmania, the ship would be calling at Melbourne and there were other seamen on board who were interested in selling their briefs.

Carter and Morcom on the *Orontes*

With that opportunity presenting itself, McNeill and Carter took the evening train to Melbourne. On board they met Bill Orr, the leader of the Miners' Federation, who had known Carter since his time in Lithgow during the Depression. Arriving in Melbourne, they declined the offer of a drink and instead asked Orr to introduce them at the CPA's Melbourne headquarters. There they met Tom Hills, a well-known waterfront activist, who invited them to stay at his place until the *Orontes* put into port.

When the ship arrived in Melbourne, Hills went aboard and found that one of the two volunteers who had boarded in Sydney had changed his mind. He had left the vessel and returned to Sydney, which had created suspicions about the other, Morcom, the veteran of the Adelaide Beef Riot and treasurer of the NSW CPA. Morcom had bought the brief of a seaman called Connor and did not want anyone else to attempt the same ploy as he felt it would attract unnecessary attention and cruel his own chances of success. In the hierarchy of the CPA, Morcom was much more senior than McNeill and Carter and his view held sway.

---

[3] Inglis, *Australians*, p. 130.

Thwarted, Carter, who had scrimped and lived frugally to save money for the journey, borrowed additional funds from the CPA in Melbourne on the understanding that it would be repaid by the CPA in Wollongong. With this money he bought a ticket and joined Morcom, who Carter felt to be a "very, very capable fellow", on the voyage as a fare paying passenger. Without the funds to buy a ticket McNeill was left in Melbourne, where he was soon joined by Young who had made his own way down from Sydney.

As a senior CPA official, Morcom set out on his journey with instructions from the Central Committee to "study military strategy and tactics as much as possible" so that, on his return, his understanding and experience could be placed at the disposal of the CPA. He had been keen to go to Spain since the conflict had started and, on his departure, thanked the party for letting him go. It was intended that he be a correspondent for the *Workers' Weekly*, which he described as the "official organ" of the Central Committee.[4]

With Carter and Morcom (posing as Connor) aboard, the *Orontes* departed Melbourne on 15 March. It called at Adelaide and then at Fremantle where joining it as passengers were Donald Bradman and the Australian cricket team, who were cruising to Britain for the 1938 Ashes tour.[5] The presence of the Australian cricketers meant the ship's journey to Europe was covered in great detail by the Australian press. Among other titbits, the press reported that Bradman came down with a sore throat and was confined to his cabin, the bowler Ted White had £15 stolen from clothes left in the changing room while he was taking a swim, and that the team enjoyed a sherry party with the ship's captain.

As was the custom, the ship called at several ports, including Colombo, where the Australian cricketers played a one-day match against the locals, and Aden, where the players visited a bazaar and viewed what were advertised as mermaids. In Egypt they toured the pyramids, while at Naples the cricketers visited Pompeii and were impressed by the grandeur of the smoking Vesuvius. They were amazed at the extensive

---

4   RGASPI 545/6/68/175/19-25; *Workers' Weekly*, 13 December 1938, p. 1.
5   *West Australian*, 22 March 1938, p. 15.

pro-Mussolini propaganda, with militaristic slogans like "Believe, Obey, Fight!" painted on almost every wall. The team witnessed the dictator's military might and saw warships, submarines, and squadrons of aircraft. Reaching France, the cricketers were guests at a reception in Nice and then entertained themselves by playing roulette in a Monte Carlo casino.[6]

Rather more seriously Morcom, who had "got the wind up" about being detected while posing as the seaman Connor, left the voyage at Toulon to make contact with the French Popular Front who he thought could get him into Spain. This improvisation proved successful and Morcom crossed the Pyrenees to arrive in Spain on 22 April. He was quickly identified as a "leading functionary of the CPA" and evaluated by the senior officers of the International Brigades to be a "very well-developed and experienced militant type".[7]

Carter stayed aboard the *Orontes* to arrive at Southampton on 20 April, disembarking the next day at London's Tilbury Docks. With only six shillings in his pocket, he decided to take advantage of the opportunity vacated by Morcom. Impersonating Connor, he collected £14 pounds in wages from BHP ("Brand new notes they were!"), telling the pay clerk that he had lost his papers in a drunken fight during the stop in Egypt. He then made contact with the Communist Party of Great Britain, presented his CPA credentials and left his suitcase with the Committee for Spanish Relief for safekeeping. Under the Communist Party's auspices, he travelled with a small group of Englishmen and Irishmen to Paris, where he passed a medical, then to Lyon and the border.

The group of volunteers, about eight in total, crossed into Spain by hiking over the Pyrenees. Halfway across, one of the group, an English taxi driver, sprained his ankle. Carter had to help carry him into Spain. On arrival they met with Spanish officials:

---

[6] *Daily News*, 14 April 1938, p. 5; *Daily Telegraph*, 15 April 1938, p.16, *The Age*, 16 April 1938, p. 11.
[7] RGASPI 545/6/68/175/19-25.

> You sat at a table and they gave you the option. "Righto, you want to sign? If you sign up you're here for the duration of the war or until you get killed. But it's not too late. If you decide to go back, we'll give you protection, right back to the border." And that's how fair they were, they gave you that option.

Having carried the taxi driver over the mountains, Carter was more than a little irritated to see his burden exercise the option to change his mind and return.

Carter arrived in Spain on 25 April, Anzac Day, and travelled through to Barcelona. He found it an attractive city as he described in a letter back to Wollongong:

> It is a beautiful town and it is a shame to see the wilful destruction done by the rebel forces. They bombed it about a week ago. We are on patrol in the hills looking for rebel observers. Believe me they are hills too. The chief food is horse flesh and beans.[8]

McNeill on the *Melbourne Star*

Stuck in Melbourne, McNeill and Young, with Hills' assistance, spent the next couple of weeks hunting around the Melbourne waterfront, trying and failing to secure spots as crew members on a ship departing for Britain. McNeill slept on the floor of Hills' home and persevered,[9] while an exasperated Young gave up and travelled to South Australia to try his chances from there. Eventually, McNeill and Hills met an Irish seaman who, after a few drinks, boasted that he had assisted a former heavyweight boxer, Colin Bell, to stowaway on a voyage to Australia. Having "blown his bags out" with this story, he agreed to help McNeill stowaway.

The *Melbourne Star* was due to sail in a few days. On 6 April, the afternoon of its departure, the Irishman had the "shivers" and was in "fear and trembling" about the undertaking he had made which he

---

[8] *Illawarra Mercury*, 2 September 1938, p. 5.
[9] Tom Hills - Wendy Lowenstein, NLA Bib ID 6094510.

could not keep. One of the ship's firemen, a man referred to only as Robbie, stepped in and undertook to manage McNeill's stowaway passage. McNeill paid him £5 for his trouble. It was McNeill's first time at sea and it would be an ordeal.

The *Melbourne Star*, of the Blue Star Line, had been launched in 1936. With a gross tonnage of 12,805 tons, it was a refrigerated freighter that transported agricultural produce, including cases of fruit and carcases of beef and lamb, from Australia and New Zealand to consumers in Britain. Although built and operated as a cargo ship, it also carried fare-paying passengers. A typical journey started in Melbourne, visited Fremantle, and then crossed the Indian Ocean to Africa with calls at Lourenco Marques (now Maputo), Natal, East London, Port Elizabeth and Cape Town, before steaming up the Atlantic to London.[10]

Photo 10 – To get to Spain, McNeill stowed away on the *Melbourne Star*. (Harry Issell, State Library of Victoria)

As there were four men in a cabin working across different shifts, the plan was that McNeill would always be able to find a bunk to occupy.

---

[10] Blue Star Line Brochure Australian Service ANZ No. 5 1/1/1938 – 15M, Fraser Darrah Collection.

He could mess with his new companions as well. On the first night at sea though, a young British stowaway was found aboard and placed under arrest. He was to be put off at Fremantle. After this incident, the other firemen no longer wanted to take the risk of accommodating McNeill and told him he'd have to find somewhere else. Despite this setback:

> *Robbie was an organiser and had plenty of guts. He escorted me down one flight of steps onto a second deck, lifted up a manhole and climbed down some steps, about 30 feet, into what was the tail end of the ship, where the bilges were. This was just inside from the screws; they were bilges but they were comparatively dry. I stayed there during the daylight hours, and at night time he lifted up the hatch and I came up and slept in his bunk. That went on for about five weeks.*[11]

McNeill would have breakfast in the mess, take some sandwiches for lunch and sit in the darkness by himself, listening to the thrumming of the engines for hour after hour, for 14 to 16 hours a day. It was, he said in Spain, like "solitary confinement with the roar of machinery the only company".[12] Before long, the ship's grapevine ensured that everyone, apart from those in authority, knew there was a stowaway on board. No one disclosed his presence even during episodes when the ship was thoroughly searched. At a stop in Africa, there was a scare about another potential stowaway.

> *My mate came bounding down the steps. He said to me "It's on now! You've got to get down there. They'll turn over everywhere."*
>
> *I said, "What's doing?"*
>
> *"There's a couple of Africans, Black Africans, come aboard and there's one bloke not been discovered. They'll turn over this place lock, stock and barrel until they find him."*
>
> *It turned out that half an hour later this bloke appears – so the panic was off. But I was down there just the same.*

---

[11] The account of McNeill's journey to Spain is from the WL interview.
[12] Letter from Phil Thorne to Nettie Palmer, 19 August 1938, Aileen Palmer collection, 6759, Box 1, National Library of Australia.

On another occasion, the problem was a canary.

> One of the crew in my cabin had taken a canary on board, and you were not supposed to take them outside Australia or bring them into England, and all this sort of business. So, there was a search on about that and I can remember the bloke dashing down, opening it up and letting the canary fly through the cabin. This was about 1000 miles at sea. Poor thing.

After a journey of five weeks, the *Melbourne Star* arrived in London at King Albert's dock on 11 May.[13] One of the firemen, a Liverpool Irishman that McNeill remembered as a "real good type of bloke", took him ashore, flashed a pass through the gate and gave McNeill the fare to Covent Garden. Arriving there on a bus, a policeman directed him to King Street where the Communist Party's headquarters were located. Here he hoped to meet Pollitt, the leader of the party.

From England to Spain

With a letter of introduction from the CPA, McNeill arrived to find the office closed. The only person present was the manager of the bookshop and he was closing up for the day. McNeill knew no one in London and had almost no money, so the manager of the bookshop offered to take him home. The pair departed for a Communist Party branch meeting in Holland Park where McNeill met a man who had a brother working at Port Kembla.

The next day McNeill returned to the Communist Party's offices to find Pollitt away, but in his stead he met Willie Gallacher MP, the communist member for the Scottish constituency of West Fife in the House of Commons. Gallacher escorted him to an office in Litchfield Street where recruitment for the International Brigades was handled. There he met Robbie Robson, who was managing the process and who arranged for McNeill to have a medical examination by a pair of doctors.

The voyage, made under such circumstances, had left McNeill emaciated

---

[13] The *Melbourne Star* was to have an eventful life as an anti-fascist freighter. During the Second World War it was damaged while participating in convoy runs to relieve Malta and was eventually sunk by U-129 in the Atlantic. See Taffrail, *Blue Star Line at War 1939-1945*, Slough, 1973, pp. 143-5.

and weak and the doctors were hesitant to clear him. McNeill admitted that he "hadn't fared the best" during the journey from Australia. He told the doctors that he "wasn't in the best of nick but would improve with a bit of food and fresh air". With that assurance, the doctors passed him fit for service.

With his years of party service recognised, McNeill was put in charge of a group of eight and left the next day for France, travelling on a weekend ticket. In Paris, he met the contacts he had been given and was subjected to another medical examination. This examination was by a German Jewish doctor who had fled from Hitler. This doctor found McNeill frail, underweight and under-nourished and would only pass him as fit to serve if he agreed to stay in Paris for a further week, "on good food, plenty of milk, lay off the wine and women, and build myself up".

The others in the group left Paris the following day. McNeill was allocated a billet and given meal tickets for a local seamen's restaurant. After a week "knocking around" Paris, he gained some weight and was feeling stronger. He was called to a briefing with a large group of volunteers which included another Australian, Kevin Rebbechi, and English volunteers George Wheeler and Jack Jones (who would later become a powerful British trade union leader). An instructor who could speak 13 languages undertook a roll call which showed that there were men from countries all over Europe. When Australia was called out, everyone looked around at McNeill– they wanted to find out who the Australian was.

The men were then given their instructions: they were to arrive at the train station separately, not to gather in large groups, not to converse, and to bundle any belongings in brown paper bags that could be tucked under their arms. McNeill thought the last instruction "was the stupidest thing imaginable because it was a dead giveaway. There were 70 or 80 people and all with brown parcels?" The men travelled from Paris and alighted together at Arles. From there they were bussed to the French border town of Perpignan that had decorated a municipal garden with a "great big dirty hammer and sickle, about twenty feet in circumference, right in the centre. It was a communist town".

They waited in a communist-owned hotel and were then moved to a farm a couple of miles from the border. As the fascists knew about this route and had shot at previous groups, another subterfuge was attempted to confuse any hostile observers. A dozen or so local people mingled with the group and McNeill had a "little blonde" snuggle up to him during the bus trip. Once at the farm they were fortified with a meal of country food and robust French wine. After darkness fell a Spaniard appeared, told the men to take off their shoes and put on the gaiters they'd been issued with. They were to cross into Spain by hiking over the Pyrenees. Instructions were strict. They were to walk in single file, three feet apart. There was to be no smoking, no talking and they weren't to make the slightest noise. They had to crawl across a railway bridge on their stomachs, then start to ascend the mountains. It was a tough slog. Four of the men were so exhausted by the ordeal that they had to be carried. McNeill remembered:

> *You'd go up one peak and you'd think, "Well, thank Christ that's over." Then in front of you there'd be another huge valley, and another peak a bit higher. And that went on time after time.*

At one point in the trek the group paused to rest. A nightingale's performance of birdsong, high in the moonlit mountains, left the men enchanted. After an overnight trek, the group arrived on Spanish soil. They were taken to a peasant's house where they met several Spanish soldiers, shared some cigarettes and washed in a mountain stream. Trucks transported the men to Figueras where they were quartered in an old monastery decorated with an arch that read *Resistir es Vencer* (To resist is to conquer). Their first Spanish meal was a tasty macaroni, enjoyed with a sour red wine.[14]

At Figueras, McNeill was registered in the British Battalion by Arthur Olorenshaw, a musician, member of the Communist Party of Great Britain and the battalion's adjutant. McNeill presented his CPA credentials, and Olorenshaw noted his long record of political and union activism and assessed him as being a "good working-class type" who seemed to be "thoroughly reliable" with a "good political

---

[14] George Wheeler, *To Make the People Smile Again*, Newcastle upon Tyne, 2003, pp. 42-44.

understanding".[15] He was placed in the battalion's Machine Gun Company No. 5, soon to be re-organised into Company No. 2, under the command of Jack Nalty, once an officer with the Irish Republican Army.

Photo 11: Jim McNeill in Spain, 1938. (Illawarra Museum)

Photo 12: Jim McNeill in Spain, 1938. (Illawarra Museum)

---

[15] RGASPI 545/6/68/203.

Bill Young

Arriving in Adelaide, Young continued with his attempt to get to Spain. William John (Bill) Young was born on 18 October 1900 at Kingston, Tasmania, to Douglas and Susanna, a family that managed to combine Douglas' membership of the Labor Party with Susanna's strict Methodism. She disapproved of dancing, gambling, drinking, extra-marital sex and Papists. Bill received seven years of public schooling, before starting his working life in a jam factory.[16]

On 14 September 1918, just one month short of his eighteenth birthday, Young enlisted in the Australian Imperial Force at Hobart. He had blue eyes, brown hair, stood five feet nine and a half inches and weighed 146 pounds. His time in the army was short, as he was discharged on 1 November 1918 following the discovery of a "misstatement as to age" on his attestation paper. He had lied and rather than wait a month until he was 18, made himself a year older than he was.[17]

After this debacle, Young left Hobart for the mainland where he worked in factories, mines and as a timber worker. A member of the Australian Workers' Union, he joined the Railwaymen's Union when constructing lines in Victoria. He returned to the family home in Hobart in 1925 with a pregnant Adora Shaw who was accompanied by her own son, Kevin. Later that year Bill and Adora's son, Keith William (Billy or Keithy) Young, was born.

Young found employment at the Risdon zinc smelter as a stripper, a hard and dirty job removing zinc from electrolytic plates. The Risdon smelter was, at the time, the world's largest. The family lived in a company-owned house in Tower Road, New Town, but there was hostility between Susanna and Adora, and the marriage failed in 1928. Departing Tasmania, Adora took Kevin, but left Billy with his father. Soon after, Young and Billy left Hobart for Sydney. Billy never saw his

---

[16] Lynette Silver and Billy Young, *Billy: My Life as a Teenage POW*, Binda, 2016, p. 4; and RGASPI 545/6/218.

[17] NAA: B2455.

mother again and believed she died in Sydney.[18]

Young rented a room for himself and Billy in a terrace on Albion Street, Surry Hills, then a crime-ridden slum district adjoining Sydney's Central station, and began living on his wits. With his brother he ran a billiard hall cum SP bookies' operation, pitched himself as a street photographer, and peddled fruit and vegetables on the streets. He took work as an ironworker when it was available. As the Depression deepened, Young fell into a criminal milieu and became well-known to the courts.

His first prison sentence was at Cootamundra in October 1928, a penalty of seven days for vagrancy. A more serious offence occurred in April 1931 when he attempted to cash a £100 cheque. The cheque was in the name of Carey, a tea broker, and it was forged. Young was found guilty of uttering. He told the court that his wife was dead, and he had a five-year-old son to care for: "I haven't twopence to my name. I did not go around with a gang of men." The judge noted this, agreed that Young was not one of those men who defrauded small shopkeepers and women, but still sentenced him to six months' on each charge, to be served concurrently. His mug shot shows him handsome in a shabby suit and hat; his facial expressions betray no sign of him being perturbed about being in custody. Now 30, he was fully grown at 5 feet ten and 1/8 inches and had filled out to a solid 168 pounds. His hair was still brown and in the years since 1918 his eyes had apparently changed from blue to brown.[19]

More short-term imprisonments followed over the next two years, with Young twice convicted for stealing. He served three months in both 1932 and 1933 for habitually consorting with reputed criminals. In Long Bay he met Carter, and the two idled their time away while working in the prison workshop making coir mats.[20] Billy was only five

---

[18] Silver and Young, *Billy*, p. 6.

[19] Silver and Young, *Billy*, p. 9; NSW State Archives RNCG-617-1-[17/1500]-25675; *Sydney Morning Herald*, 9 May 1931, p. 6.

[20] NSW State Archives RNCG-617-1-[17/1500]-25675; Joe Carter – Amirah Inglis, Amirah Inglis Collection, Noel Butlin Archives, Australian National University; Joe Carter-Laurie Aarons, Mitchell Library, State Library of New South Wales, MLOH 628/5.

at the time of his father's incarceration for uttering. Each time his father went away Billy was placed in an orphanage or cared for by friends who ran a stand at Paddy's Markets. When Young returned, he gave Billy a shiny new coin, telling him he had found it under a cabbage.[21]

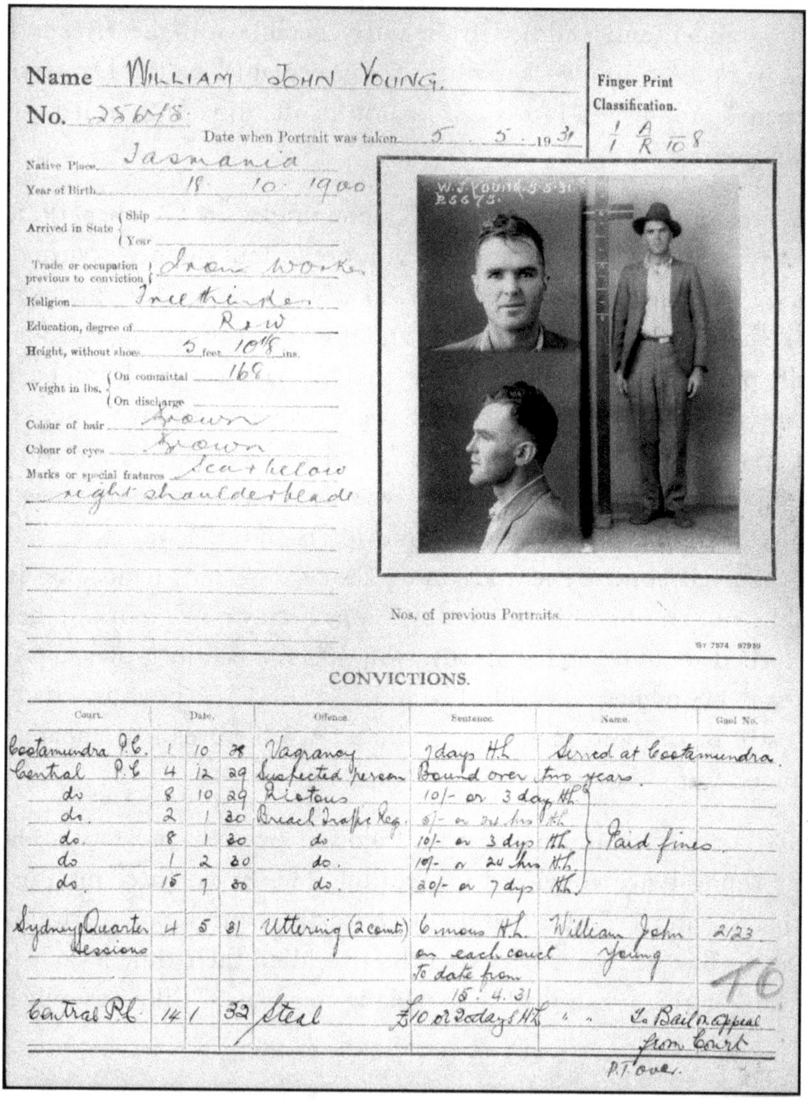

Name WILLIAM JOHN YOUNG.
No. 25673
Date when Portrait was taken 5 . 5 . 1931
Finger Print Classification. 1/1 A/R 10 8
Native Place Tasmania
Year of Birth 18 . 10 . 1900
Arrived in State { Ship / Year }
Trade or occupation previous to conviction Iron worker
Religion Freethinker
Education, degree of R & W
Height, without shoes 5 feet 10⅛ ins.
Weight in lbs. { On committal 168 / On discharge }
Colour of hair Brown
Colour of eyes Brown
Marks or special features Scar below right shoulderblade

Nos. of previous Portraits

CONVICTIONS.

Court.	Date.			Offence.	Sentence.	Name.	Gaol No.
Cootamundra P.C.	1	10	28	Vagrancy	7 days H.L.	Served at Cootamundra.	
Central P.C.	4	12	29	Suspected person	Bound over two years.		
do	8	10	29	Riotous	10/- or 3 days H.L.	Paid fines.	
do.	2	1	30	Breach Traffic Reg.	5/- or 24 hrs H.L.		
do.	8	1	30	do	10/- or 3 dys H.L.		
do	1	2	30	do.	10/- or 24 hrs H.L.		
do.	15	7	30	do.	20/- or 7 dys H.L.		
Sydney Quarter Sessions	4	5	31	Uttering (2 counts)	6 mons H.L. on each count to date from 15 . 4 . 31	William John Young	2/23
Central P.C.	14	1	32	Steal	£10 or 20 days H.L.	" " To Bail on appeal from Court	

P.T. over.

Photo 13 – Bill Young's prison record. (Museums of History New South Wales – State Archives Collection)

[21] Silver and Young, *Billy*, p. 17.

During these years, Young also joined Jimmy Sharman's Boxing Troupe, a travelling entertainment which was a feature for decades at agricultural shows in country towns and annual shows in the big cities. It provided a line-up of boxers who took on all-comers in prize-fights that the audience bet on. Boxing paid well, at least a pound a fight, and honed Young's fight skills. He used those skills in street brawls with the New Guard. McNeill remembered that Young was good with his fists and "could deal it out, left and right" when the New Guard attacked CPA and Unemployed Workers' Movement meetings. Young was broad shouldered and as "strong as a lion". He joined the Unemployed Workers' Movement in Glebe and was active in its efforts to assist those faced with evictions.[22]

Young joined the CPA in February 1935, having convinced the party that his days of petty crime were over. Billy remembered his father as an "enthusiastic zealot" whose faith was "immediate and absolute". His heroes were Lenin and Stalin, and he became a dedicated seller of the *Workers' Weekly*. As the global political situation worsened, he pasted posters calling for a boycott of Japanese-made goods and daubed the walls of the Ultimo power station with "Hands off Abyssinia". With Billy as his lookout, he painted the Spanish Republican slogan "They shall not pass" on a wall near the Wentworth Park greyhounds racing track.[23]

Young supported the seamen's strikes of 1936 and in 1937 was elected the chair of the West Sydney Section of the CPA. When the CPA made it known that volunteers for Spain were required, Young needed little persuasion. He sent Billy to his grandmother in Hobart and went, as he put it, to "offer my services to the Spanish government in their fight against Fascism which I hate".[24]

In Adelaide, Young haunted the wharves of Port Adelaide seeking a vacancy aboard a ship so he could work his way to Europe. He heard from one seaman that there were two others about to abandon their

---

[22] Ibid., pp. 19-24; WL interview.
[23] Silver and Young, *Billy*, p. 24.
[24] RGASPI 545/6/218.

posts on a cargo ship, the *Port Nicholson*, but on the morning of 9 April, the date of its scheduled departure, the two were still aboard. Determined to finally get away, Young learnt the ship's layout from his contact. He made it aboard, but then could not locate his friend. He snuggled himself into a coal heap used to fire the boilers and waited for the ship to get to sea.

After several days, he emerged, bewhiskered and blackened, and tried, in a voice made croaky by the coal dust, to speak to the trimmer tending to the boilers. The startled man had been on a heavy drinking binge while in Adelaide and had to be assured by Young that he was only a stowaway seeking a drink of water and was neither a demon nor an apparition caused by the *delirium tremens*. Young was cleaned up, given a shower and overalls, and presented to the captain. The skipper, after giving Young a lecture on the dangers of stowing away, offered him a job. The two seamen who had been threatening to desert their posts had done so just as the ship was departing. This had left the ship's establishment two short, so the captain was keen to have Young as part of the crew. His engagement was backdated to the date of departure from Port Adelaide; that is, Young received wages for the days he spent hiding in the coal heap.[25]

Arriving in England in late May, Young made his way to the Communist Party's offices in London to be told that the next contingent of volunteers would not be departing for at least a week. Forsaking sightseeing, Young spent his days selling the *Daily Worker* on the streets of London. He eventually arrived in Spain on 14 June 1938.[26]

Margot Miller

McNeill, Morcom, Carter and Young were not the only Australians in Spain. Some 70 Australians went to support the Spanish Republic, although the exact number is not known. Women provided medical and nursing services or carried out administrative and support roles. One,

---

[25] WL interview; *Workers' Weekly*, 30 August 1938, p. 3.
[26] WL interview; RGASPI 545/6/68/175/178.

Margot Miller, a 24-year-old Sydney copywriter, survived being shot in both legs on the Aragon front when she went to aid a wounded soldier. She shared her ordeal with the *Australian Women's Weekly*:

> We were crossing an open space behind the line when rebel machine guns opened on us. I felt a terrible crack on the leg and stumbled into a ditch, which was much too shallow for comfort. Militia men from the front trench crawled over with a stretcher. They rolled me on to it and ran back in a hail of bullets. Death seemed so inevitable that I was too numb to be frightened.[27]

In later years, under her married name of Margot Bennett, she wrote a series of crime thrillers that were praised by Graham Greene and Julian Symons. She maintained her interest in left-wing politics and supported the Campaign for Nuclear Disarmament. She died in 1980.[28]

Jack Garcia

Members of Australia's Spanish community also returned to fight for democracy in their homeland. Jesus Garcia Montero, known as Jack Garcia, had arrived in Australia in 1915 from Asturias. He laboured on a railway in the Northern Territory before moving to Innisfail, Queensland, where he worked as a boilermaker at the Goondi Sugar Mill. Taking six months leave from his job, he paid his own fare to Spain. He was injured in battle and returned home, where a welcome reception was organised by the Innisfail Spanish Relief Committee.[29] The *Johnstone River Advocate and Innisfail News* provided an account of his remarks to the gathering:

> Mr Garcia spoke of the very heroic part taken by the civilians behind the lines. Food was terribly scarce, and young and old were suffering in silence, so that the men at the front could have sufficient food and clothes to be able to resist the enemy, which was supplied with everything they

---

[27] *Australian Women's Weekly*, 26 December 1936, p. 11.
[28] *The Times*, 6 December 1980, p. 14.
[29] Inglis, *Australians*, p. 116.

required. He said if only people would realise that the sum of 2/- per week would feed and clothe thousands of children and old people they would no doubt sacrifice a few drinks or a pleasure trip now and again.

Mr Garcia was overcome, and could not continue any longer.[30]

Jack Franklyn

Most of those who went to fight were working-class men like Dickinson and McNeill, who had lived tough lives on the economic margins of society. Many, but not all, were members of the CPA, their lives scarred by the despair and humiliation that the Depression's unemployment inflicted on the Australian working class. They knew little of Spain's history, culture or economy, and could not speak either Spanish or Catalan. As internationalists, they straightforwardly comprehended the war as part of the global struggle against fascism.

Jack Franklyn was one of these men. Born in Blackburn, England, on 4 August 1897,[31] he received a primary school education. During the Great War he joined the British Army and served with the Duke of Cornwall's Light Infantry on the Western Front.

After the war, he went to sea. His voyages included trips to Canada and the USA, where he was imprisoned for 17 months in Bellefonte, Pennsylvania. He told friends his time behind bars was due to a case of mistaken identity. According to the story, he was thumbing a ride and an old Ford stopped to pick him up. At the next town they were greeted by police, with guns drawn, who stopped the car. Its occupants had robbed a gas station before they decided to give Franklyn a lift. The perpetrators tried to convince the judge that Franklyn was not part of the robbery, but protestations from them and from Franklyn himself

---

[30] *Johnstone River Advocate and Innisfail News*, 38 June 1938, p. 1.
[31] Franklyn sometimes gave his place of birth as Sydney, but at the 1945 inquest into his death it was stated that he had been born in Blackburn, England.

were to no avail and he had to serve time.³²

Photo 14: Jack Franklyn, 1938. (Australian National University Archives Centre)

Released in 1928, Franklyn made his way to Australia, where he joined the CPA and the Friends of the Soviet Union in 1933. In addition to the usual fare of Marx, Engels and Lenin, his political thinking drew on his reading of Upton Sinclair, Joseph McCabe, Voltaire, John Strachey and Robert G. Ingersoll. Much of his party work was concerned with the distribution of literature, which he undertook in Canada, where the Canadian Communist Party was illegal. Active in the seamen's unions of Australia and New Zealand, he was involved in street fights with scabs and police during strikes. In the Northern Territory he prospected for

---

32 RGASPI 545/6/68. A 2024 application to the Pennsylvania Department of Corrections established that "records we had pertaining to this individual would have been destroyed in accordance with the Department of Corrections' Records Retention Schedule".

tantalite at Lady Moulden's mines. He campaigned for better conditions for the unemployed in Darwin before being "railroaded" to Perth.[33]

He worked his way to Europe as a seaman and crossed the Pyrenees to arrive in Spain on 20 November 1937. His objective was to "fight fascism with the International Brigade". While still a new recruit, he faced disciplinary action for singing after hours and was confined to barracks for five days. While he considered the choral infraction to be minor, he accepted his punishment stating that he understood that "one must accept rigid discipline to be a true anti-fascist".[34]

Franklyn's interest in literature was not confined to reading and singing. He co-wrote the *Song of the British Battalion* with an American, Joe Frankel, and also composed a poem that was sent back to the *Workers' Star*, a CPA paper published in Perth.

Spain

A rough and rugged country,
Red poppies growing wild,
An emblem there in splendour
Where proletarians died.

They came from every nation
To fight the valiant cause.
For freedom and democracy
These heroes did not pause.

Spanish soil has been invaded,
Foreign Fascists, filth and scum
Had sought new fields to conquer.
They thought we would succumb.

---

[33] RGASPI 545/6/68; Palmer and Fox, *Australians in Spain*, p. 37.
[34] RGASPI 545/6/68.

But Franco, doom awaits you!
Our cause can never fail!
All Spain will be united,
Your crime shall not prevail.[35]

---

[35] *Workers' Star*, 19 August 1938, p. 1.

10

Stuck like flies

After the Battle of Jarama the war had gone badly for the Republic. While there were successes, such as the humiliation of the Italians at Guadalajara, the overall course of the war was clear. Thwarted in his attempt to encircle Madrid, Franco had struck north with a major offensive in the Basque country. This offensive, which included the destruction of Guernica by Hitler's Condor Legion and Mussolini's *Aviazione Legionaria*, succeeded and the major industrial and port city of Bilbao fell on 19 June 1937. Earlier, divisions within the Republican government led to street fighting in Barcelona, as a struggle was fought out between competing elements of the anti-fascist coalition.

On 6 July, the Republic launched its first major offensive of the war and took Brunete, a town 30 kilometres west of Madrid. This initial success was reversed and the town was retaken by the fascists. By the time fighting ground to a halt in late July, the Republic had suffered 25,000 casualties and lost large quantities of equipment. Franco could rely on a steady flow of materiel from Italy and Germany to replenish his supplies, but the policy of non-intervention meant the Republic could not readily re-supply itself.

Another Republican offensive was launched in August across the Aragon front. Many men and more equipment were lost at places such as Belchite for little or no strategic gain. In December, the Battle of Teruel began and was fought in freezing temperatures. Initial Republican successes were halted and then reversed at a terrible cost during bitter winter fighting. Before Republican forces could regroup, Franco launched an attack across the Aragon Front which made effective use of superior artillery and air power. The fascists advanced eastwards in what became a Republican rout. On 15 April 1938 the fascists succeeded in reaching the Mediterranean, splitting the Republic in two, with Catalonia isolated from Madrid and Valencia.[1] Franco then started advancing south, towards Valencia.

McNeill and his circle of Australians arrived in Spain as the strategic situation facing the Republic was deteriorating. On the major battlefields Republican forces had suffered a string of defeats, the flow of foreign volunteers into Spain was drying up, and Spanish recruits were being enlisted into the International Brigades to bring units up to strength. There were shortages of food, oil, medical supplies and arms. Barcelona had been subjected to sustained bombing by the Germans and Italians and there were thousands of refugees to be fed and housed. Political tensions in the government were growing and war-weariness was weakening morale.

Elsewhere, there seemed to be declining interest in the war with the international community's attention focused on other developments, like Hitler's annexation of Austria. There was no indication that Britain would ever depart from its support for non-intervention and the flow of supplies from the Soviet Union, which was probably already dwindling, was being choked off by the German and Italian navies.[2] Stalin had seen there was no serious prospect of cooperating with Britain and France to oppose fascism and was drawing his own lessons. If the Western powers were willing to use the farce of non-intervention to abet the destruction of Spanish democracy, what would they do should Hitler now turn east?

It was in this context that the Republic's leaders decided to mount a major new offensive, which would become the Battle of the Ebro. It would have a number of goals. Militarily, it would relieve pressure on Valencia. Politically, demonstrating that the Republic maintained its ability to fight would be good for domestic morale and there was the hope that victory on the battlefield might revive international

---

[1] Beevor, *Spanish Civil War*, pp. 319-327.
[2] Tremlett, *International Brigades*, p. 456.

interest in assisting the Republic. But beset as the Republic was by problems, an offensive on the scale contemplated was what the military historian Antony Beevor has called "a monumental gamble against very unfavourable odds".[3] This was especially so given that previous Republican offensives had mostly ended disastrously.

The alternative course of action was to go over to the defensive and avoid large-scale engagements where the fascists' superior artillery and German and Italian air power had proven to be so decisive. Strong defensive positions could be used to launch harassing raids and support guerrilla actions with the aim of prolonging the conflict until a wider European war broke out – a war that seemed increasingly inevitable. Despite this plausible defensive alternative, the Republic's leaders decided that their best option was to stake all on an offensive in the hope of securing a spectacular victory that would demonstrate to both domestic supporters and international observers that the cause was not lost.

A large Army of the Ebro, totalling 80,000, was formed by extending the age of conscription to both younger and older men. The 16-year-old conscripts were known as the *quinta del biberon*, the baby's bottle call-up.[4] Commanded by the communist officer Juan Modesto, a former woodcutter who had trained at the Frunze Military Academy in Russia, the new army was impressive. It had been equipped with 25,000 tons of Soviet war materiel secured when the border with France was temporarily re-opened after Hitler had taken Austria. A shortage of artillery remained a weakness, with the Republicans possessing as few as 150 guns. Some of these were virtually antiques, being pieces from the nineteenth century.[5]

---

[3] Beevor, *Spanish Civil War*, pp. 346-7.
[4] Ibid., p. 345.
[5] Ibid., p. 347.

Training

As part of these preparations, the Australians were sent to different training camps. Franklyn was spared the frozen horrors of Teruel and sent instead to the training base at Pozo Rubio, near Albacete, where he studied and passed his exams to work with telephone and radio systems. He also acquired knowledge of the heliograph and was appointed to the Transmissions Company. His initial impression was that the spirit of democracy in the Republican Army was "quite different" from that of the British Army he had served in during the Great War.

> *The international comrades along with their Spanish brothers are the finest disciplined soldiers I have ever seen, and I spent three and a half years in the last war; and their morale is 75 per cent higher, because their fight is for world democracy and not for the parasite class.*[6]

Franklyn met Charlotte Haldane, the secretary of the Spanish Relief Committee's Dependents Aid Committee who was accompanying Paul Robeson, the renowned American singer, on his tour of Spain to sing for the International Brigades. As a man who enjoyed singing himself, Franklyn reported that Robeson sang "some very fine songs" and was "vastly popular with the Internationals".[7] Robeson said that he "sang with my whole heart and soul for these gallant fighters of the International Brigade". He campaigned for the Republic and made a radio broadcast explaining his stand:

> *Every artist, every scientist, must decide now where he stands. He has no alternative.... The artist must elect to fight for Freedom or for Slavery. I have made my choice. I had no alternative.*[8]

In April 1938 Franklyn wrote to the CPA, telling them that he was now in the Attlee Company. The No. 1 Company of the British Battalion had changed its name after receiving a visit from Attlee, now the leader of the British Labour Party. Franklyn told the CPA that he was fully engaged in "building strong fortifications which the fascists will

---

[6] *Workers' Star*, 6 May 1938, p. 6.
[7] Ibid.
[8] Paul Robeson, *Here I Stand*, London, 1958, pp. 60-1.

never penetrate". His main concern was to see the early defeat of the Chamberlain government as he felt that only with a strong Labour government in Britain can we "get the war material that is badly needed and bring this heroic fight to a victorious finish".[9] He wrote again, probably in early July, reporting that he had met McNeill and Young. He was feeling part of "a splendid, mechanised, highly trained army whose morale is 100 per cent higher than the fascists".[10]

Morcom's "steady and reliable" qualities were recognised on his arrival. He was transferred from the British Battalion's base at Figueras and sent to a training school for non-commissioned officers. He maintained his dedication and commitment and compared himself to Alexei Stakhanov, the Soviet miner who with his prodigious output was the personification of a productivity campaign in the USSR. Morcom wrote home to friends:

> *Training is very intensive & one has to devote [oneself] full time to study.*
>
> *I am an activist – a Stakhanovite of the army. Activists pledge themselves, among other things: – to rapidly assimilate military science – to know all the weapons of conflict – to fight without rest against provocateurs, wreckers, etc. – to assist others in knowing the science of war – to care for our arms with our life – to raise the political level of others – to assist in liquidating illiteracy – to study and learn the Spanish language – promise to be a model soldier, and with our arms, our life & our honour as anti-fascists to fight for the independence of Spain.*
>
> *The above are a few of our guiding principles. So, you see I am still a full-time functionary.*
>
> *The fascists bombed a village two miles from here two days ago, & their planes pass over every day.*[11]

---

[9] *Workers' Weekly*, 10 June 1938, p. 3.
[10] *Workers' Star*, 19 August 1938, p. 1.
[11] Letter from Morcom to Mary Lamm dated 10 July 1938, Tom and Mary Wright Collection, Z267/Box 17 Noel Butlin Archives, Australian National University.

Morcom remained a dedicated servant to the cause and submitted a self-criticism that identified public speaking as a weakness but nonetheless promised to undertake a lecturing tour on his return to Australia.[12] He was appointed to the Battalion's No. 4 Company and became its communist party secretary. The *Workers' Weekly* reported his arrival in Spain with Morcom stating he had come to "do his bit for democracy".[13]

Carter, whose experience with firearms was hitherto restricted to shooting kangaroos, volunteered for a machine gun company that was officered by German anti-fascists.[14] The unit was to be used to counter any breakthroughs the fascists might make through the Republicans' lines. Carter was sent to a training camp on the coast, overlooking the Mediterranean. He found the Republic was desperately short of supplies.

> *I never had a full uniform, sometimes you had a pair of trousers, a pair of shoes if you were lucky, never a full uniform. Food was short – half a loaf of bread, a cup of lentils and occasionally a little mule meat.*
>
> *Our training consisted of three bullets for the machine gun and three bullets for the rifle, twice a week.*[15]

Training with men from all over the world including Italians, Americans, Canadians and Poles, Carter regarded his fellow International Brigaders as the "cream of the working-class. Not only brave, but intellectuals, of all descriptions and all nationalities".[16] One of the intellectuals serving in the British Battalion at this time was James Jump, a journalist and poet, from Liverpool, England. Serving alongside men like Carter, he came to the conclusion that he could "never make a real soldier" and "was only intellectually an anti-fascist".

> *All around me were men who had suffered poverty and unemployment, and the degradation that accompanied those two evils. These were men*

---

[12] RGASPI 545/6/68/175/19-25.
[13] *Workers' Weekly*, 15 July 1938, p. 3.
[14] *Workers' Weekly*, 9 December 1938, p. 3.
[15] *Tribune*, 16 July 1986, p. 16.
[16] Joe Carter – John Clements, Imperial War Museum, IWM 3812.

> *capable of hatred and revenge. To them, fascism was an extension of capitalism, under which they had suffered hardship and humiliation. They had not become socialists through reading* Left Review *or the* New Statesman.[17]

Carter, who had used his fists while on the track in Australia and picked up a few boxing tricks in his Lithgow gymnasium, became friends with an American ex-bantamweight boxer. Boxing was keenly followed by the volunteers who cheered as they heard the news of the heavyweight championship rematch bout between Joe Louis, "the Brown Bomber", and the German Max Schmeling. Fought in June 1938, the contest was thickly overlaid with politics. Schmeling was seen as a representative of the Nazi regime. Louis, an African American, was embraced by White Americans as the nation's champion who contested the Nazi dogma of the supremacy of the master race. Schmeling suffered a humiliating first round defeat by technical knockout.[18]

Carter was trained on the Russian-supplied Maxim machine guns. He found them a capable weapon, but heavy and hard to handle ("You had to be a horse, half a horse"). He also handled a Czechoslovakian weapon:

> *I finished up with an air-cooled light machine gun, Czechoslovakian, a beautiful little rifle – if you could call anything deadly beautiful.*[19]

After enlisting at Figueras, McNeill was transported to the Montblanc Training Base, about 120 kilometres southwest of Barcelona, where he trained alongside Americans of the Lincoln Battalion. The men were issued with an odd assortment of giggle suits, the simple khaki clothing worn in lieu of a formal uniform. One volunteer said it made them look

---

[17] James R Jump, *The Fighter Fell in Love: A Spanish Civil War Memoir*, London, 2021, p. 134.

[18] Joe Carter – John Clements, Imperial War Museum, IWM 3812; Joe Carter – John Shipp, Wollongong University Archives, B16. For an example of the political coverage of the fight see 'Louis packed a vengeance punch: big fight a racial war', *Labor Daily*, 24 June 1938, p. 1.

[19] Joe Carter – Amirah Inglis, Amirah Inglis Collection, Noel Butlin Archives, Australian National University; Joe Carter – John Shipp, Wollongong University Archives, B16.

like "extras in a Charlie Chaplin film".[20] At Figueras, the men had been provided with beds, towels and soap, but conditions at Montblanc, inside another old church and monastery, the Convent de la Mercé, were more primitive. Instead of beds the men slept on palliasses infested with lice.

Photo 15: McNeill (centre, no cap) at the Montblanc training base, 1938. (Tamiment Library and Robert F. Wagner Labor Archives, New York University)

The training became more intensive, with the men instructed on the tactics to be used in mountain fighting and how to advance effectively as a team. The quality of the food deteriorated as they adjusted to what would be the rigours of the front. Montblanc, a walled medieval town, could only offer a tasteless, monotonous diet, with what one volunteer described as "small shrivelled fish with glazed eyes, cooked in oil drums". After training, the men entertained themselves with football matches, and visits to the town's cafes. Some braved the fear of disease to patronise the town's brothel. More soberingly, the wounded returning from the front came through Montblanc, confronting the new volunteers with the reality of war.[21]

---

[20] Wheeler, *To Make the People Smile Again*, p. 48.
[21] John H. Basset, 'International Brigader', in Philip Toynbee, (ed) *Distant Drums*, London, 1976, pp. 134-5.

McNeill was reading the *Workers' Weekly*, keeping in touch with local news, and appreciative of the £23 collected by the Spanish Relief Committee at Wollongong and Corrimal. In his first letter back to the Wollongong CPA, McNeill maintained a thoroughly positive outlook:

> The weather is great, nice and warm, just the kind of days one would like to spend at Towradgi. Cigarettes are scarcer than usual. I am fortunate in being a non-smoker. I am doing fine with guns, and am feeling fit, and more convinced of victory for the Spanish forces than ever, the more I see of the Spanish government supporters.[22]

Young, on his arrival, encountered McNeill and Franklyn. In Barcelona he met Mrs Alice Holloway, secretary of the NSW Women's Auxiliary of the Australian Railways Union, who was undertaking a tour after visiting Moscow to witness the May Day parade.[23] Young was based in the "beautiful Spanish hills" where he practised target shooting, hitting "three bulls out of five at 300 metres" during his first session. This success prompted him to promise the CPA that he'd send them "a fascist scalp or two".[24] His anti-fascist fervour was as strong as ever and he wrote home to report on the devastation caused by modern warfare:

> One place we passed through had been bombed the day before, and 26 women and children had been killed.
>
> I will never forget the sights I saw coming through Spain to join my battalion. Small towns and villages had been bombed by German and Italian fascists. They are nothing but sadists, just ruthless killers of women and children.[25]

Ahead of the Battle of the Ebro the British Battalion was based on the outskirts of the village of Marca, where the men built themselves perfectly camouflaged crude shacks or *chabolas*, from whatever local materials were to hand. The camp was in a small valley overlooked by

---

[22] *Illawarra Mercury*, 2 September 1938, p. 5. Towradgi is a beachside suburb of Wollongong.
[23] *Sydney Morning Herald*, 23 September 1938, p. 5.
[24] *Workers' Weekly*, 13 September 1938, p. 3.
[25] Ibid.

a flat-topped mountain faced with dramatic cliffs of white stone. The blunt white-sided mountain was promptly nicknamed *La Mola* (The Tooth) and the camp given the nickname of *Chabola* Valley.[26] On cloudy days, mist would fall slowly from the mountain like a majestic waterfall. The camp was visited by well-wishing dignitaries including Jawaharial Nehru and his daughter Indira, two future prime ministers of India. The Brigaders greeted their special guests with cries of "Long live Indian independence".[27]

McNeill was impatient to fight, but trusted his commanders would send the unit into action "when everything is ready and we'll be much more efficient". When the company was not training, it was forging strong relationships with the local community by helping farmers in the fields. McNeill helped build a bomb shelter in the school grounds to provide protection for the children.[28] To maintain morale a fiesta was held with football, boxing and athletic events. The local community participated in the festivities and fruit, chocolates and champagne were distributed. What had been a successful and morale-building day ended in tragedy when, after the completion of a competition that displayed how quickly the men could set up their machine guns, a local youth was somehow killed in a firing mishap.[29]

The first accounts of McNeill's and Carter's arrival in Spain were published in Australian newspapers in August 1938. The reports recounted McNeill's dramatic stowaway journey and conveyed his call for renewed efforts by Australian anti-fascists to have the arms embargo lifted. If non-intervention continued, McNeill predicted "a long and bloody struggle before the people win out".[30] For an anxious audience, he provided information on the Australians he had seen in Spain. He reported that like Dickinson and another Australian who had died, Jack 'Blue' Barry, he was serving in a machine gun company. Dickinson and Barry he said, had earnt "imperishable names" for themselves. Carter

---

[26] Angela Jackson, *At the Margins of Mayhem*, Pontypool, 2008, p. 20.
[27] Ibid., pp. 88-90.
[28] Ibid., p. 76; *Workers' Weekly*, 7 October 1938, p. 3.
[29] Wheeler, *To Make the People Smile Again*, p. 59.
[30] *Steel & Metal Worker*, 26 August 1938.

said the "spirit of the Spanish people has to be seen to be believed. The more the fascists bomb them, the more determined they become to win the war."[31]

The Battle of the Ebro

By the time these reports were published, readers were already aware that the Republic had launched a major offensive across the Ebro, a river that flows through Catalonia. The offensive had begun a few minutes after midnight during the night of 24-25 July. The Republic staged an audacious and largely successful crossing of the river using small rowing boats and pontoon bridges. Catching the fascists by surprise, the Republicans made swift progress across a wide front that stretched for 80 kilometres. The British Battalion experienced no difficulty in making the river crossing, with Franklyn saying they had "crossed the river like cats, not a hitch anywhere".[32]

Once over the river they pushed on and in the first 24 hours advanced 25 kilometres to the outskirts of Gandesa, an important transport hub that commanded several vital roads. Reacting to the Republic's initial successes, Franco quickly pulled troops from other areas to send as reinforcements. This redistribution of forces meant the Republic had, at least initially, achieved its goal of easing the pressure on Valencia. The two armies then settled down to fight the last major engagement of the war.

McNeill had been injured even before the attack had started. On 22 July, while marching with his company to an assembly area, a soldier in another company dropped a grenade. A dozen men were injured with McNeill receiving what he regarded as "only slight shrapnel wounds" to the face, left eyelid, ear, leg and foot. Not all the shrapnel could be removed, and he would feel a small piece in his eyelid for the rest of his life.[33]

---

[31] *Workers' Weekly*, 30 August 1938, p. 3; *Labor Daily*, 19 August 1938, p. 4.

[32] *Workers' Star*, 28 October 1938, p. 1.

[33] RGASPI 545/6/69/196; WL interview; *Workers' Weekly*, 16 September 1938, p. 3.

The front line for the British Battalion ran through the Cavalls and Pandols mountain ranges lying just east of Gandesa. These are jagged mountain ranges, with steep rocky slopes sparsely covered with stunted trees and low spiky shrubs. The Battalion was attempting to take a crucial hill in the Cavalls, known as Hill 481, which was the key to Gandesa.

There was savage fighting for control of Hill 481, which had a distinctive rounded peak as its pinnacle. The British named it "The Pimple" while German Brigaders called it the "Hill of Death". The fascists dug in on the top of Hill 481 with observation posts, barbed wire, and machine gun nests and had artillery that allowed them to shell the Republican positions. The Condor Legion used the battle to practice the screaming dive bombing of its Stukas. The Republican soldiers had rifles, grenades and machine guns, but no mortars or artillery. They bit on pieces of wood, hung around their necks, as they endured the terrifying bombardment.[34] The patches of bare rock on the steep mountainside made digging in nearly impossible, and the best most of the Brigaders could do was to use rocks to construct parapets and firing positions.[35]

Morcom was killed on the first day of fighting.[36] He was reported as missing and his body was not recovered.

Young, also at the forefront of the attack, met Franklyn on 26 July while filling his water bottle from a well. He told Franklyn "I got four fascist b_____s today and I'll bump a few more off tonight." Young was, as the *Workers' Weekly* triumphantly reported, in the thick of the Ebro battle. He was dead by the time the report was published in Australia.[37]

McNeill recalled the battle and the death of Young:

> *Ebro was a turning point because if we had planes, tanks, guns and sufficient supplies, we could have swept the fascists from their stronghold. Our supplies were petering out. We had two or three planes*

---

[34] Beevor, *Spanish Civil War*, p. 359.
[35] Jump, *The Fighter Fell in Love*, p. 131.
[36] *Workers' Weekly*, 28 October 1938, p. 3.
[37] *Workers' Weekly*, 11 October 1938, p. 3.

that came over against a myriad of the fascists. They were like bees swarming over all our positions. It was one huge armada of planes bombing hell out of us every yard we went.

We were held up at a great granite hill, encrusted with ironstone – it would turn a pick even trying to dig into it – and it was the depot for all the reinforcements, all the munitions and supplies the fascists needed. And it was there they held us - forever more as it turned out. But we made valiant attempts to take this hill, what became known as 481.

It was on this hill, 481, that Lewis Clive and Bill Young met a barrage of machine gun fire on about the eighth attempt to take this hill and both of them were killed in the same burst of fire.

We weren't able to bury either of them because they advanced almost within grenade-throwing range and the fascists beat us back. They remained out there and we weren't able to get any further up.[38]

Remembered by McNeill as a "marvellous thrower of the hand grenade", Young had become friends with Lewis Clive, who was said to be even better with a grenade. Educated at Eton and Oxford, Clive was a Labour Councillor on the Kensington Borough Council, active in the Fabian Society and had won a gold medal in the coxless pairs rowing event at the 1932 Olympic Games. He was regarded by McNeill as a member of the aristocracy.[39]

While socially they were worlds apart, both Clive and Young were politically committed men. A fellow Etonian described Clive as "incorrigibly idealistic". McNeill said that Young had often stated that he was prepared for "anything coming his way as long as he first got a crack at the fascists".[40] Carter said that "Bill got hit right in the head. Big game bastard he was".[41] In an appraisal written after the battle, the

---

[38] WL interview.
[39] Thomas, *Spanish Civil War*, p. 547; WL interview; https://olympics.com/en/athletes/lewis-clive accessed 10 June 2024.
[40] Tremlett, *International Brigades*, p. 485; *Workers' Weekly*, 1 November 1938, p. 3.
[41] Joe Carter – John Shipp, Wollongong University Archives B-16.

International Brigades recorded that Young's personal conduct had been excellent, he was "very brave under fire" and his "conduct was that of a party member and soldier".[42]

The news that Morcom and Young were missing took months to make its way to Australia. It arrived in letters from McNeill and Franklyn. McNeill said that there had been no trace of either since they had gone over the top to make an unsuccessful charge: "whatever their fate, they were prepared for it, and they played a heroic part in the struggle against fascism".[43]

In an act of respect, the National Congress of the CPA elected Morcom, who was missing but not yet declared dead, to sit in absentia with Stalin and Mao on the party's presidium.[44] The CPA eventually confirmed the deaths of Young and Morcom on 13 December 1938, proclaiming that "Australia will never forget".[45] The *Workers' Weekly* published a poem dedicated to Morcom's memory before Christmas, and another for Young in February 1939.[46]

Young's son Billy, now an orphan, was back in Sydney and billeted by members of the CPA who rallied around to provide for him.[47] The Happy Times Social Club organised a Christmas social. Billy received a bicycle, watch and other gifts, including a holiday at Blackheath. A columnist in the *Workers' Weekly* wrote:

> *Everyone will sympathise with young Keith. He certainly had a Daddy to love and to be proud of. Wipe those eyes, Keith, hold your head up bravely, sonny boy. Show the world that you are a Bolshevik, too, a true son of your father.*[48]

---

[42] RGASPI 545/6/68/177.
[43] *South Coast Times*, 28 October 1938, p. 19.
[44] *Workers' Weekly*, 22 November 1938, p. 1.
[45] *Workers' Weekly*, 13 December 1938, p. 1.
[46] *Workers' Weekly*, 20 December 1938, p.2; *Workers' Weekly*, 17 February 1939, p. 2.
[47] Silver and Young, *Billy*, p. 34.
[48] *Workers' Weekly*, 13 December 1938, p. 2.

His guardians were veteran communists Stan Moran and Jack McPhillips. He was sent to Corrimal to live with Sam Blakeney, a retired coal miner and keen lawn bowler, and his wife. In 1941 Billy, like his father before him, lied about his age and joined the 2nd Australian Imperial Force. Unlike his father, his underage status was not detected. With the fall of Singapore, Billy became a teenage prisoner of war. He survived the Sandakan death march to return to Australia and died of covid in 2022.[49]

The deaths of Morcom and Young were part of the terrible price the British Battalion paid while trying to take Hill 481. Conditions were appalling, with fighting occurring through the intense heat of a Spanish summer. Food and water were scarce and basic hygiene was difficult to maintain. Lice soon infested the troops. The rock of the mountain range shattered when hit by bullets and shells, raining the men with sharp stone splinters. Conditions for the wounded were dreadful. The men were tormented by swarms of flies and a plague of rats attracted by the stench of dead bodies and excrement.

After two weeks of fighting the advance was clearly stalled, Gandesa had not been taken, and on 7 August the British Battalion was withdrawn for ten days of rest. It had only 150 men left out of 558. Having halted the Republic's advance and established supremacy in the air, Franco's troops now went on the offensive and launched a slogging, hill by hill advance through the hard, mountainous terrain. Their mission was to recover every piece of the territory they had lost in the first phase of the battle. The orders for the Republicans were to "Resist, Fortify and be Vigilant",[50] and to entrench themselves at every opportunity. Some Welsh and Scottish miners thought McNeill must have been a coalminer when they saw him trench digging with a pick and shovel: "My experiences at gold and tin prospecting stand me in good stead."[51]

Carter and Franklyn were fortunate not to be killed. Franklyn, a telephone linesman during the attack on Hill 481, admitted he was

---

[49] Silver and Young, *Billy*, p. 35; *Sydney Morning Herald*, 21 May 2022, p. 3.
[50] Tremlett, *International Brigades*, p. 485.
[51] *South Coast Times*, 28 October 1938, p. 19.

extremely lucky to survive after being the target of machine gun fire.

> *The beret I am wearing has two holes in it where a bullet whistled through behind the neck. I must try and keep it for a souvenir. I can have a good laugh every time I look at it, and say to myself, boy, that was a close shave.*[52]

He endured the ordeal of the Pandols and retained his ideological resolve to oppose fascism:

> *The Fascists did their utmost to smash our ranks and morale, using avion en masse – 50 bombers in the air at one time, fighter planes swooping down at us and strafing us with light bombs and machine gun fire, and artillery pounding away at us with trench mortars and 75-pounders. I wish with profound sincerity I could present a picture to you of the everlasting courage in which our gallant comrades (both Spanish and Internationals) faced Franco's last throw of the dice.*[53]

Photo 16: Bert Bryan and Jack Franklyn (obscured) fighting on Hill 481. (Australian War Memorial, AWM2023.312.1)

---

[52] *Workers' Weekly*, 11 October 1938, p. 3.
[53] *Northern Standard*, 27 January 1939, p. 5.

Franklyn was, according to his sergeant, John Dunlop, an accountant from Edinburgh, "quite a character" who was "nuts on bridge". With his enthusiasm for the game unleashed, Franklyn used to cajole a group of bridge players to sit "half the night and half the day in a dugout under an olive tree playing bridge". Franklyn regaled his British comrades with stories of his adventures prospecting across outback Queensland and the Northern Territory and painted "quite an attractive picture of life in the Australian bush".[54]

Carter had the experience of a shell landing a few feet from him. Luckily, it was a dud and failed to explode. Writing to the Port Kembla Ironworkers', he recounted seeing the fascists machine gun a Republican pilot who was coming down behind their lines in his parachute. They could have easily taken the pilot prisoner, but "there is nothing too low for the fascists to do".[55] Carter admired the bravery of Harry Bourne, a London Jew, who he said was a great working-class fighter. After suffering an injury to his leg, Bourne rebuffed offers of assistance. He told the men, "Your best job is to kill those fascist bastards – as many as you can!"[56] Carter also fought alongside a young Italian university student who had come from America:

> *I told him to get down and bring some ammunition up. He said, "Jesus, mate, I'm frightened." I said, "Well, you're no more frightened than I am, don't kid yourself about that..*
>
> *Anybody that wasn't frightened was born real mad or something.*[57]

Franklyn and Carter were both eventually wounded. Franklyn was subjected to heavy shelling while fighting on Hill 666 in the Pandols. A piece of shrapnel hit him in the cheekbone, just below his right eye, and he was hospitalised in Barcelona and Olot. He saw no further action. Carter recalled the fighting retreat through the Pandols as where the fascists "kicked the shit out of us and drove us back".

---

[54] John Peter Cowan Dunlop - Conrad Wood, Imperial War Museum, IWM 11,355, Reel 11.
[55] *Workers' Weekly*, 18 October 1938, p. 3.
[56] Joe Carter – John Clements, Imperial War Museum, IWM 3812.
[57] Ibid.

Suffering from dysentery, he was injured when a burst from a machine gun went over his head, just missing him, but hitting the rock surface behind him. He was hit in the arm by a ricochet and was sent back for medical attention when his arm started to "blow up".

> *I got two aspros, laid down for a couple of days and it went down. Being young, I suppose, helps.*[58]

Events elsewhere were now moving rapidly. The European crisis surrounding Hitler's designs on Czechoslovakia was reaching a climax. On 21 September the leadership of the Spanish Republic used the occasion of a speech to the League of Nations to announce an immediate withdrawal of all international volunteers. The number remaining was, by this time, so low that it was a concession of limited military value. The aim of the gesture, however misplaced, was to pressure the British and French into either forcing Franco to match the gesture by sending his Germans and Italians home too, or to finally accept the absurdity of non-intervention and provide the Republic with practical support and so check the advance of the Axis powers.[59] Neither aim was realised.

Earlier in September the British Battalion had been transferred to the front near Corbera. Very different from the mountains, this was rich agricultural country, with picturesque plantings of cherry and peach trees. There were groves of olive trees, terraced grapevines and rolling fields marked out by low stone walls. The withdrawal announcement reached officers of the XV International Brigade on 22 September. They decided to proceed with what had been planned for the next day and to tell the men this was to be the British Battalion's final action. The last day's fighting opened with the fascists launching a massive artillery barrage. Casualties during the day were heavy and McNeill was among them:

> *We went into the attack early in the morning, at dawn. We knew they were going to attack and we decided to cushion the attack so we went into an advanced position. And then we saw their tanks advancing and we knew we were goners if we remained where we were.*

---

[58] Joe Carter – John Shipp, Wollongong University Archives B-16.
[59] Tremlett, *International Brigades*, p. 502.

> *It was part of our plan to go about 300 yards in advance and then if we were forced back to retreat, 300 yards behind and take up our real position. On the way, in that 300 yards, I was hit in the leg, and I was a cot case. I was laying out there, bullets going all around me, and I crawled down, there was a terraced grapevine, and I got down behind the first terrace, about 18 inches, and I was quite safe.*[60]

McNeill was conscious and fortunate not to be alone in no-man's land, as there were others also sheltering in the protection provided by the low terrace. He had been hit by a machine gun bullet through his left calf. Fortunately, it missed the bone. He was shot at midday and lay, with a self-applied tourniquet, through the remorseless heat of the long afternoon. Any movement in the grapevines attracted snipers so McNeill said the group was "stuck like flies on a flypaper" and could not move from where they lay.

> *Grapes were hanging on the vines around me, but the slightest move resulted in a burst of fire that kicked up the dust unpleasantly close, so I couldn't use the grapes to quench my thirst.*[61]

Despite his efforts to keep the leg moving, it stiffened and when darkness settled on the battlefield McNeill found that he could only crawl away. As he was escaping, a shell blew him into the air and he was hit in the left buttock by a piece of shrapnel. This wound was bleeding more heavily than the calf wound. Still carrying his rifle and ammunition case, he was picked up by Canadian and Spanish soldiers on patrol who carried him 300 metres to a dug-out dressing station. Another shell landed ten feet from them, but it failed to explode. McNeill gave credit for this piece of fortune to the saboteurs disrupting the production of munitions in the fascist countries. After treatment in the dug-out he was carried two kilometres "over terrible rough ground" to an ambulance which transported him to a nearby hospital.[62]

---

[60] WL interview.
[61] *Workers' Voice*, 19 November 1938, p. 2.
[62] *Workers' Weekly*, 18 November 1938, p. 3; *Steel & Metal Worker*, 18 November 1938, p. 1.

The British Battalion's resources were spent. No matter how brave, courageous and determined its fighters were, they could not match the fascists' artillery and air power. Casualties were heavy. On the Battalion's final day of action 106 men went into battle and only 58 returned.[63] One of the dead was Nalty, the commander of McNeill's machine gun company. The next day what remained of the British Battalion assembled for a roll call. McNeill was not there and, in the post-engagement confusion, he was assumed to be missing and feared killed. On 5 October, Pollitt, having returned from a trip to Spain, sent a cable to the CPA: "Jim McNeill reported missing feared killed Ebro action September 23."[64]

The news was reported in Australia as McNeill having been killed on the Ebro battlefield. The *Labor Daily* reported that McNeill, "a popular Port Kembla ironworker", had been killed in action. The *Workers' Voice* said that McNeill had been one of the Australian labour movement's best fighters and that the ardent anti-fascist had "died with rifle in his hand". The *Illawarra Mercury* noted his role in the leadership of the Port Kembla Ironworkers' and was slightly more conservative in its reporting, headlining "Corrimal Resident Reported Killed in Spanish War".[65] The news must have weighed heavily on his family and friends, who told the papers that he was "a splendid type of Trade Unionist".[66]

---

[63] Tremlett, *International Brigades*, p. 506.
[64] *Workers' Weekly*, 7 October 1938, p. 1.
[65] *Labor Daily*, 7 October 1938, p. 2; *Workers' Voice* 26 October 1938, p. 4; *Illawarra Mercury*, 7 October 1938, p. 12.
[66] *South Coast Times*, 7 October 1938, p. 13.

11

A deferred casualty

News of the arrival of Carter and McNeill in Spain had been greeted with loud applause at a meeting of the Port Kembla Ironworkers'. In a message to the union, McNeill said that the Spanish unions, whether industrial, peasant or co-ops, were "the bitterest fighters of fascism". The union sent £2 to the pair to provide a little comfort while the Illawarra Trades and Labour Council sent them a message of support, confident that they would "worthily uphold the democratic traditions of the South Coast workers".[1] Letters from both Carter and McNeill were regularly published in *Steel & Metal Worker*, and in newspapers which detailed their adventures in articles such as "Putting Port Kembla on the Map of Spain!"[2] Another gave an account of McNeill's meeting with the portly Marty, who McNeill thought to be a "wonderful physical specimen".[3]

While they were in Spain, activity in support of the Republic continued in Wollongong. The Spanish Relief Committee held film nights in Bulli, Corrimal and Wollongong that showed the "havoc caused by aerial

---

[1] *Illawarra Mercury*, 19 August 1938, p. 16; *Workers' Weekly*, 6 September 1938, p. 3; *Steel & Metal Worker*, 26 August 1938.

[2] *Workers' Weekly*, 7 October 1938, p. 3.

[3] *Workers' Weekly*, 16 September 1938, p. 3.

bombs". The screening in Bulli was subject to attempted interference by the authorities, which led to a protest by the Miners' Federation, but the Wollongong screening proceeded without difficulty and raised more than £20 for the cause.[4]

Nor was Spain confined to Wollongong's screens. On the stage, Sydney's New Theatre League, a drama troupe closely associated with the CPA, visited the Wollongong Town Hall and performed *Remember Pedrocito*, a play written by the American John Loftus. It has two of Franco's soldiers, Pablo and Juanito, coming to the realisation that they are fighting for the wrong side. After their captain kills Pedrocito, a young boy, they execute him and make for the Republic's lines. A sturdy piece of agitprop, Loftus has Juan say: "All the fighting isn't done with guns."[5] A reviewer thought that while the production had weaknesses, it was generally well done, and praised the performance of Victor Arnold, an actor who was said to look Spanish.[6]

Dick Whateley

The Spanish Relief Committee also arranged for Dick Whateley, a returned International Brigader, to address a conference convened by the Illawarra Trades and Labour Council. A Melbourne seaman who had worked his way through Mexico, Colombia, Brazil and Paraguay, Whateley had felt himself drawn to the Spanish people.[7] Labelled by Esmond Romilly, an English writer-soldier in his book *Boadilla*, as an "Australian tramp" who was 30 but looked 40, Whateley had been one of the first Australians to make it to Spain where, as part of the German-based Thalmann Battalion, he had taken part in the critical early battles to defend Madrid.[8]

---

[4] *Illawarra Mercury*, 14 April 1938, p. 10; *South Coast Times*, 8 April 1938, p. 9.
[5] A copy of the script can be found in the Mitchell Library, State Library of New South Wales, Collection 01: New Theatre records, 1914-1990, Call Number MLMSS 6244 Series 8 Box 139.
[6] *Illawarra Mercury*, 2 September 1938, p. 2.
[7] Palmer and Fox, *Australians in Spain*, p. 40.
[8] Esmond Romilly, *Boadilla*, (1937), London, 1971, p. 41.

Described as a "young man of slight build suffering from nervous shock", the *Illawarra Mercury* quoted Whateley's account of the war: "I have watched a school blown sky-high by Franco's bombers. Cathedrals were bombed and priests, nuns and worshippers killed."[9] Soon after his visit to Wollongong, Whateley suffered a breakdown and was reported to be a "physical and nervous wreck as a result of his service in Spain". He was instructed not to read any news about the war and the Spanish Relief Committee opened a fund to support him.[10]

Nettie Palmer, an Australian writer who had been in Spain at the outbreak of the war and had returned to Australia to become a mainstay of the Spanish Relief Committee, said that he seemed a "disembodied dreamer, standing just inside a forest". Another friend, the writer and Spanish Relief Committee activist Len Fox, said that to most people "he was just a vague, dreamy person who sometimes stood for minutes on end without saying a word".[11] Whateley suffered additional bouts of ill health and in March 1943 collapsed with acute pneumonia. He was treated in Lidcombe State Hospital, which he regarded as a "filthy blot". While there he argued with an anarchist cook about the CPA's position on the war. After the doctors gave up hope he told a friend: "I refused to die. I didn't want to die before fascism was finally defeated." He survived but never fully recovered and died in Liverpool Hospital in September 1943. Palmer regarded him as a "deferred casualty of Spain".[12]

After reports arrived that Barcelona had been bombed, the Illawarra Trades and Labour Council sent a message of sympathy to the Republic. A reply from Spain was received:

> *Sincerest thanks in the name of the Government and mine, for your*

---

[9] *Illawarra Mercury*, 10 June 1938, p. 7.

[10] *Workers' Weekly*, 26 August 1938, p. 4.

[11] Letters from Nettie Palmer to Len Fox, 11 November 1941 and 3 October 1943, in the Len Fox papers 1852-2001, Mitchell Library, MLMSS 8085 Box 26; Len Fox, *Broad Left, Narrow Left*, Chippendale, 1982, p. 42.

[12] Letter from Whateley to Len Fox, 4 June 1943, in the Len Fox papers 1852-2001, Mitchell Library, MLMSS 8085 Box 26; *Workers' Weekly*, 26 August 1938, p. 4; Palmer and Fox, *Australians in Spain*, p. 40; Inglis, *Australians*, p. 201.

> kind interest in the Spanish people's cause, which is also that of the world.
>
> Democracy must result victoriously.
>
> *Dr Negrin*
>
> *Prime Minister*[13]

The concerns expressed in Wollongong were not simply rhetorical, as the trade unions were also acting on their anti-fascist beliefs. In July, a member of the Seamen's Union of Australia, Herman Stieglitz, was arrested on board the *Aeon*, a cargo steamship, while it was docked at Port Kembla. The young man was to be deported, having earlier abandoned his position on another vessel to avoid returning to Germany where he had been arrested for being a trade unionist. The threatened deportation had prompted a stop-work meeting by the Waterside Workers' Federation. Resolutions opposing the deportation were carried by the Port Kembla Ironworkers' and the Board of the Southern Miners. The Lyons government quickly reversed its deportation decision and allowed him to stay in Australia.[14]

This issue was resolved speedily, but by the end of the year, the anti-fascism of the Wollongong trade unions was to bring them into direct collision with the Australian government and BHP.

---

[13] *South Coast Times*, 8 April 1939, p. 19.

[14] *Canberra Times*, 22 July 1938, p. 4; *Workers' Weekly*, 22 July 1938, p. 4; *Labor Daily*, 23 July 1938, p. 5.

12

You are legend

McNeill spent most of his recovery in hospitals at Girona and Mataró and appreciated the care he received:

> Clean white walls, beds, sheets, linen and blankets, with really beautiful and charming Spanish girl nurses working at top pressure to relieve the suffering of the wounded, and the best food that can be obtained in war-stricken Spain, all form a vivid contrast to the putrid stench of dead men and mules, dirt, lice and ceaseless action against the fascists, who were sending everything over they had.[1]

McNeill's reaction to the withdrawal of the International Brigades was one of dismay and regret. He said that while the men badly needed a spell, they would like to have remained until the fascists were driven right out of Spain.[2] His mood would not have been lifted by reading that Neville Chamberlain, the British Prime Minister, had returned from Munich waving a piece of paper which he claimed had secured "peace for our time". While Chamberlain's agreement with Hitler was greeted positively in Australia, McNeill was unlikely to have been fooled. He had previously dismissed Chamberlain's diplomatic manoeuvrings with the comment: "What new swindles is Chamberlain hatching?"[3]

---

[1] *Workers' Weekly*, 15 November 1938, p. 3.
[2] *South Coast Times*, 11 November 1938, p 8; *Illawarra Mercury*, 2 December 1938, p. 4.
[3] *Workers' Weekly*, 21 October 1938, p. 3.

His suspicions would not have been allayed by the patient in the bed beside him in the Mataró hospital. An aviator with the Condor Legion who spoke fluent English, Otto had been shot down while bombing Barcelona.

> He boasted to us what idiots we were for fighting for Spain. They were just going to be a vassal and Hitler was going to go on to conquer the world. So, they freely tipped that, one of the Condor Legion, and I believed him.[4]

Farewell to the International Brigades

The withdrawal of the International Brigades was accompanied by a succession of celebratory farewells, fiestas, dances and processions. Carter took part in a farewell ceremony held in the Vila Engracia at Las Masies, an event addressed by Prime Minister Negrin, who announced that after the war was won the International Brigaders would be granted Spanish citizenship. It was a deeply emotional event, captured in an iconic series of images by the photographer Robert Capa. Volunteers like Carter could return home, but the German, Austrian, Italian and Czechoslovakian volunteers had no homes to go back to. Carter wrote:

> Modesto, who fought with the International Brigade on many fronts and knew us intimately, broke down while he was speaking and had to brush the tears from his eyes.
>
> Negrin spoke of how the Spanish government appreciated the International Brigade's heroic fight for Spanish independence with telling force. He concluded by saying that after the war is won 'Spain will be yours.'
>
> It is at moments like this that one is once again filled with regret at leaving such a country before the final victory when the fascists will be swept into the sea.[5]

---

[4] WL Interview.

[5] *Information Service*, 28 December 1938, p. 3.

McNeill and Franklyn were in hospital and missed this event but were well enough to participate in a grand farewell procession staged in Barcelona on 28 October in front of a crowd estimated at 200,000. A moment of lasting meaning for many of the men, McNeill wrote a detailed description of the parade in a letter to his mother:

> We had a magnificent parade in Barcelona, in which the whole of the International Brigade took part. Artillery, machine guns, tanks, mobile anti-aircraft, armoured cars, infantry machine guns mounted on motor cycles, watched us pass. Overhead the sky swarmed with planes. The light ones swooped down the spacious squares almost to our heads. High up the chasers and bombers lent a grim aspect to the proceedings as they patrolled the skies. But Franco's pilots never pick a fight with ours. Raining bombs on women and children and unprotected little towns like Corrimal and Bulli is his speciality.
>
> We marched nine abreast, headed by massed bands, with our flags and banners denoting the battles we had fought in. In front a huge 25ft banner told Spain we would continue to fight for aid for her in our own countries and against Fascism.
>
> The huge crowds went wild with enthusiasm. They cheered and shouted to us till they were hoarse, and clapped till exhausted. As our banners came into view the crowd cheered us to the echo. Hundreds of beautiful girls rushed out from the pavements and hugged and kissed us.
>
> It was a memorable occasion, and reached a climax when we dipped our colours passing Premier Negrin and La Pasionaria of the government. The people showered on us the beautiful flowers of Spain, and the scene will remain with us forever.[6]

In a letter jointly signed by McNeill, Carter, Franklyn and a New Zealander, Herbert "Bert" Bryan who had fought alongside Franklyn on Hill 481, the men followed strict Stalinist orthodoxy and said that the parade also showed the marvellous unity of the Catalonian people who

---

[6] *Daily News*, 14 December 1938, p. 5. A newsreel of the two farewells can be viewed: https://www.youtube.com/watch?v=xtJO_OG2MRk

had survived "such a struggle against the fifth column and the POUM".⁷ It was during this procession that La Pasionaria, the iconic communist leader, made her famous farewell to the International Brigades:

> *From all peoples, from all races, you came to us like brothers, like sons of immortal Spain; and in the hardest days of the war, when the capital of the Spanish Republic was threatened, it was you, gallant comrades of the International Brigades, who helped save the city with your fighting enthusiasm, your heroism and your spirit of sacrifice. And Jarama, and Guadalajara, Brunete and Belchite, Levante and the Ebro, in immortal verses sing of the courage, the sacrifice, the daring, the discipline of the men of the International Brigades.*
>
> *Mothers! Women! When the years pass by and the wounds of war are staunched; when the memory of sad and bloody days dissipates in a present of liberty, of peace and wellbeing; when the rancour has died out and pride in a free country is felt equally by all Spaniards, speak to your children. Tell them of these men of the International Brigades.*
>
> *Recount for them how, coming over seas and mountains, crossing frontiers bristling with bayonets, sought by raving dogs thirsting to tear their flesh, these men reached our country as crusaders for freedom, to fight and die for Spain's liberty and independence threatened by German and Italian fascism. They gave up everything – their loves, their countries, home and fortune, fathers, mothers, wives, brothers, sisters and children – and they came and said to us: "We are here. Your cause, Spain's cause, is ours. It is the cause of all advanced and progressive mankind."*
>
> *You can go proudly. You are history. You are legend.*⁸

From the parade McNeill took a small paper flag of the Spanish Republic, attached to a light wooden stick, as a souvenir. He also collected a hand-mirror, backed by a photograph of La Pasionaria, castanets decorated with ribbons of the colours of the Republic, a scarf and a shawl, postcards and a calendar for 1939 signed by other International Brigaders. He received a silver lapel badge and a *Carnet de Honor* (Card

---

⁷ *Information Service*, 28 December 1938, p. 2.
⁸ The full speech can be found in Tremlett, *International Brigades*, pp. 513-4.

of Honour) that recognised his service with the International Brigades. He preserved and cherished these mementoes for the rest of his life.⁹

As a long-term member of the CPA's Propaganda Department, McNeill was aware that his correspondence would be used in Australia to promote the cause for which he was fighting. His letters also had to be cleared by the International Brigades' own military censors. Unsurprisingly, the letters often conveyed an unreliable enthusiasm, best exemplified by one that appeared in the *Workers' Weekly* headlined "Great Ebro Victory Over Fascists" which absurdly claimed, against all military facts, that the retreat back across the Ebro was part of the original intention and plan.¹⁰

By the middle of November, the fascists had recovered all the territory that they had initially lost. Only then did McNeill feel uneasy about the likelihood of the Republic's ultimate defeat.¹¹ The Battle of the Ebro had cost the lives of at least 60,000 men on both sides. The Republic had lost enormous amounts of materiel, including 200 aircraft and 1800 machine guns. It was a devastating setback that exhausted the Republic's military capability. Defeat was now inevitable.¹²

Leaving Spain

In November, McNeill was in the small town of Castelfulit. He spent his time reading Frank Pitcairn's *Reporter in Spain*. Pitcairn was the pseudonym of Francis Claud Cockburn, a communist journalist who reliably followed the orthodoxy of the Comintern. His reports in the *Daily Worker* were savaged by Orwell in *Homage to Catalonia:* "They would be credible only if one knew nothing whatever of the facts."¹³ While McNeill was reading Pitcairn's book, the Republic was putting the leaders of the POUM on trial.¹⁴

---

9   These items are part of the McNeill Collection in the Illawarra Museum.
10 *Workers' Weekly*, 6 January 1939, p. 3.
11 WL interview.
12 Thomas, *Spanish Civil War*, p. 561.
13 Orwell, *Homage*, p. 121.
14 Thomas, *Spanish Civil War*, p. 568.

As part of their demobilisation, the International Brigaders completed detailed questionnaires set by the Spanish Communist Party and the International Brigades' War Commissariat about their backgrounds and experiences in Spain. Asked by the International Brigades what lessons McNeill would take home, he wrote:

> *The need for clear understanding of international fascism. I have learnt what people can suffer courageously when they are fully conscious of what they are fighting for, namely to retain their liberty and to retain the conditions they had commenced to enjoy under their Popular Front government and the need for crushing all traitors who organise opposition against the democratic program of government.*[15]

McNeill was assessed as being a "good cadre" who had done his job "very well and in a quiet manner". The questions asked by the Spanish Communist Party were more politically pointed. One asked if he ever held political positions contrary to the Communist Party's line or had relations with Trotskyists. Having already seen a Scottish Brigader imprisoned for Trotskyism, and perhaps by now aware of Marty's obsession with spies and the show trials being staged in Moscow, McNeill answered with a clear "No". He said he had come to Spain to "Fight against fascism, for democracy." Detailing his own political background, he did not mention his extensive involvement with the IWW, which was a sensible omission given that Trotsky's enthusiasm for the IWW, as it operated in America, was known.[16]

In his responses to the questionnaires, Carter admitted that he had been expelled from the CPA in 1931. His explanation was that this had been for drunkenness, not because he had been gaoled for theft. His commanding officer took care to note that he was sober and had "definitely overcome the weakness for which he was expelled". The assessment praised him for being a "very fine comrade and very sincere" who could be developed as a propagandist. Promotion to the rank of corporal had been under consideration. Asked his views of the International Brigades, Carter responded that he felt the Brigaders to

---

[15] WL interview; RGASPI 545/6/68/182-209.
[16] Mcintyre, *The Reds*, p. 86; RGASPI 545/6/68/182-209.

be the "advanced workers of their countries" who had "the courage to fight for their class under any conditions". He did feel though, that the officers needed special training.[17]

Franklyn was judged to be a "decent chap" with a good class consciousness, although displaying a "rank & file tendency". He thought his employment prospects as a seaman in Australia were poor, as he felt he would be victimised for his union and political work. He remained keen to explain to the "masses of Australia the Spanish struggle against fascist invasion by Mussolini and Hitler". He felt that the International Brigades had been "undaunted" and had shown "heroic courage alongside their Spanish brothers".[18]

After the farewell in Barcelona, the men had expected to promptly depart Spain. Instead, the British Battalion waited for more than a month in the town of Ripoll, close to the border with France, to be repatriated. While there, McNeill, Carter and Franklyn were joined by other Australians including Lloyd Edmonds and Kevin Rebbechi, and two New Zealanders, William Murn Macdonald and Bert Bryan, all being outside the tight circle of the CPA in Sydney and Wollongong.

The brave antipodean warriors assembled for a group photograph. Haggard and tired, the men were veterans of a defeated army and the standard bearers of a lost cause. The strain of their battlefront ordeal is shown on their stern, unsmiling faces. They are dressed in mismatched clothing, several wear berets, and an emaciated Rebbechi is in a raincoat. A Spanish flag was given to McNeill and Franklyn by the Popular Front for presentation to Miles, the general secretary of the CPA.[19]

---

[17] RGASPI 545/6/68/42-49.
[18] RGASPI 545/6/68/56-64.
[19] *Workers' Voice*, 4 February 1939, p. 2.

Photo 17 – International Brigaders from Australia and New Zealand at Ripoll, awaiting repatriation from Spain, 1938. Top L-R: Kevin Rebbechi, Lloyd Edmonds, William Murn Macdonald, Joe Carter; Bottom L-R: Jack Franklyn, Bert Bryan, Jim McNeill. See Appendix 1. (Alexander Turnbull Library, Wellington, New Zealand)

There were practical and diplomatic arrangements to be made to enable the British Battalion's repatriation, but the waiting dragged on and the men became impatient. Carter blamed Chamberlain for the delays, believing that the Conservative Prime Minister was hoping that Franco would take the opportunity to bomb the assembled left-wing fighters into oblivion.[20] McNeill believed that Chamberlain would prefer to see the British Battalion "under the soil of Spain" rather than have it return to Britain and work for the defeat of his government.[21] Franklyn joined a delegation which travelled to Barcelona to call on the British Consul and establish the reasons for the delay. The Consul

---

[20] Joe Carter – Amirah Inglis, Amirah Inglis Collection, Noel Butlin Archives, Australian National University.
[21] *Workers' Voice*, 18 January 1939, p. 2.

reported to London that the men believed that they were being misled and had fallen "into a dangerous mood". To avoid any "disagreeable incidents" he acted to expedite their departure.[22]

On 6 December, just over 300 International Brigaders departed Ripoll to arrive at the International Station at La Tour-de-Carol for the journey through France. Edmonds and Rebbechi were too ill to travel and stayed behind in hospital. The departure left Franklyn heartbroken.

> *I shall never forget that memorable morning. I happened to be gazing out, looking at the Pyrenees Mountains high up in the air, when I saw a lovely little Spanish house near the railroad tracks. Just outside, only a few yards from it, stood a Spanish peasant woman, symbolic of her race, standing upright to attention, fist tightly clenched, upraised in Salud to our battalion.*
>
> *As the train crossed over into French territory, to be quite frank, I was choking, that old lady was 70 if she was a day. There she stood until we were out of sight and I held my fist up till I could see her no longer.*
>
> *That old lady, who was quite near a land of full and plenty, was practically starving, yet she could stand there on that cold morning and show her hatred of fascism, raise her fist in clenched salute, and cry "Viva is International!"*
>
> *That last silhouette of Spain will stay in my memory as long as I live.*[23]

In Spain, food had been scarce, but in a France not ravaged by civil war it was plentiful. At a station on the French side of the border the men gorged on butter, cheese, omelettes, fruit, coffee, wine and English chocolate.[24] The men expected their next stop to be in Paris, but by December 1938 the Popular Front government of France was collapsing under the strain of divisions over the war in Spain and the Munich agreement. This fraught political situation likely explains

---

[22] *Workers' Star*, 20 January 1939, p. 4; NAA: A2910, 433/1/85 PART 1.
[23] *Workers' Star*, 20 January 1939, p. 4.
[24] Ibid.

why their train was diverted away from Paris, a disappointment for the International Brigaders who had anticipated being greeted by their supporters in the city of light.

In London

Instead, the men had to wait until the next evening, when their train arrived at Victoria Station, London, to be greeted by an official party of parliamentarians, trade union leaders and thousands of well-wishers. In scenes which the newspapers said had not been witnessed since the end of the Great War, thousands of people broke through police cordons to embrace the men. The crowd greeted them with cries of "Down with the Chamberlain government! Long live the Spanish Republic!" Speeches of welcome and congratulations were made with Attlee describing the International Brigaders as "heroes of the democratic faith".[25] The men then formed up in orderly ranks and a procession of thousands, led by a bugle band, marched to the Co-op Hall in Whitechapel where the veterans were feted with a reunion banquet. Carter reported that the meal was wonderful, and "we certainly did credit to it".[26]

The British and Irish veterans dispersed, returning back to their homes. The Australians though, were effectively destitute and still had to travel from London back to Australia. McNeill, Carter and Franklyn were joined for the journey home by three other Brigaders, Charlie McIlroy, Charlie Walters and Charlie Riley, the latter two having been repatriated earlier because of the seriousness of their injuries.

The six men were billeted across London with supporters of the International Brigade Dependants and Wounded Aid Committee. This relief organisation had already been supporting Riley and Walters and on 18 November made the first approach to the Australian government to assist with the men's passage home. The Australian

---

[25] *The Argus*, 9 December 1938, p.11.
[26] *Workers' Weekly*, 3 January 1939, p. 3 and *Workers' Star*, 28 January 1939, p. 1.

High Commission referred the matter to Canberra and in a cable dated 1 December, before McNeill, Carter, Franklyn and McIlroy had left Spain, Prime Minister Lyons agreed to their repatriation.

Subsequently, the men also requested advances of £10 each to cover expenses, including new underclothes and incidentals. This was also approved by Lyons and the men, having signed declarations agreeing that they would repay the cost of their passages and the advances, were provided with certificates of identity and booked on the *Maloja* to depart Tilbury for Australia on 6 January 1939.[27]

This left the men to spend Christmas in London. McNeill and Franklyn were billeted with Mr and Mrs Longhurst, Communist Party members active in the co-operative movement. McNeill found the Longhursts to be "wonderful people" who treated the men well. The Australians were starting to recover from the deprivations experienced in Spain with McNeill gaining more than 10 kilograms while in London. He said that every time they passed a shop window displaying foodstuffs, someone would say, "If that were only in Barcelona or Madrid!"[28]

McNeill and Franklyn also spent time with Tommy Bloomfield, a Scot who had been captured at Jarama and had witnessed the killing of Dickinson. After suffering harsh treatment while imprisoned, Bloomfield had been released in the prisoner exchange on condition that he not return to Spain. He broke this pledge and was back with the British Battalion in time to take part in the Ebro fighting. The trio posed for a formal portrait which shows a friendly Franklyn in his beret and a stern Bloomfield in his forage cap flanking a drawn and evidently greying McNeill.

---

[27] NAA: A2910, 433/1/85 Part 1.

[28] *Workers' Star*, 20 January 1939, p. 4; *Workers' Star*, 3 February 1939, p. 1; *Workers' Weekly*, 24 January 1939, p. 1.

Anti-Fascists

Photo 18: Jack Franklyn, Jim McNeill and Tommy Bloomfield (L-R) in London, c1938. (Illawarra Museum)

The men also enjoyed the hospitality of the Haldanes, a prominent family that had devoted itself to the Republican cause. Charlotte Haldane had worked at the recruitment centre in Paris helping volunteers make their way to Spain. She became well known to the International Brigaders for her explicit lectures on the dangers of venereal disease.[29] Her husband, the communist biologist Professor J.B.S. Haldane, was famous for his scientific contributions including the development of the primordial soup theory on the origins of life. So famous was the Professor that he was known by his initials alone. J.B.S. visited Spain several times, and rather haplessly tried to assist. He was the man who took it on himself to instruct Dickinson's men in the use of the absent Mills hand grenades. One of the men observed that there was "something rather touching in the idea of this very great and brilliant geneticist trying to make what contribution he could to our cause".[30] The Haldanes' son, Ronald, aged just sixteen, had joined the International Brigades in November 1936, telling his

---

[29] Richard Baxell, *Forged in Spain*, London, 2023, pp. 152-3.
[30] Gurney, *Crusade*, p. 77.

mother he was a suitable recruit because he had done physical training at school.[31] Ronald was shot in the arm at Jarama but survived to be repatriated to England.

Charlotte Haldane invited the Australians to her home a few days before Christmas, where they enjoyed a festive turkey dinner. She had just returned from a tour of China where she had seen Mao's Red Army conduct itself in an impeccable manner. She pressed the men, on their return home, to warn Australians that their country would soon be attacked by the Japanese.[32] Nor was this the only warning that the men received of an impending war. Immediately prior to their departure they met with Pollitt who told them he expected war in Europe to break out by March.[33]

On the cold morning of 6 January 1939, the six men boarded a train at St Pancras to take them to the Tilbury docks. A crowd gathered on the platform to farewell them. Songs were sung and the Australian and Spanish flags were waved. A representative of the Australian Associated Press presented them with cartons of cigarettes, the *Daily Worker* photographed them looking grave in their London overcoats, and the long trip home commenced.[34] On boarding the *Maloja* they found among their fellow passengers a party of German-Jewish refugees who were fleeing from Hitler.

While their ship was steaming across the Indian Ocean, Barcelona fell to the fascists.

---

[31] Brome, *International Brigades*, p. 18.
[32] Joe Carter – Amirah Inglis, Amirah Inglis Collection, Noel Butlin Archives, Australian National University.
[33] WL interview.
[34] *Workers' Star*, 3 February 1939, p. 1; *Daily Worker*, 7 January 1939, p. 4.

13

A noble stand

McNeill was unaware that his family and friends back in Australia feared him dead. His family contacted the CPA for more information, but beyond the initial advice received from Pollitt it had none to share. Two brothers then contacted the Italian consul in the hope that McNeill had been taken prisoner by the Italian forces fighting for Franco. The consul blithely assured them that there were no Italian forces fighting in Spain.[1]

The news that McNeill was injured, and not dead, came with letters he wrote home from his hospital bed. The *South Coast Times* of 11 November conveyed McNeill's account of how he was hit, accompanied by assurances that he was recovering and could now "hobble with the aid of two sticks".[2]

It was news greeted with relief in Wollongong. The Port Kembla waterside workers had already contributed £100 to Spanish relief, a considerable sum for its time, and in September the men resolved to levy themselves another £100 by Christmas. The union stated that the death of Australians fighting fascism in Spain had "blazoned a name for the Australian working class" and "arouses our most sincere feelings to the point of admiration. In honour of our comrades that have made the supreme sacrifice, we will resolve to carry on the fight more bitterly against fascism both at home and abroad."[3]

---

[1] WL interview.
[2] *South Coast Times*, 11 November 1938, p. 8.
[3] *Maritime Worker*, October 1938, p. 3.

The leadership of the waterside workers saw fascism as a global phenomenon and believed that Australia was not somehow exempt from its dangers. In its newsletter, *Maritime Worker*, the union decried the alarming growth of fascism across the world. Spain was where workers were "fighting in defence of their country and democratic liberty" against Franco who was receiving the "open assistance and collaboration from his backers, Mussolini and Hitler". In China the Japanese were inflicting atrocities on an innocent population. This meant that Australians had been forced to realise, the editorial proclaimed, that "fascism is not confined to Europe but is within striking distance of our own shores". The editorial was buttressed with an article by Attlee detailing his recent trip to Spain. The Labour leader wrote that non-intervention had made the British government "an accessory to the murder of democracy in Spain".[4]

The *Dalfram*

On the same day that news of McNeill's survival was published, the Port Kembla waterside workers, under the leadership of the CPA's Ted Roach, carried a resolution confirming that because of the "unprovoked and murderous attack" by the Japanese against China, it had decided to "assist the Chinese workers in their fight against Fascist Japan".[5] Four days later, a tramp freighter, the *Dalfram*, docked at Port Kembla's No. 4 jetty, ready to be loaded with 7000 tons of pig-iron bound for Kobe, Japan, as an initial tranche of a contract for 23,000 tons. The 180 waterside workers at Port Kembla refused to complete the loading of the ship, triggering a major industrial dispute. The dispute was extraordinary as it was a political stand against fascist aggression, and not the usual industrial dispute about wages or working conditions.[6]

---

[4] *Maritime Worker*, April 1938, p. 4 and p. 11.

[5] Rupert Lockwood, *War on the Waterfront: Menzies, Japan and the Pig-iron Dispute*, Sydney, 1987, p. 110.

[6] Jon White, 'The Port Kembla Pig Iron Strike of 1938', *Labour History*, No. 37, November 1979, p. 63.

The dispute escalated into a matter of national importance. The Lyons government insisted that it, and not the Port Kembla waterside workers, would determine Australia's trade and foreign policies. After a month-long stand-off, BHP, which had the export contract with Mitsui for the pig-iron, announced that it was standing down 4000 steelworkers. The economic impact of this, in a town of Wollongong's size, was devastating. Layoffs made for a grim Christmas for the entire community, including the small businesses and traders who were dependent on the wages of the waterside workers and steelworkers.

In the middle of this dispute, another letter from McNeill arrived congratulating the waterside workers on the action they had taken to protect the young German seaman from deportation to the "torture camps of Hitler". McNeill saw the Port Kembla workers as providing a "practical demonstration of the far-reaching international value of such actions" in helping "to beat back the union-breaking hordes of fascists".[7] Citing fears of severe punishment in Hitler's concentration camps, more German seamen would abandon their ships at Port Kembla in 1939.[8]

While the *Dalfram* dispute was underway, the New Theatre returned to Wollongong and performed Betty Roland's short play *War on the Waterfront* before an audience of waterside workers. The piece centred on a dramatized confrontation between a waterside worker and the might of BHP:

> BHP: *What business is it of yours where the cargo goes to? It's your job to load it and ask no questions.*
>
> JOE: *Oh yes, Adolph? Since when was I born deaf and dumb?*
>
> BHP: *Will you get on with your work?*
>
> JOE: *Not me, governor. I'm not going to make money out of the blood and suffering of helpless Chinese men and women. I leave all that sort of thing to you.*

---

[7] *Workers' Weekly*, 6 December 1938, p. 3.
[8] *Daily News*, 1 February 1939, p. 2.

> BHP: *You'll find what it means to try your puny strength in international affairs. I'll break you and I'll cripple you for years.*
>
> JOE: *Perhaps you will, but, by God, not before I've made things pretty hot for you. There won't be a single man or woman in Australia who won't know all about the dirty game you're up to. Iron ore is banned, so you turn it into pig-iron and you ship it out and dodge the law that way, Mister BHP, the fattest hog in Australia. Got your belly full of Chinese corpses, haven't you.*[9]

The New Theatre sought permission to perform the biting work in Sydney's Domain, and when this was refused proceeded to perform it anyway in front of an enthusiastic audience of 2000. The performers were subsequently fined £5 each for defying the ministerial refusal made by the Minister for Agriculture, Albert Reid (Country Party).

As the *Dalfram* dispute dragged on into 1939, Attorney-General Menzies visited Wollongong in an attempt to obtain a resolution. As an envoy of a government seeking to resolve a dispute about the arming of an aggressive fascist state, Menzies was a provocative choice. Just weeks before he had made headlines with his public support for Nazi Germany's re-armament.[10] A hostile crowd greeted him in the middle of Wollongong with cries of his new sobriquet, "Pig-iron Bob". In the Town Hall Menzies met with Wollongong's union and political leaders. Roach told him that the union feared the pig-iron, if exported, may return as "destructive missiles fired at the inhabitants of the South Coast". Menzies responded that the government would not be coerced by a minority but, if the *Dalfram* was loaded, then the government would review its policy regarding the export of pig-iron.[11]

---

[9] Betty Roland, 'War on the Waterfront', *Communist Review*, February 1939, pp. 110-114.

[10] *Sydney Morning Herald*, 12 December 1938, p. 11.

[11] *Illawarra Mercury*, 13 January 1939, p. 6.

Photo 19 – Attorney General Menzies (aka Pig-iron Bob) in Wollongong, January 1939. (Fairfax Photographic Archive)

This was to be the basis of the eventual settlement, with the *Workers' Weekly* hailing the dispute as "spectacular, unselfish and historic". Placing it in an international anti-fascist context, the paper contended that it was Chamberlain, Lyons and Menzies who were betraying the national interest to Hitler, Mussolini and the Mikado, while working men stood against the fascist aggressors.[12]

The CPA was not alone in lavishing praise on Wollongong's anti-fascist strikers. Sir Isaac Isaacs, a former Chief Justice of the High Court of Australia and from 1931 to 1936 the Governor-General of Australia, had read *Mein Kampf* and wrote a pamphlet warning Australians of the need to make preparations for a looming war. He wrote of the strike:

For myself, I honour the men who stood out as long as they could,

---

[12] *Workers' Weekly*, 24 January 1939, p. 2.

and those who supported them. They went far, and with sincerity of heart and purity of motive, sacrificed much to vindicate, for the whole Australian community a general humanitarian sentiment, and the right to insist on personal freedom of conscience where unrestrained by law.

I believe that Port Kembla with its studied, but peaceful and altogether disinterested attitude of the men concerned, will find a place in our history beside the Eureka Stockade, with its more violent resistance of a less settled time, as a noble stand against executive dictatorship and against an attack on Australian democracy.[13]

The strike lasted ten long weeks and cost the workers of Wollongong £100,000 in forgone wages.[14] Here was a community traumatised by its Depression experiences of mass unemployment, the collapse of its trade unions and clashes with the New Guard. It was a community that, by 1938, had recovered with a renewed commitment to stand up for itself and others.

Japan was seen as a direct threat to Australia. One of the goals of the strikers and their supporters was to disrupt the war preparations of an aggressor nation. Australia's role in supplying Japan's war industries became a national issue, tagging the future Prime Minister Menzies with a humiliatingly appeasing nickname that, much to his chagrin, he would never shake off.[15] As for the *Dalfram* itself, it continued its work as a tramp steamer until it was torpedoed off the coast of Madagascar by a German U-boat in 1943.

As the International Brigaders traversed the Indian Ocean, an anonymous sonnet was published in Sydney's *Daily News*. The poet, who it transpired was Len Fox of the Spanish Relief Committee, recognised the *Dalfram* dispute as embodying the same determination to fight for freedom that was demonstrated in the men's service in Spain.

---

[13]   Isaac Isaacs, *Australian Democracy and Our Constitutional System*, Melbourne, 1939, pp. 15 and 25.

[14]   White, 'Port Kembla', p. 74.

[15]   Russell Ward, *A Nation for a Continent: The History of Australia 1901-1975*, Richmond, 1977, p. 229.

Jim McNeill and his mates in the Spanish Civil War

RETURN OF THE INTERNATIONAL BRIGADES

We hold our heads high reading of these men
Who marched, laughing, against the black battalions of death
And saved Madrid— though they alone know how — in the hours when
Liberty had to be fought for in the last ditch with the last breath.
We bend our heads low, remembering others whose eyes
Will never see gums over the lonely camp again.
Stretching their strange limbs to the Southern skies —
Barry, Baynham, Hynes — and all who died for liberty in Spain.

The Brigades come home, their crowded chapter ended,
Men branded with scars won defending freedom's flame
On Spain's red soil as on Eureka's hill.
We turn from these Australians who defended
In far lands our heritage to find the same
Proud spirit burning at Port Kembla still.[16]

---

[16] *Daily News*, 26 January 1939, p. 6.

14

The future will raise monuments

On 2 February 1939, while the Republic was entering its death throes, the Spanish Relief Committee organised a memorial service in Sydney for those Australians who had died in the conflict. The names of Dickinson, Morcom and Young were listed among those who "died fighting for Democracy and Freedom". More than 600 people attended the ceremony in the Assembly Hall at Wynyard with Reeve, Dickinson's IWW mentor, seated in the front row. Reverend Purnell led the service, Chopin's *Funeral March* was played, and a minute's silence observed. Speeches were made by well-known identities including the activist Jessie Street, the journalist A.F. 'Bluey' Howells who had recently returned from a visit to Spain, and International Brigader Sam Aarons. Afterwards, those attending walked to the Martin Place Cenotaph to lay wreaths.[1]

The international situation had grown ever more disturbing. In Europe, Hitler had dismembered Czechoslovakia, taking the Sudetenland and was readying to occupy what was left. Legions of Nazis had unleashed *Kristallnacht*, a bout of murderous terror on Jews living in Germany, Austria and the Sudetenland. Japan was continuing its war on China and had used poison gas to win the Battle of Wuhan.

---

[1] *Sydney Morning Herald*, 3 February 1939, p. 7; *Daily News*, 3 February 1939, p. 2; Inglis, *Australians*, p. 187; A.F. Howells, *Against the Stream: The Memories of a Philosophical Anarchist 1927-1939*, Melbourne, 1983, p. 165.

Anti-Fascists

All these developments had repercussions in Australia. The *Dalfram* strike put Australia's response to Japanese aggression on the national agenda. A fear existed that Hitler's next territorial demand would be for the return of the colonies, including New Guinea, which had been stripped from Germany at Versailles. The potential for Nazi Germany to occupy New Guinea was perfect material to alarm the Australian public and the prospect generated numerous frightening press articles. The *Workers' Weekly* and the *Labor Daily* predicted that Chamberlain and Lyons would again be only too eager to appease Hitler. The *Sydney Morning Herald* editorialised that handing New Guinea over to the Nazis would make it "a pistol pointed at our head".[2]

Concerns about the servile appeasing instincts of the Australian government were scarcely allayed by the rebuke given by Prime Minister Lyons to the visiting British novelist H.G. Wells. Lyons took exception to Wells' description of Hitler as "a certifiable lunatic", observing it was to be regretted that Wells had made "disparaging remarks about the leaders of other nations" while a visitor in Australia.[3]

Even as late as July 1939, after Franco had secured his final victory in Spain, after Germany had seized all of what had been Czechoslovakia and abandoned the Anglo-German Naval Agreement, obeisance to the dictators continued. Menzies, who had become Prime Minister in April subsequent to the death of Lyons, was unabashed in his praise of Hitler:

> *History will label Hitler as one of the really great men of the century.*

And:

> *Hitler has proved himself a great man and a tireless worker.*[4]

His approach to the international situation on the eve of the outbreak of war was asinine:

> *You gain nothing by imputing low or improper motives to your*

---

[2] *Labor Daily*, 12 November 1938, p. 1; *Workers' Weekly*, 15 November 1938, p. 1; *Sydney Morning Herald*, 14 November 1938, p. 10.

[3] *Sydney Morning Herald*, 6 January 1939, p. 9.

[4] *Mirror*, 15 July 1939, p. 17.

opponents. What the whole world needs is a lot more good sense and understanding.[5]

In Perth

This then was the political climate that faced the International Brigaders when the *Maloja* arrived at Fremantle on 7 February 1939. The men had left the country against their government's wishes, often secretly, sometimes under assumed identities or as stowaways. Now they were publicly hailed as heroes. The Spanish Relief Committee launched a major publicity campaign and staged numerous events to raise money and promote the cause.

Before docking, the men were greeted by a speeding launch flying streamers in the purple, red and gold of the Spanish Republic. In response, the ever-musical Franklyn, in his black beret, standing straight and strong, produced his soldier's mouth organ, threw back his head and played the marching song of the International Brigades. His comrades stood with their fists raised in salute, a gesture intended to typify, as the *Workers' Star* explained, "the international working class in its undying fight against fascism… with the rising sun on their faces and courage and determination in their hearts, the heroic International Brigaders returned home to Australia".[6]

A photograph taken on board shows the six men properly attired in coats and suits; their arms linked in solidarity. A dapper McNeill in a three-piece suit holds the Australian flag, Franklyn, McIlroy and Riley wear their berets, and between them the men carry a sash and the flag of the Spanish Republic.[7] Standing proud, they look happy to be home.

---

5   *Daily News*, 17 July 1939, p. 2.
6   *Workers' Star*, 10 February 1939, p. 1.
7   *Chronicle*, 16 September 1939, p. 32.

Photo 20: Returning home on the *Maloja* are (L-R) Jim McNeill, Charlie McIlroy, Charlie Riley, Charlie Walters, Jack Franklyn and Joe Carter. See Appendix 2. (State Library of Western Australia b2377462_1)

Photo 21: Informal group shot on the *Maloja*. Standing (L-R) are Joe Carter, Charlie Walters and Jim McNeill. Sitting (L-R) are Jack Franklyn, Charlie McIlroy and Charlie Riley. (Illawarra Museum)

From Fremantle they took a train to Perth. One thousand people greeted them at the station, showering the returned heroes with flowers. Posing for photographs, McNeill held a placard that read "Arms and Food for the Spanish People". A banner proclaimed:

> *Long Live the Spirit of the International Brigade*
>
> *They Shall Not Pass*
>
> *Welcome Home From Spain – Aussies!*
>
> *We Salute You*[8]

Photo 22: The returning International Brigaders are welcomed at Perth's railway station. (State Library of Western Australia b2377462_6)

Prominent figures from the Spanish Relief Committee and CPA made speeches of welcome. A truck mounted with loudspeakers and banners carried the men to a lunchtime meeting in the centre of Perth where

---

[8] Accounts of the welcome are provided in *Daily News*, 8 February 1939, p. 2; *Workers' Star*, 10 February 1939, p. 1; *The West Australian*, 8 February 1939, pp. 21-2; *The Argus*, 8 February 1939, p. 13.

McNeill and Franklyn gave speeches detailing the destructive power of German and Italian bombers. Franklyn said it was the duty of all democratic people to "unite before it is too late". McIlroy added that unity and strength were needed to counteract the work of fascist agents in Australia.

That evening a reception was hosted for them at the Fremantle Trades Hall, where they heard speeches from the future Premier of Western Australia, John Tonkin, other Labor parliamentarians and trade union leaders. Acting as the group's spokesperson, McNeill gave press interviews decrying the policy of non-intervention and outlining the renewed commitment the men felt to assist Spain. A letter to Prime Minister Lyons, signed by each of returned men, was publicly released. It appealed for justice for Spain and the provision of relief for Spanish refugees. Pointedly, the men proclaimed their status as volunteers:

> *You, more than anyone else in Australia, are aware of the fact that we Australians left our home to fight for the Spanish Government without the knowledge or sanction of your Government. We, then, were volunteers in the full meaning of the word.*
>
> *We urge that the Australian Government should make some immediate grant to aid the thousands of Spanish refugees who stream across the French frontier and face the cold of a European winter without food or shelter, and that you raise your protest against the inhuman slaughter of refugee women and children by German and Italian airmen.*[9]

In Adelaide

The *Maloja* sailed for Adelaide where the group was paraded through the city in cars displaying Spanish Relief Committee banners. They met the Lord Mayor at the Adelaide Town Hall and were feted with a luncheon at the Rechabite Hall on Victoria Square attended by representatives of the trade unions, Labor Party, Left Book Club, Women's Non-Party

---

[9] NAA: A461, J420/1 Part 1.

Association and other sympathetic organisations.

Each of the men gave an address. Walters said that the democracies had much with which to reproach themselves, explaining that the fascists had brought 30,000 Moorish tribesmen to Spain: "Their reward was loot, drink and plenty of white women". McIlroy described doctors performing operations without anaesthetics and of small children dying of hunger. Franklyn detailed the crippling shortage of weapons, assuring his audience that if properly armed the Republic "could easily overcome Franco's army and the fascist hordes". Riley and Carter both detailed their anti-fascist motivations. Riley called on the Australian people to unite and resist fascist tyranny and aggression. Carter said that he had joined the International Brigades to defend freedom and democracy, and in fighting for the workers of Spain he was also fighting for Australia.[10]

Back in Adelaide almost ten years after leaving it, McNeill spoke emotionally of Dickinson, describing him as being well known "as a champion of the cause of the unemployed" who died in an "act of resolute bravery". Dickinson was, McNeill said, "a champion of the oppressed and exploited" who "died as he lived – undaunted to the end". There was no mention of how Dickinson had been prosecuted and imprisoned for publishing newspaper articles during his time in Adelaide.[11]

The report in the Labor Party's weekly newspaper, the *Workers' Weekly Herald*, was accompanied by a poetic tribute, "A Good Rebel", written by the pseudonymous James O'Sincerity, which recalled Dickinson's time on the stump and equated his political activism in Adelaide with his service and death in Spain.

---

[10] *Workers' Weekly Herald*, 17 February 1939, p. 3

[11] *Workers' Weekly Herald*, 17 February 1939, p. 3; *Mail*, 11 February 1939, p. 2.

Anti-Fascists

A Good Rebel

Bolshie, a rebel –
    They dubbed him so –
Out on a soap-box
    Years ago!
He strove for justice
    By day and night,
Fought for the outcasts
    An endless fight.
O, little he cared
    For scoffing eye,
As he sent his words
    To passers-by.
"Our land, it is rich.
    We want", he said,
"The right to labor,
    The right to bread.
"Homes for our children
    Where want's unknown –
"Some hours of leisure
    To call our own".
He struck for labor
    An honest blow –
A rebel they called him
    Years ago.

There flashes the news
    Of him again –
Now for the toiler
    In Bloody Spain –

There, facing a squad –
A murd'rous crew –
He throws his challenge –
"To Hell with you!"
With eyes to the front,
Back to the tree –
He died for the likes
Of you and me!

After lunch the men recorded an interview about their Spanish experiences. The CPA had recently taken to producing gramophone records which could be posted across Australia and played at party meetings and events. It is not clear if a record of this interview was ever produced and distributed.[12]

In Melbourne

When the *Maloja* arrived in Melbourne on 12 February, the welcomes continued. A luncheon was held in the banqueting hall of the Hotel Victoria, a venue that had to be hastily booked when the original venue, the tea room in the Buckley and Nunn department store, proved too small to accommodate the large number of acceptances.[13] The need for a larger venue was an indication of public support, as was the collection of £115 at a public meeting, chaired by Nettie Palmer, held in the Apollo Theatre. McNeill addressed the crowd:

> *We pledged ourselves to return to Australia to bring about the overthrow of the reactionary Chamberlain and Lyons governments and set up a democratic Labor government. We came back to build up a great army of workers for the Spanish Relief Committee, and force a lifting of the arms embargo.*[14]

---

[12] Joe Carter – Amirah Inglis, Amirah Inglis Collection, Noel Butlin Archives, Australian National University.

[13] *The Age*, 13 February 1939, p. 13.

[14] *Workers' Voice*, 18 February 1939, p. 4.

Before they landed, the men were interviewed aboard the *Maloja* by Norman Banks of radio station 3KZ, which broadcast from Melbourne's Trades Hall. The interview, part of Banks' popular "Voice of the Voyager" program, generated calls of complaint from the public and also an intimation of concern from the Postmaster-General, a ministerial post held by Archibald Cameron, a member of the Lyons Ministry.[15] For 3KZ ministerial attention was disturbing as Cameron had recently, in an astonishing act of political censorship, cut the transmission of Sydney radio station 2KY after he objected to its pro-strike coverage of the *Dalfram* dispute.[16]

In Sydney

The main focus of the SRC's publicity campaign was the men's arrival in Sydney, where a round of celebrations was planned. A leaflet was circulated that placed Spain in the patriotic tradition of the Eureka Stockade and the Anzacs. Supporters were encouraged to be at Pyrmont's wharf 20 at 7.30am on 16 February "to give an Aussie welcome to these great fighters for democratic liberty". Hundreds assembled to see a streamer-clad pilot boat escort the *Maloja* to its berth. The crowd burst into song, singing "For They are Jolly Good Fellows", "The Red Flag", and "Advance Australia Fair". Police were required to control the crowd which surged aboard to congratulate the men with handshakes and embraces. Riley was photographed in his singlet, displaying a bullet wound. There were speeches of welcome from dignitaries including J.B. Miles (CPA) Gordon King (Illawarra Trades and Labour Council), James Mackie (a Port Kembla ironworker), Edgar Ross (Miners' Federation) and a "coloured seaman" from the *Dalfram* whose name was not recorded.[17]

Speaking on behalf of the men, McNeill said they were sad to leave Spain and their places on the front lines "while our heroic brothers lie forever in the warm heart of the Spanish soil". Dickinson and the other

---

[15] Inglis, *Australians*, p. 188.
[16] Lockwood, *War on the Waterfront*, pp. 172-6.
[17] *Workers' Weekly*, 14 February 1939, p. 1; *Workers' Weekly*, 17 February 1939, p. 1.

Australians left behind, he said, "lie forever amid the olive groves and grape fields in the hills and valleys of Spain".[18]

McNeill was presented with a bouquet of flowers in the Republic's colours (yellow hyacinths, purple roses and red gum tips) by a woman who told him she had cried on reading that he had been killed.[19] From the wharf, the men travelled in a procession of decorated cars through the city to the Hotel Metropole for morning tea and press interviews.

That evening 2000 people packed into the Sydney Town Hall to show the men that Australia was, as the *Workers' Weekly* proclaimed, "proud and honoured to welcome them home". McNeill said they had received cables of welcome from 96 different organisations and were pleased with the broad nature of the support. Speaking through cheers, Maurice Blackburn MP (Labor), who was visiting from Melbourne, predicted:

> *The future will raise monuments to many men who today are unknown. They will be raised to men who have died for freedom and who have risked their lives for freedom.*[20]

A resolution declared with "joy and pride", that the men had given "valiant service in defence of Spanish and world democracy".[21] A collection raised £172 and the anti-fascist tone of the evening was complete when a group of sailors, who had jumped ship rather than sail the *Dalfram* and its pig-iron to Japan, was presented to the enthusiastic crowd.[22]

Activity was intense over the following week. The men spoke in the Domain, on radio stations 2KY and 2BL, and at meetings across Sydney. On Saturday they were part of a showboat night cruise around Sydney Harbour. Passengers were entertained by a choir of young German and Austrian refugees, who were described as being of much more Aryan

---

[18] *Workers' Weekly*, 17 February 1939, p. 1.
[19] *Daily News*, 17 February 1939, pp. 1-2.
[20] *Workers' Weekly*, 21 February 1939, p. 1.
[21] *Daily News*, 17 February 1939, p. 1.
[22] *Workers' Weekly*, 21 February 1939, p. 1; Minutes of the Spanish Relief Committee, 22 February 1939, Phil Thorne Collection, Noel Butlin Archives, Australian National University.

appearance than either Hitler or Goebbels.²³

Amidst the round of celebrations, there were several sour notes. The Australian government chose not to make an official acknowledgement of the anti-fascist service of Australians in the International Brigades. The Minister for External Affairs, Billy Hughes, who had been a vociferous advocate for Australia's participation in the Great War, declined to attend any of the welcomes on the ground that his presence would contravene the policy of neutrality and imply that the Australian government approved of the men's participation in the fighting.²⁴ The NSW Police made their interest in the men known. A plainclothes officer took a verbatim record of the proceedings at the Town Hall, and in an echo of the Adelaide free speech campaign, officers collected names after McNeill solicited donations for Spain while addressing a crowd in the Domain.²⁵

There were sections of society that were less than admiring. An article in the Catholic church's *Southern Cross* referred to the International Brigades as "the scum of all nations", while Father Richard Morrison wrote that the Brigaders were the "scum of the earth":

> *Scum, scum, scum – don't you hear the beat of the drum?*
>
> *Scum of the earth, scum of the earth.*²⁶

In Wollongong

On 27 February, after more than a week of welcomes and receptions in Sydney, McNeill and Carter took the train to Wollongong. Arriving in the early evening, they were greeted by a pipe band that led them in a procession to a civic reception given by the Mayor of Wollongong. Another Wollongong alderman, Rex Connor, the future Whitlam government minister, said that McNeill and Carter had seen things they

---

23 *Daily News*, 16 February 1939, p. 2.
24 *Sydney Morning Herald*, 15 February 1939, p. 17.
25 *Daily News*, 17 February 1939, p. 1; *Workers' Weekly*, 21 February 1939, p. 4.
26 *Southern Cross*, 10 March 1939, p. 17; *Southern Cross*, 4 August 1939, p. 17.

would be glad to forget but had proved themselves true internationalists. McNeill responded with a declaration that they loved the Illawarra and would not like to see things happen in Wollongong that had happened in Spain. Carter said that by fighting fascism in Spain, they were just pushing the enemy farther away from Wollongong. Across the Illawarra the men enjoyed handsome greetings with the Port Kembla Ironworkers' hosting a smoko at the Soldiers' Memorial Hall.[27]

The six *Maloja* veterans met with the executive of the Spanish Relief Committee and each indicated a willingness to continue to work for the cause. McNeill and Carter undertook a tour of the Hunter Valley, speaking at public meetings in Kurri Kurri, Cessnock and Newcastle.[28] Without training in public speaking, giving speeches to large gatherings did not come easily to the men. McNeill, with his background in the IWW and activism in the Ironworkers' union, was regarded as the most effective speaker, but Carter struggled.

> *It was very, very hard to get up and speak. You're trembling. You don't know what to say. We had brilliant meetings, big meetings, sympathetic meetings, good people, and we didn't know how to…*
>
> *I'd rather be in the front lines than get up in the Apollo Theatre with all these people and not know what to say.*[29]

After speaking from the CPA's platform in the Domain, Carter was approached by officials who proposed that he join the army and apply his battlefield experience as an instructor.

> *When we hit Sydney the army, officials of the army, knowing that the war was coming on, they came down and said "What about joining the army as instructors?"*
>
> *When we went to Spain, we were scoundrels…Now, what did they want to do? They wanted us to become instructors.*

---

[27] *South Coast Times*, 3 March 1939, p. 19; *South Coast Times*, 17 March 1939, p. 7.

[28] *Newcastle Morning Herald and Miners' Advocate*, 17 March 1939, p. 15.

[29] Joe Carter – Amirah Inglis, Amirah Inglis Collection, Noel Butlin Archives, Australian National University.

It's a funny thing how they change – when it suits them![30]

Carter declined the army's offer and did not serve in the Second World War, a decision about which he later expressed regret.[31]

Ken McPhee

McNeill and Carter were not the only, nor the first, Port Kembla steelworkers to return from the Spanish Civil War. Kenneth "Ken" McPhee was born in 1913 and had grown up in Manly, NSW. He went to sea at 15 and while a sailor had "learned the rudiments of Communism and the hypocrisy of religion". He was at the forefront of the seamen's strike in 1936 and after it was lost found himself unable to secure further berths. He took a position as a rigger at the Port Kembla steelworks and became the treasurer of his local communist party unit.

His time in Wollongong was short as later in 1936 he was able to secure a position as a seaman and departed for England. Soon after arriving he took a position on the *Llanstephan Castle* which was working the around Africa route. While aboard and listening to the wireless he heard about the International Brigades. Determined to join the fight, he jumped ship in Marseille and made his way to Spain, arriving on 20 January 1937.[32] He went into action on 12 February at Jarama with the No. 1 Company. He was wounded but managed to survive the carnage. He also fought at Brunete, where he was shot through the shoulder and lung. He was repatriated to England and then worked his way back to Australia aboard the dredge *Kerimoana*.[33]

He was welcomed with a reception organised by trade unions and the Spanish Relief Committee. It was attended by the Spanish Consul, Senor Baeza, and Alderman Donald Grant MLC. A leading member of the IWW during the Great War, Grant had been imprisoned, along

---

[30] Joe Carter – John Clements, Imperial War Museum, IWM 3812.
[31] Joe Carter – Amirah Inglis, Amirah Inglis Collection, Noel Butlin Archives, Australian National University.
[32] RGASPI 545/6/68/140.
[33] RGASP 545/6/53/22; *Labor Daily*, 15 August 1938, p. 1.

with Reeve, as one of the Sydney Twelve. After his release he joined the Labor Party and would be elected to the Australian Senate in 1943. Grant told McPhee: "You have held up the honour of democrats of this country."³⁴ McPhee replied that he had gone to Spain:

> *Because the Spanish people were fighting for freedom and if we couldn't help them through our governments at least I could help by fighting with them.*³⁵

Hailed as a hero for his service under fire as a messenger, McPhee said:

> *That is nothing. You ought to have seen the two Australian nurses at the Battle of Jarama. For 10 days they worked night and day through a continual bombardment. They are the bravest people I've ever seen.*³⁶

McPhee served in the merchant navy during the Second World War and placed himself in serious danger by doing so. There were 30 ships in Australian waters lost to enemy action. At least 654 people died, with others suffering serious injuries. The vessels carrying ore for BHP were called 'death ships' because they sank so quickly.³⁷ The fatality rate for members of the Seamen's Union of Australia was higher than that suffered by Australia's fighting forces.³⁸ McPhee survived and in the post-war years maintained his trade union activism.³⁹ He worked as a ferry master on Sydney Harbour and died in Sydney in 1968. At the news, 120 waterside workers stood in silent tribute.⁴⁰

---

[34] *Labor Daily*, 16 August 1938, p. 5.
[35] *Workers' Weekly*, 19 August 1938, p. 2.
[36] *Labor Daily*, 16 August 1938, p. 5.
[37] Patricia Miles, *War Casualties and the Merchant Navy*, https://www.environment.nsw.gov.au/maritimeheritageapp/research.aspx?id=51 accessed 27 March 2024.
[38] Australian War Memorial, Merchant Navy – Second World War, https://www.awm.gov.au/articles/encyclopedia/merchant_navy accessed 30 March 2024.
[39] *Tribune*, 20 May 1953, p. 10.
[40] *Tribune*, 21 August 1968, p. 11.

15

A reactionary, imperialist war

On 2 March 1939, following the lead of Britain and France, Australia formally recognised Franco as the head of the Spanish government. Madrid was taken when what remained of the Republican army surrendered on 28 March and the war ended on 1 April. In almost three years of fighting 600,000 people had died. About 100,000 had been murdered or summarily executed. Some 5000 of the 35,000 International Brigaders were either killed in action or died of disease. Rather than live under Franco's fascism, 340,000 Spaniards became refugees. The non-communist leaders of the Republic, including Azana and Negrin, found refuge in democratic countries including France and Britain; La Pasionaria made her way to Moscow. Exile for the defeated supporters of the Republic was prudent given that Franco presided over 200,000 executions during the next four years.[1]

As the affairs of the Spanish Relief Committee wound down, the returned International Brigaders returned to the realities of everyday life. Carter and Franklyn obtained employment on the wharves. Carter travelled around Australia, working port to port, before returning to Wollongong. He became a stalwart of the CPA and worked on the wharves at Port Kembla for decades. Franklyn also travelled to different ports before gaining a place in Sydney. The Australian government sent a number of letters seeking repayment of the funds expended to repatriate them. Both Carter and Franklyn ignored the requests for payment and officers from the Commonwealth Investigation Service followed up with personal visits to their homes.

---

[1] Thomas, *Spanish Civil War*, p. 606; Beevor, *Spanish Civil War*, p. 390; Tremlett, *International Brigades*, p. 510.

Franklyn told the constables that his financial position was unsound and he had "no intention of ever paying the money" as he considered it the duty of the Australian government to provide a person stranded in a foreign country with their passage home. Carter took the matter up with James "Big Jim" Healy, general secretary of the Waterside Workers' Federation, who took the matter to Eddie Ward MP, a prominent Labor parliamentarian from inner Sydney. Requests for repayment then ceased.[2]

McNeill returned to his cottage in Wilga Street, Corrimal. The prestige attached to being a veteran of the Spanish Civil War meant that his involvement in the CPA's campaigns continued to be promoted. Both Carter and McNeill participated in a protest held in Wollongong against the government's plan to establish a national register, which the labour movement suspected of being a contrivance to surreptitiously introduce conscription. Plans for a boycott of the register, led by the Australian Council of Trade Unions, were well advanced but abandoned after Menzies made concessions including establishing a register of wealth as well as of manpower.[3]

Their experiences in Spain meant that McNeill and Carter had credibility when Wollongong's civic leaders met to discuss the question of what sort of civil defence measures the town required. Present at the meeting were political, business, union and community figures. It was an opportunity for the union leaders to reflect on the correctness of their stand against supplying Japan with war materials. The civic fathers heard from Carter about houses in Potts Point and Toorak that had solid, effective, bomb proof *refugios,* and that therefore so should the houses of the "real Australians who make the country go". He called for the construction of bomb shelters in the streets of Wollongong.[4]

---

[2] NAA: A367, C50142; Joe Carter – Amirah Inglis, Amirah Inglis Collection, Noel Butlin Archives, Australian National University.

[3] *Illawarra Mercury,* 21 July 1939, p. 6; Mcintyre, *The Reds,* pp. 382-3.

[4] *Illawarra Mercury,* 19 May 1939, p. 9. Construction of several air raid shelters in Wollongong commenced in 1942.

Nazi-Soviet Non-Aggression Pact

Local concerns about civil defence reflected the darkening international situation. Days after securing what was left of Czechoslovakia, Hitler started pressing territorial claims on Lithuania, which promptly gave up the city of Memel. His next demand was upon Poland. Indicating that there was to be no departure from Australia's support for appeasement, Menzies said that Hitler's demands about the Polish Corridor warranted "sympathetic consideration".[5]

On 17 April, Stalin offered Britain and France a military alliance that would bring each nation into war if any of them were attacked by Hitler. It took Britain six weeks to reply and even then only to suggest talks. Negotiations commenced, but dragged on slowly. Britain sent a relatively junior delegation to Moscow for talks that finally commenced on 12 August. Stalin had long been suspicious of the motives of the democracies. He believed they were attempting to contrive a war between Germany and the USSR, which he was desperate to avoid. Stalin's purges had wreaked slaughter through the leadership of the Red Army which was in no position to fight a war.[6]

On 23 August, Stalin executed an extraordinary volte-face and instead of continuing negotiations with Britain and France, signed a Non-Aggression Pact with Germany. The world was astonished. With Hitler's eastern front secure, war in Europe was now certain.

Stalin's Soviet Union had been the most trenchant opponent of Nazism and the two had armed opposing sides in the Spanish Civil War. Now they were in alliance. Communist parties around the world grappled with the news. How were they to explain the pact to their members, given that many had been attracted to communism precisely because of its previously resolute opposition to fascism?[7]

In Australia, prominent CPA members were "stunned" and "shocked"

---

5   *The Herald*, 29 April 1939, p. 1.
6   Richard Overy, *Russia's War*, Great Britain, 1998, pp. 43-6.
7   Evans, *The Third Reich in Power*, pp. 693-4.

by the signing of the Non-Aggression Pact.⁸ Some resigned in protest, others slipped quietly away. Betty Roland, the playwright of *War on the Waterfront*, was expelled for her "political and moral cowardice".⁹ Most members though stayed loyal to the party as they came to terms with events that none had anticipated.¹⁰

The CPA's attempts to understand what was happening, and provide leadership as to how developments should be interpreted, were befuddled. A first claim, that the Nazi-Soviet Non-Aggression Pact "can contribute very much to world peace", was rendered embarrassingly obsolete when, within days, Hitler invaded Poland and the Second World War began.¹¹ Many of the *Luftwaffe* pilots attacking Poland had been members of the Condor Legion and had acquired their skills and tested their tactics while fighting in Spain.¹²

Citing as precedents its support for China in its struggle against Japan and for Republican Spain against the fascists, the initial policy of the CPA was to support, in every way, the struggle of Poland against "enslavement by the Nazi beasts".¹³ On 17 September, the Red Army crossed Poland's eastern border and occupied the territory allotted to Stalin under the secret terms of the Non-Aggression Pact. This meant that the CPA's support for Polish independence contradicted Stalin's actions and was immediately unsustainable. So, yet another position was required and on 21 September the CPA's Central Committee decided:

> *In the new situation in relation to Poland some formulations hitherto used, such as the support for the struggle of Poland for independence, are no longer appropriate.*

---

8   Stuart Mcintyre, *The Party: The Communist Party of Australia from heyday to reckoning*, Crows Nest, 2022, p. 37.
9   Ibid., p. 39.
10 Mcintyre, *The Reds*, p. 389.
11 Communist Party of Australia Records, Mitchell Library, State Library of NSW, MS 5021 Box 5, Central Committee Circular 157, 23 August 1939.
12 Richard J. Evans, *The Third Reich at War*, London, 2008, p. 3.
13 Communist Party of Australia Records, Mitchell Library, State Library of NSW, MS 5021 Box 5, Central Committee letter to all districts and branches, 4 September 1939.

Instead, it was to be understood that the USSR had saved national minorities - Ukrainians and White Russians - from Nazi slaughter, and from domination by the "so called Poland".[14] In October the Central Committee was consoling itself with the thought that the Nazi-Soviet Non-Aggression Pact could provide a lasting peace in Europe if only politicians accepted that "It is unreal to say 'Hitler's word cannot be depended upon.'" The CPA wanted to see an international conference convened that would consider Hitler's proposals.[15]

By November, the CPA had fully embraced the position of the Comintern. The party declared the war against Hitler an imperialist conflict, a line strictly maintained until German forces attacked the USSR in June 1941. The CPA held an interpretation of events favourable to the Soviet Union and attacked Curtin and other "reactionary Labor leaders" who "have gone bankrupt and have crossed over to the camp of the imperialists" by actively supporting the war against Hitler.

> *The war was a reactionary, imperialist war which should have been opposed right from the beginning by all parties of the Communist International.*
>
> *It is more essential than ever that the Party be mobilised for the most resolute struggle against the war.*[16]

Because of its "duty to explain and popularise the role of the Soviet Union",[17] circumstances became even more challenging for the CPA following the Red Army's invasion of Finland on 30 November 1939. Despite indisputable evidence to the contrary, the CPA claimed that this invasion had not actually happened. Instead, the Red Army and the Finnish Peoples' Army were merely jointly engaged in purging Finland

---

[14] Communist Party of Australia Records, Mitchell Library, State Library of NSW, MS 5021 Box 5, Central Committee Circular 176, 21 September 1939.

[15] Communist Party of Australia Records, Mitchell Library, State Library of NSW, MS 5021 Box 5, Central Committee Circular 188, 6 October 1939.

[16] Communist Party of Australia Records, Mitchell Library, State Library of NSW, MS 5021 Box 5, Central Committee Circular 221, 29 November 1939.

[17] Communist Party of Australia Records, Mitchell Library, State Library of NSW, MS 5021 Box 5, Central Committee Circular 180, 28 September 1939.

of "war provocateurs and the Mannerheim clique".[18] This was a ludicrous lie and led to sustained hostility towards CPA activities and speakers. All of this culminated in the Menzies government's decision of 27 May 1940 to declare all communist organisations illegal, their activities and publications being "prejudicial to the defence of the Commonwealth or the efficient conduct of the war".[19]

McNeill's friends in Wollongong immediately conformed to the CPA's line on the war. The Illawarra Trades and Labour Council, which had previously so forcefully proclaimed its anti-fascism, carried a resolution declaring that the war with Nazi Germany "is a struggle between rival Imperialist groups, whose sole concern is the maintenance and extension of their territorial and economic possessions". It wanted to see peace negotiations with Hitler commenced at the first opportunity. Roach, who had led the waterside workers in their anti-fascist industrial actions, said that military service trainees "should fight for better conditions for the workers, not for huge profits for warmongers".[20] McHenry, who McNeill had worked with in the Ironworkers' union, told Wollongong's 1940 May Day crowd that "their objective should be to get together, show a solid front and recognise only one enemy – the capitalist".[21]

Joining up for the Second World War

McNeill was a loyal member of the CPA, but he demonstrated that his anti-fascist convictions were deeply and sincerely held. Perhaps drawing on the authentic rebelliousness of his Wobbly past, he simply disregarded the sophistries and lies of the CPA and immediately volunteered to serve in the 2nd Australian Imperial Force. Applications for enlistment opened at the Wollongong Drill Hall with the recruiting officers saying they were seeking applications from men aged between

---

[18] *Tribune*, 22 December 1939, p. 1.
[19] Mcintyre, *The Reds*, p. 396.
[20] *Illawarra Mercury*, 9 February 1940, p. 11.
[21] *South Coast Times*, 3 May 1940, p. 5.

20 and 35, who would "represent the cream of Australian manhood".[22] McNeill joined up immediately. He would later say that his motivation for signing up was:

> The hatred of fascism and stuff like that bloke in hospital [Otto, the German pilot] saying they were going to conquer the world.[23]

He was only a few months shy of 40 years old and so almost five years beyond the desired age. To ensure he was accepted, he lied on his attestation papers and made himself six years younger than he was, giving his date of birth as 8 January 1906. After a medical examination McNeill was declared fit for service.[24]

Nor was his age the only fiction he gave to make himself an attractive recruit. He stated that he had served with the forces of the Spanish Republic from 1937 to 1938, when in fact the records of the International Brigades show that he, Carter and Morcom all arrived in Spain during April and May 1938, and newspaper reports carried letters from him stating that he had left Australia only in 1938.[25] Perhaps he felt that exaggerating his recent military experience would help secure a favourable appraisal from the recruiting officer.

In the first months of the war the CPA was the target of attacks by soldiers who believed that a communist speaker had referred to them as "five bob a day murderers". Despite the claim being denied, antagonism lingered. The red flag was ceremoniously burnt by servicemen and there were violent confrontations between soldiers and CPA members in Sydney's Domain. In Melbourne and Brisbane soldiers clashed with communists at street meetings.[26]

In November 1939, the Military Board, responsible for the administration of Australia's military forces, issued commanding officers with detailed and secret instructions about communism: "the allegiance

---

[22] *Illawarra Mercury*, 6 October 1939, p. 1.
[23] WL interview.
[24] NAA: B883, NX4888.
[25] *Labor Daily*, 19 August 1938, p. 4.
[26] Mcintyre, *The Reds*, pp. 389–394.

and obligations of a Communist to the Communist International are entirely incompatible with the loyalty and duty of a soldier". The manual set out the process to be followed in investigating an active communist, who it said can "only be regarded as a subversive propagandist and potential agent for both espionage and sabotage".[27] The Military Board would have been humiliated to know that the CPA obtained a copy of their manual and circulated a typescript of its contents.[28]

Other communists who joined the Australian Imperial Force were discharged once their party membership became known. There is no record of McNeill's CPA membership ever being investigated or raised as a concern, even though his political affiliation had been widely publicised and was certainly no secret. With the fictions around his age and length of service in Spain accepted, and his membership of the CPA unacknowledged, his enlistment proceeded. On 3 November he was taken on strength with the 2/3rd Australian Infantry Battalion at a newly established training camp at Ingleburn, NSW. This battalion was part of the 16th Australian Infantry Brigade, which in turn was part of the 6th Australian Infantry Division of the 2nd Australian Imperial Force.

Gavin Long, the general editor of the *Official History of Australia in the Second World War*, considered why men volunteered. Possible motives he identified were that they were adventurers, held an ardent loyalty to England, were bored or unskilled and in need of a job. His conclusion is nobler and emphasises the volunteers were "conscious of a peculiarly compelling duty to the State and their fellow men". The *Official History* also described the impact of political developments on those who supported the Spanish Republic and who admitted the Nazi-Soviet Non-Aggression Pact left them feeling "bewildered" and willing to stand aside while they waited to see how the war developed.[29]

McNeill did not stand aside. Consistent with the idea of selflessness,

---

[27] Military Board, *Military Manual for Dealing with Subversion in the Armed Forces*, 1939, p 4. A typescript is in the CPA records in the Mitchell Library, State Library of New South Wales, ML MS 5021, Box 85.

[28] Mcintyre, *The Reds*, p. 466.

[29] Gavin Long, *To Benghazi*, Canberra, 1961 (revised edition), pp. 56-60.

his motivation for enlisting was his well-established hatred of fascism. He had fought the New Guard in the streets of Sydney, then been shot on a Spanish battlefield by Franco's fascists, and so it was entirely predictable that he would be among the first Australians to volunteer to fight Hitler. Having previously ignored his government's position on the Spanish Civil War, he now defied his party's position on the Second World War, and was ready to return to Europe to again fight fascism. It was as the writer Ernest Hemingway had predicted when the American International Brigaders departed Spain: "No good men will be at home for long."[30]

Nugent Bull

McNeill was not the only Australian veteran of the Spanish Civil War to be part of the Second World War. Nugent Bull, a devout Catholic and a member of the Campion Society in Sydney, was unique as the only Australian to fight for the fascists in Spain. He was schooled at Marist High School and St Joseph's College in Sydney, and was active in the Old Boys' society which described him as "breezy irrepressible Nuge". He regularly attended the Domain to support Catholic speakers and heckle those of the left. An enthusiastic sportsman, he was friends with the Australian test cricketer Bill 'Tiger' O'Reilly. He managed his family's undertaking business in Newtown and also did the accounts for Luna Park.[31]

Ideologically motivated by his Catholic anti-communism, he travelled to Spain in 1937 and enlisted in the Joan of Arc battalion of the Spanish Foreign Legion. His brigade's motto was "Long Live Death!" and he fought in the freezing cold temperatures of the battle for Teruel, but fell ill and was transferred to a transport unit for the final offensive against Barcelona in early 1939. His letters home showed that he

---

[30] Ernest Hemingway, 'Milton Wolff', in Jo Davidson, *Spanish Portraits*, New York, c1938. No pagination.

[31] Inglis, *Australians*, p. 123; J. Keene, 'An Antipodean Bridegroom of Death: An Australian with Franco's Forces in the Spanish Civil War', *Journal of the Royal Australian Historical Society*, Vol. 70, Part 4, April 1985, p. 251.

took great interest in political developments in France, decrying the influence of "Masonic Jewry" which he felt was running the country. He predicted France would soon be engulfed in a war against "Atheistic Communism".[32] As for Britain, Bull thought "the stamp of the governing classes is pronouncedly Jewish".[33]

He participated in Franco's triumphant victory parade through Madrid and travelled to Morocco where he received an honourable discharge. He then went to Britain and, after a frustrating search for full-time employment, joined the RAF's No. 149 Squadron as a gunner. He took part in raids over Germany and bombed factories that had produced weapons for Franco and were now doing so for Hitler. He died on 9 September 1940 when, during an electrical storm, his Wellington bomber crashed into the English Channel.[34]

After news of his death appeared in the Australian press, the Bull family received a spiteful letter which illustrated the intense and bitter emotion that the war in Spain had aroused:

> *That he should be killed fighting against those he fought with in Spain is a just fate.*[35]

---

[32] Keene, *Antipodean Bridegroom*, p. 261.
[33] Keene, *Fighting for Franco*, p. 108.
[34] Judith Keene, 'Bull, Joseph Nugent Palmer (1908–1940)', *Australian Dictionary of Biography*, National Centre of Biography, Australian National University, https://adb.anu.edu.au/biography/bull-joseph-nugent-palmer-12827/text23157, published first in hardcopy 2005, accessed online 6 December 2023.
[35] Inglis, *Australians*, p. 204.

16

Soldiers of democracy

The conditions encountered by McNeill and the other recruits at the Ingleburn camp were primitive and reflected Australia's overall lack of war readiness. Roads were unformed, huts were not finished, kitchens and meat houses were not fly-proof, and latrines not properly functional. There were no medical supplies.[1] Sir Earle Page MP, a doctor, Gallipoli veteran, former leader of the Country Party and bitter critic of Menzies, visited the camp and criticised its sanitation arrangements. He said the risk of an epidemic was great and that the army needed to install a septic system or sewerage.[2]

Agitation by communists was not needed to create disgruntlement in a camp that was "wet" for officers and "dry" for the ranks. Meals were inadequate and there were complaints about the prices charged at the canteens, which were operated by a private contractor. The men's response to the extortionate prices was powerful; a canteen was burnt to the ground. Embarrassingly for the army, the NSW Police had to attend along with reporters from Sydney's newspapers. The men's direct action prompted an investigation that brought a positive result. The army took control of the canteens and cut prices in half.[3]

The men slept on palliasses and in the absence of proper uniforms, the army issued clothing that had been in storage since the First World War. Like the International Brigades, the Australian Army suffered from a lack of equipment. The 16th Brigade waited two weeks before

---

[1] AWM52 8/3/3/1, Diary for 4 November 1939.
[2] *Sydney Morning Herald*, 28 November 1939, p. 13.
[3] *Daily Telegraph*, 21 November 1939, p. 1; *Daily Telegraph,* 6 December 1939, p. 9.

receiving their rifles. Training concentrated on drilling, digging, and long route marches. On one occasion the 2/3rd marched from Ingleburn to Austinmer, north of Corrimal, so the men could enjoy a swim in the surf.[4]

While the men were slogging through their training, being shown sexual health films like *Damaged Goods*, entertaining themselves with sport, boxing tournaments and vaudeville shows, a political debate was stirring about what should be done with them. The British War Office wanted the Australian 6th Division sent overseas as soon as possible. Though Australia was nominally at peace with Japan, the Labor Opposition publicly expressed foreboding about Japan's aggressive intentions, a concern expressed privately in military and government circles. Would it not be more prudent to keep the men at home to defend Australia?

In late November, Menzies announced the 6th Division would be deployed overseas. On 4 January 1940, a farewell parade was held through the streets of Sydney. An estimated 250,000 people lined the streets and climbed onto shop awnings to cheer the 6000 marching soldiers. The *Daily News* reported that among the multi-coloured streamers and boxes of confetti, there were both tears and cheers. What had been a collection of volunteers was now looking like a proper army.

> *Sun-tanned and fit, with arms swinging in rhythmic precision and bayonets gleaming, Australia's new army marched with all the spirit and zeal of the men of 1914-18.*
>
> *Wearing their new-type uniforms, with long trousers and gaiters, and carrying rifles and fixed bayonets, the men moved off on schedule from Prince Alfred Park.*[5]

The first convoy carrying part of the 6th Division departed Sydney on 9 January for the Middle East where their training was to continue. McNeill was not with them; he had been transferred to the Army Service Corps, responsible for logistics and transport. His contingent was scheduled to follow several months later.

---

[4] Peter Charlton, *The Thirty-Niners*, South Melbourne, 1981, pp. 43-48.
[5] *Daily News*, 5 January 1940, p. 5.

In convoy

McNeill's second voyage to Europe to fight fascism was very different from his first. He was to board, not stowaway on, the ship known to the military by its code name of *X1*, and to the world as the *Queen Mary*, the largest and fastest passenger liner in the world. Launched in 1936, the *Queen Mary* was in New York when war broke out. Requisitioned by the British Admiralty, the ship arrived in Sydney on 16 April. Too large to be docked at any of Sydney's wharfs, it was moored off Bradleys Head. Works began to convert her from a luxury liner capable of accommodating 2100 passengers, into a troop ship that could carry 5000 soldiers. Hundreds of workers from the Cockatoo Docks and Engineering Company were ferried out to work in continuous night and day shifts to effect the transformation. Luxurious fittings were removed, multi-tiered bunks and hammocks installed and the work was completed on 3 May.[6]

McNeill and the Army Service Corps embarked on 4 May. The men woke early and breakfasted at 4.15 am. A parade was held in the cold darkness at 5.00 am and a train transported them from Ingleburn to the city. From a wharf at Pyrmont they were ferried out to the *Queen Mary*.[7] The ship was one of seven passenger liners assembled in convoy to transport 18,200 troops from Australia and New Zealand to the Middle East. It departed Sydney on 5 May and headed to sea to rendezvous with the liners coming from New Zealand. Once formed up, the convoy headed south, escorted by three war ships, the *Australia*, *Canberra* and New Zealand's *Leander*, and was joined by another liner that departed from Melbourne.

The convoy stopped at Fremantle where the men on all the ships, other than the *Queen Mary*, enjoyed shore leave in Perth before departing Australia. Missing out on a shore interlude made for a sour mood on the *Queen Mary*. The soldiers staged a protest in the dining room which nearly degenerated into a riot.[8] The generally depressed atmosphere

---

[6] Peter Plowman, *Across the Sea to War*, Dural, 2003, p. 118.
[7] Michael Clarke, *My War 1939-1945*, Toorak, 1990, p. 130.
[8] Plowman, *Across the Sea*, p. 129.

was not lifted by the news that Germany had commenced the Battle of France and launched attacks across Holland, Belgium and Luxembourg.

The convoy set out across the Indian Ocean towards Ceylon (Sri Lanka). Bad weather made some men sea sick and there was alarm when a whale was mistaken for a submarine. On deck, the men did physical exercises and rifle drills. Leisure time was passed with tournaments of boxing, draughts and chess, lectures, and a revue, *Smiling Thru*. More informally, gambling was rife. The soldiers also wanted souvenirs and could not be restrained from purloining crockery, ash trays and any other items branded with the mark of the *Queen Mary*.[9]

Mid-journey, the speed and totality of Germany's successes in Europe saw the convoy alter its course. Arriving at Cape Town, South Africa, on 26 May, the *Queen Mary* anchored outside the harbour. The men gathered on deck and watched the crew on a nearby tanker, costumed in tribal attire, perform some vigorous dances for them. It was a welcome that seems to have set the tone for the visit to Cape Town. After brooding on being denied shore leave at Fremantle, the men were determined to enjoy themselves.

Poor weather made it difficult for tug boats and lighters to transport the men between ship and shore. Only 418 out of 2,500 men taking leave on the first day returned to the ship. Many managed to return the following day and were described as being mostly sober, "although in all stages of sartorial disorder". After dealing with rumours that the Chinese orderlies were about to mutiny, the officers called a ship's muster that showed more than 1000 men were absent without leave. Parties of officers set out to retrieve the men from prison lock-ups, bars and brothels. McNeill's service record shows that he was absent without leave for 45 minutes on 27 May and punished with an admonishment.[10]

On 31 May the convoy headed north. While the Australians and New Zealanders had been revelling in Cape Town, the situation in

---

[9] Clarke, *My War*, pp. 150-6; Plowman, *Across the Sea*, p. 134.
[10] NAA: B883, NX 4888.

Europe had worsened. The British Expeditionary Force and Allied forces retreated to Dunkirk to be rescued by Operation Dynamo, the heroic evacuation. Britain, with its Empire and Dominions, stood alone. As the convoy journeyed north, Churchill addressed the House of Commons with the speech that has gone into history - "We shall fight on the beaches" - and pledged to never surrender. Although not told their new destination, it must have been clear to the men they were going to defend Britain from invasion.

In the tropics, the temperature and humidity increased. Conditions aboard the ship, designed as it was to keep passengers snug while they travelled across the North Atlantic, became increasingly difficult.[11] Given the troops' escapades in Cape Town, it can have been no surprise that what was euphemistically called a "short arm parade" was conducted to address the widespread incidence of sexually transmitted disease. Also unsurprisingly, there was no shore leave granted during the stay in Free Town, Sierra Leone. The men did trade with locals who paddled dugouts to the ships and swapped baskets of fresh fruit for the *Queen Mary's* blankets, sheets and towels.

Leaving Free Town, the convoy made for Britain, escorted by the *Hood*, the pride of the Royal Navy, the aircraft carrier *Argus* and eight destroyers. The final stretch of the journey passed through dangerous waters; a point made clear when the convoy witnessed a recently torpedoed ship aflame in the ocean. The poet Kenneth Slessor, working as a war correspondent, was aboard the liner *Mauretania* and recorded the scene:

> *The great red flames and the spouts of smoke could be clearly seen, and she appeared to be standing bows up almost vertically in the sea. A fascinating but awful sight.... News of the submarine's presence in the neighbourhood made everyone jumpy.*[12]

---

[11] Robert Lacey, *The Queens of the North Atlantic*, London, 1973, p. 81.
[12] Plowman, *Across the Sea*, p. 142.

In Britain

On 16 June, the convoy arrived in Gourock, Scotland. Messages of welcome from the King and Anthony Eden, the Secretary of State for War, were read to the men. Their arrival came as Britain faced its worst crisis of the war. Germany had occupied Paris; Italy had entered the conflict as an ally to Germany, and the outlook across Europe and in the Mediterranean was seriously bleak. The troops evacuated from France had abandoned most of their equipment, so the forces Britain did have were not fully equipped. The arrival of thousands of Australians and New Zealanders was welcome news, and to lift the public's morale the British government worked to ensure that it was extensively reported in the press. A fawning article in *The Times* was typical of the coverage:

> *It was the grandest convoy in all history. The ships made a wonderful picture of might and majesty as they arrived and took up their anchorages.*
>
> *The men are as good to look at as they are refreshing to talk with – men of splendid physique and free minds, ideal soldiers of democracy. In conversation all were anxious first to hear the latest about the war.*
>
> *There was not the smallest sign of gloom or despondency when they learned how grave was the news. One received the impression, indeed, that it did not particularly surprise them – almost as if they took it for granted that without Australia and New Zealand we could hardly expect to be getting on very well. It will take a lot to disconcert the Anzacs.*[13]

The Australians were based at camps around Salisbury Plain in England's south. McNeill was assigned to the Austforce School at Tidworth Park to undertake training as an infantry leader. Through the rest of 1940 he was in postings at a depot in Bulford, Australian Imperial Force Headquarters at Amesbury Abbey, and then back to the Army Service Corps. During this period the Battle of Britain was fought and troop encampments were among the *Luftwaffe's* targets. Camps quartering Australians were attacked on numerous occasions, although

---

[13] *The Times*, 21 June 1940, p. 7.

they suffered no significant casualties. The commander of the Condor Legion, Wolfram von Richthofen, was now in command of *Fliegerkorps VIII* and responsible for attacking targets in England's south. Given his first-hand experience of Germany's aerial power, McNeill was probably the only Australian who fully anticipated and understood the reality of the ordeal that the British people were to face in the blitz.

Spain was clearly on McNeill's mind because he made contact with other International Brigaders and was quickly co-opted onto the National Executive of the International Brigade Association, an organisation of veterans, where he worked with Peter Kerrigan and Sam Wild. Kerrigan had been the British Battalion's political commissar and a correspondent for the *Daily Worker*, while Sam Wild had fought at Jarama and been the commander of the British Battalion during its final months of fighting. The association raised money, published a magazine, *The Volunteer for Liberty*, and ran campaigns in support of Spanish refugees and other former members of the International Brigades who were being held in camps in Vichy France, across North Africa and in Spain itself.[14]

The association agitated for veterans from the Spanish Civil War to be properly treated in Britain's forces, as there were cases of men being refused admission when they sought to enlist, or being drummed out when their commanders heard they had fought with the International Brigades.[15] The association also organised social functions and McNeill attended what was promoted as a Grand Fiesta at London's Conway Hall which featured a running buffet, dancing to a Musicians' Union band, and a cabaret show starring Andrea and Rosita, who were "famous Spanish specialty dancers".[16]

McNeill sought out Tom Wintringham, commander of the British Battalion at the Battle of Jarama, and met with him in his London apartment. McNeill had not served under Wintringham and the

---

[14] Letter from McNeill, dated 22 July 1965, in the Saffin Collection, State Library of Victoria, MS SEQ Box 15.
[15] Hughes, *They Shall Not Pass*, p. 223.
[16] A promotional leaflet is in the McNeill Collection in the Illawarra Museum.

meeting seems to have been about Dickinson who Wintringham said was "one of the most fantastic personalities he had met". This praise was probably not just Wintringham providing solace to a comrade, as in his memoir of the war, *English Captain*, he nominated Dickinson, who he described as a Grimsby man (Wintringham had also been born in Grimsby), as "one of my most promising officers".[17]

In September 1940 McNeill was at the Australian Imperial Force Headquarters when Churchill paid a visit. Playing on the power of the Anzac legend, the British Prime Minister gave the Australians a typically stentorian address which was well received by the troops.

> *Speaking to you in the name of the British Parliament and the people, I express to you our deep gratitude not only because we know you would fight to the death – for after all no one wants to live forever – but because of the encouragement it gives us here, now that we are all alone.*
>
> *We are certain that the divisions sent from Australia will preserve the same glorious reputation which made them renowned twenty-five years ago and which caused the Australian Corps to be recognised by friend and foe alike as unsurpassed in all the valorous manhood of Europe.*[18]

By the end of 1940 the RAF had defeated the *Luftwaffe's* attempt to gain control of the skies above Britain and the threat of invasion had eased. The Australians were now needed elsewhere and the War Cabinet decided to send them to the Mediterranean, the Middle East and North Africa. The first units departed on 15 November. By this time, the limitations imposed by McNeill's age and war wounds must have been evident and he stayed behind in England. Perhaps disappointed, in November and December he was absent without leave for 16 days, with the army withholding his pay for the period. He seems to have visited Kirkcaldy in Scotland as on his return he sent his mother a postcard from the town's Beveridge Park.

In January 1941, the decision not to send McNeill to the front was proven correct as he was admitted to the 3rd Australian General

---

[17] Wintringham, *English Captain*, p. 226.
[18] Long, *To Benghazi*, p. 308.

Hospital. He spent a month there before being transferred to the Red Cross' Barnett Hill Convalescent Home in Surrey.[19] By the end of February he was well enough to return to duty and in March he was, as he put it, "invalided into" the 1st Australian Forestry Company.

1st Australian Forestry Company

The establishment of the Forestry Companies was an example of the resourcefulness that war required. During the inter-war years Britain had imported much of its timber from Sweden, transported across the Baltic Sea. The outbreak of war meant that these supplies were cut off by Germany. The war effort required large amounts of timber for railway sleepers, bridge decking and the repair of structures damaged by bombing. Ample supplies were available from Canada, but timber was a bulky and low value commodity, filling space in submarine-stalked cargo ships that could otherwise carry valuable food and weapons. It was preferable for Britain to look to its own forests to meet its timber needs.

To help, Britain asked Australia, Canada and New Zealand to provide a workforce with the required forestry skills. Australia responded by recruiting forestry specialists into the Australian Imperial Force and the first units arrived in Britain in July 1940. They were supplemented by men, like McNeill, who were judged to be not suitable for duties elsewhere. The 1st Forestry Company was initially posted to Seahouses, Northumberland, and worked pine, spruce, beech and oak at the Chathill sawmill. McNeill was graded as a pioneer, before being re-graded as an axeman.[20] In 1941 the Company moved to Lockerbie, Dumfriesshire, Scotland. The size of the forests was a revelation for McNeill.

> *They were mighty big forests. Australians have no conception of England, you think it is all tied up together, but there are estates of 60,000 acres of fir forests, owned by Lord So-and-so. And rabbits! More rabbits than you could bloody well see in Australia.*[21]

---

[19] NAA: B883, NX 4888.
[20] NAA: B883 NX 4888.
[21] WL interview.

Photo 23 – 1st Forestry Company, Royal Australian Engineers. (Illawarra Museum)

The work was hard. The Australians were not used to working outdoors in the bitter cold of Scotland. Many of them had not seen snow before. Despite the harsh conditions, the Forestry Companies demonstrated their worth with record production figures. The war diary for the Forestry Group proudly noted that production by the 1st Forestry Company for the week ended 14 July 1943 was 43,870 cubic feet of sawn timber, a record for the war. The diary carefully noted that, in comparison, the record production so far achieved by the New Zealanders was 17,457 cubic feet, the Canadians 14,672 cubic feet, and Britain's own Royal Engineers 14,410 cubic feet.[22]

While the men worked in the forests and timber mills, they were still part of the military and had to maintain their preparedness. They did this through exercises with British units including the Royal Engineers and the Duke of Cornwall's Light Infantry.[23] There were

---

[22] AWM 5/32/8/1, p. 117.

[23] Francis Robert Mould, *The Dynamic Forest: A History of Forestry and Forest Industries in Victoria*, Richmond, 1991, p. 94.

drills on how to respond to a gas attack, demolition demonstrations and a mock attack on the Dumfries RAF Station. A group of Italian prisoners of war was deployed to assist in the forests and one was a veteran of the Spanish Civil War. After discovering that McNeill had also fought in that war, he made it clear that he had been conscripted and forced to go to Spain.[24]

The Australians got on well with the local communities. Rather than stay in tents or camp barracks, billets with local families were often available. After a day's work, the men relaxed in the local pub, sharing a drink and a game of darts with the locals.[25]

McNeill maintained his interest in politics. At a meeting of the Dumfries branch of the Communist Party he met Mabel Kendall, an English civil servant who had been relocated from London as part of the blitz dispersal strategy.[26] The pair were perfectly matched. Born on 9 May 1912, she had been raised by a farming family in Aspatria, a small village adjacent to the Lake District. Secretarial training at a school in Carlisle enabled her to become a highly skilled typist and shorthand stenographer. Kendall had been secretary of the St Pancras Peace Council, active in the London Spanish Relief Committee, and was also involved in the affairs of her trade union, the Inland Revenue Staff Federation, where she worked closely with the Federation's assistant secretary, James Callaghan, the future British Prime Minister.[27]

---

[24] WL interview.

[25] Justin Chadwick, 'The 'men behave well and are a credit to Australia': Australian Forestry Companies in the UK during WW2', *Sabretach*, Vol. LIX, No. 2, June 2018, p. 34.

[26] WL interview.

[27] Personal communication from Vanessa McNeill, 18 December 2023.

Photo 24 – Mr and Mrs McNeill. (Illawarra Museum)

McNeill used his leave to visit beauty spots and local attractions, including visits to Kendall's family in Aspatria. He was not always overly impressed with what Britain had to offer, as a postcard home to Corrimal indicates:

Dear Mother

This is a scene of one of the Lake District I have been able to visit and it is amongst the best in England but entirely different to anything of our own.

No Lake Illawarra or Bulli Lookout etc.

I am getting along fine and the weather is ideal. We are often stripped to the waist working in nice warm sunny days. I am receiving the papers from you regularly and a letter or two.

Regards to all.

Your loving son

Jim[28]

Jim and Mabel married on 17 January 1942 at Dumfries. News of the marriage was reported in Wollongong's newspapers as an "ardent anti-fascist" and member of the International Brigades deciding to "join the Benedicks" – an obscure Shakespearean reference to a man who marries late in life. A daughter, Vanessa Elizabeth, was born at the Creswell Counties Maternity Hospital on 9 May 1943. The McNeill – Kendall marriage was one of 120 marriages between the Australian foresters and British women, with Vanessa being one of at least 40 children resulting from these marriages.[29]

Photo 25 – Jim and Mabel McNeill with daughter Vanessa. (Illawarra Museum)

---

[28] The postcard is in the McNeill Collection of the Illawarra Museum.
[29] WL interview; *Tribune*, 29 March 1945, p. 3; *South Coast Times*, 26 June 1942, p. 10; Chadwick, 'The men behave well', p. 34.

The *Australian Women's Weekly* reported that the Australians' propensity to work stripped to the waist caused astonishment among the local residents, who thought them crazy. Going shirtless also attracted the attention of local children who, obviously impressed, returned from visits to the Australians carrying their own shirts across their arms.[30]

McNeill kept in touch with Wollongong by visiting Australia House for news while on leave in London. He sent a donation to the Illawarra Trades and Labour Council as his contribution to the Steve Best Memorial Committee. Best, the Council's secretary, had played a leading role in reviving the Illawarra's unions in the 1930s and was also the president of the Corrimal Branch of the Labor Party and the Corrimal Bowling Club. He had been killed, aged 41, in a car crash.[31]

Working in the forests and distant from the front, the men began to feel forgotten. These feelings intensified after Japan entered the war. With Australia now under direct attack, the men wanted to come home. Articles appeared in the newspapers with the men calling themselves "Australia's Lost Legion". While acknowledging the "generous hospitality" of their hosts, the homesick men told Australia's High Commissioner, Stanley Bruce, that they wanted to be recalled. One complaint was the delay in receiving letters and cables from Australia. McNeill was suitably appreciative of a small package he received from Reverend Mutton, of the St Albans Church of England in Corrimal, who sent razor blades, chewing gum, handkerchiefs, shaving soap and tooth paste. Receiving this package, McNeill told his mother that sugar was being severely rationed and was one of the best things to send.[32]

Perhaps to reassure the men that their work was making a valuable contribution to the war effort, they were read a letter from John Curtin, Australia's Prime Minister since October 1941. They received a visit from Dr H.V. Evatt, Australia's Minister for External Affairs, and from a delegation of Australian parliamentarians. Military authorities

---

[30] *Australian Women's Weekly*, 20 March 1943, p. 16.
[31] *South Coast Times*, 31 May 1940, p. 19.
[32] *Telegraph*, 15 June 1942, p. 5; The postcard is in the McNeill Collection of the Illawarra Museum.

considered it important to record enlisted men at work, and two of Australia's Official War Artists, Sheila Hawkins and Colin Colahan painted the Forestry Companies at work.[33]

Efforts to keep up morale were made with regular film nights (including *Desert Victory* and *Baptism of Fire*) and an Australian Rules football match against men from the Royal Australian Air Force (RAAF), a spectacle which must surely have confirmed to the Scots that the Australians were indeed mad. A major event was the Inter-Dominion Axemen's Carnival. Around 1200 people watched the Australians successfully pit their skills against the New Zealanders to win the Ministry of Supply Cup. Athletics events provided competition in shot put, tug of war and relay races.[34]

In the middle of 1943, the decision was made to return the Forestry Companies to Australia for future service in the Pacific theatre. A farewell parade through Lockerbie was staged on 9 November to celebrate the departure. Owing to a lack of shipping, the men's wives and children were left behind. McNeill returned to Gourock to embark with his No. 1 Forestry Company on the *Queen Elizabeth*. They crossed the Atlantic and arrived in New York to enjoy several days of leave. The Company's War Diary records that the men stayed at Fort Hamilton and that the "American people showed wonderful hospitality to members of the Company". The men travelled across America by train to San Francisco, with McNeill recording the stops made across the continent on the back of a postcard. Arriving at San Francisco the Company stayed at the Fort McDowell staging camp where they enjoyed more leave and American hospitality. On 30 November they boarded the *President Grant* for an uneventful trip across the Pacific to Brisbane. They arrived back in Australia just before Christmas.[35]

In early 1944 the Forestry Companies were sent to New Guinea, but McNeill was not with them. At 44, having suffered from gall stones in Scotland, his health was again becoming a concern. In February the

---

[33] See AWM ART 25524 and ART91201.
[34] AWM 5/32/8/1.
[35] AWM 5/32/3/1.

Medical Board placed him on the B list and transferred him to a supply depot. Suffering from emphysema and sinusitis, he was hospitalised and spent time in Sydney's Bonnie Brae and Neringah convalescent homes. On 27 December 1944 he was discharged, being "medically unfit for further military service".[36]

In Spain, Franco backed the Axis but did not formally become a participant in the war. He made submarine bases, air bases and monitoring services available to Germany, and supplied agricultural products and essential minerals like tungsten to the German war machine. Franco also allowed a Blue Division of 47,000 supposed volunteers to fight alongside the *Wehrmacht* against the Red Army and had the Spanish navy escort German convoys across the Mediterranean, but maintained a formal neutrality for Spain.[37]

At the war's end some supporters of the Republic entertained the hope that the Allies would free Europe of fascism by ousting Franco. The CPA published a booklet, *The Truth About Spain* by Archer Russell, a journalist for the *Sydney Morning Herald*, which made the case for Allied action against Franco's regime.[38] This hope was not to be realised. The western democracies were cool towards Franco's regime, with the American President Roosevelt writing that he could "see no place in the community of nations for governments founded on Fascist principles",[39] but the exigencies of the developing Cold War meant that, step-by-step, a rapprochement was made. American military bases were established in Spain from 1953. In the post-war years, Franco was free to maintain his dictatorship, execute his opponents, and provide refuge and safe passage for many former Nazis.[40]

---

[36] NAA: B883, NX4888; WL interview.

[37] Thomas, *Spanish Civil War*, p. 619; Paul Preston, *A People Betrayed: A History of Corruption, Political Incompetence and Social Division in Modern Spain 1874-2018*, London, 2020, p. 348.

[38] Archer Russell, *The Truth About Spain*, Sydney, 1945.

[39] *The Times*, 27 September 1945, p. 3.

[40] Gerald Steinacher, *Nazis on the Run: How Hitler's Henchmen Fled Justice*, Oxford, 2011, p. 266.

17

The great democratic traditions of Australia

In contrast to its extensive promotion of McNeill's service in Spain, the CPA largely ignored his service in Britain with the Australian Imperial Force. Publicising the willing participation of McNeill, one of the CPA's most high-profile anti-fascists, in a conflict that the party was dismissing as an imperialist war, would have been an awkward contradiction. Perhaps too, the party was aware of the army's anti-communism and wished to avoid provoking problems for McNeill with his superiors. For some of the time that he was in the army, the party was supressed by the Australian government, with its publications banned and its activities curtailed. Whatever the reasons, while McNeill was overseas the CPA's new newspaper, *Tribune*, mentioned him only once in a small piece that recounted his wounding in the Spanish Civil War and wished him good luck on his service in Britain.[1] But even this small item was only published in December 1941, six months after the Soviet Union had been attacked by Nazi Germany, and the CPA's attitude to the conflict had undergone yet another transformation.

Hitler's invasion of the USSR on 22 June 1941 flummoxed the CPA. *Tribune*, in its leading article published on the day of the invasion but

---

[1] *Tribune*, 5 December 1941, p. 3.

ahead of the news arriving in Australia, said suggestions that Hitler would turn east were "wishful thinking" on behalf of the USSR's enemies. There was not, the paper claimed, the "slightest evidence" that relations between Germany and the USSR were anything other than "peaceful and friendly". Up to then, the CPA saw its role as being to "fight the class enemy at home". Once the USSR had been attacked, the CPA quickly adopted a new position that supported both the Soviet Union and the democratic Allies. The war was no longer an imperialist one; it was now a people's war for the defeat of fascism, and the party supported Curtin's call for an "all-in effort". Apparently without any shame or embarrassment, the CPA declared itself to be the "leading and most active war party".[2] There was no acknowledgement that it had ever been in error.

Even before the suppression of the party was formally lifted by Curtin in December 1942, the CPA, through front committees, was using the prestige of the returned International Brigaders to support the war effort. A pamphlet was published by a CPA front, the Legal Rights Committee, with a call by Franklyn, who had enlisted in January 1942, to support the war.

> *I have joined the A.I.F. This is a People's War, a just war for freedom and progress against fascism. Because I fought against fascism as a trade unionist, as a member of the International Brigade in Spain, I know it is my duty now to fight wherever fascism rears its ugly head.*
>
> *Fascism menaces the world as it has, temporarily, overwhelmed Spain. I have enlisted because the A.I.F. to-day fights the fight of our people, of Britain, of Spain, because Australia and other free countries are pledged in alliance with the Soviet Union, the bulwark of world freedom. The A.I.F. is an anti-fascist army. I am proud to take my place in it.*
>
> *As a former member of the Communist Party, I call upon Australian workers to unite, to rally against fascism, to build the army, to swell production. The Spanish Army, ill-equipped, ill-fed and hurriedly trained, yet soon reached the peak of fighting efficiency because of its democracy. It was a People's Army fighting a People's War.*

---

[2] *Tribune*, 22 June 1941, p.1; Mcintyre, *The Party*, pp. 74-77.

> *This is the war for the utter destruction of fascism, for the extermination of the enemies of freedom, science and culture, the enemies of every Australian working class man, woman and child. It is a just war. The sadists and rapers are knocking, blood-drunk, at the door. The working class answers!*

Franklyn enlisted a few weeks after Japan had launched devastating attacks across Asia and the Pacific, and sunk the British warships *Repulse* and *Prince of Wales*. Australia was now, as the *Dalfram* strikers had feared, under direct attack. To ensure his enlistment Franklyn had, like McNeill, lied about his age and made himself five years younger than he was. His papers show that he declared his service in Spain with the International Brigades and that his right forearm was adorned with a tattoo of a scroll of flowers and a love-heart. He trained as a commando, but in his mid-forties the effort soon proved to be beyond him. He was medically discharged after little more than three months.[3]

McNeill, once back in Australia, with impeccable anti-fascist credentials and an early enlistment that prevented criticism from anti-communists, was now a useful figure for the CPA to promote. A profile in *Tribune* placed his anti-fascism in a continuum and recounted his fights with the New Guard, the killing of Dickinson, his stowaway voyage, wounding in Spain, and service with the Australian Imperial Force. The profile included his call for the opening of a second front which would relieve the Red Army but also allow his wife and daughter to join him in Australia.[4]

Australian communists basked in the reflected glory of the Red Army and the sacrifices made by the people of the USSR to defeat Hitler. Membership of the CPA surged to a record 22,052 and in 1944 the party had sufficient funds to acquire a large commercial building in the centre of Sydney as its national headquarters. Marx House, with lecture halls, meeting rooms, bookshop and cafeteria, represented the party at its peak.[5] An honour roll made by the Spanish Relief Committee was

---

[3] NAA: B883 NX 82345.
[4] *Tribune*, 2 March 1944, p. 4.
[5] Mcintyre, *The Party*, p. 12.

installed. It listed the names of those Australians who fought in the International Brigades.⁶

Memorialisation

That year's May Day celebrations were an opportunity for the party to display its strength. The *Sydney Morning Herald* reported that a record 12,000 people participated in the march, which included a large contingent from the CPA displaying flags and placards of red stars, kangaroos, and hammer and sickles. *Tribune* reported that McNeill led a small group of veterans through the streets of Sydney behind a banner that read: "International Brigaders. They fought fascism in 1936. They still fight fascism in 1944."⁷

> *Again, the applause swells for Private Jim McNeill and his 13 comrades of the International Brigade. There is deep pride in their marching. By the silent cathedral the commentator speaks of Barcelona and the epic of Madrid.*
>
> *"Labor is international", he says.*⁸

A photograph of the contingent shows the men stern and unsmiling. They are led by McNeill, in his Australian Imperial Force uniform and slouch hat, followed by Jack Franklyn, Lou Elliot (a shearer's cook from Queensland who had fought at Jarama), Peter Coll (an Irishman who had migrated to Australia after fighting in Spain), and Charlie Walters, all in their suits, wearing ties and freshly shined shoes. The other marchers are obscured, but the group does not appear to include any of the women who served in Spain as doctors, nurses or in other capacities.

---

6   *Tribune*, 30 March 1944, p. 7.
7   *Tribune*, 4 May 1944, p. 3; *Sydney Morning Herald,* 8 May 1944, p. 4.
8   *Tribune*, 11 May 1944, p. 4.

Photo 26: McNeill leads the International Brigades veterans in Sydney's 1944 May Day march. (Illawarra Museum)

The display of an honour roll and a ceremonial march of veterans were memorial practices immediately recognisable to Australians. In the years after the Great War, cities, towns and the smallest villages erected memorials and honour rolls. With funds raised by public subscription, these memorials were installed in town centres, schools, workshops and places where the community gathered, like town halls and libraries. By 1944, the marches and gatherings of Great War veterans on Anzac Day had become a central day in Australia's national calendar. The CPA, in installing an honour roll and coordinating a May Day march of International Brigaders, was emulating these widely accepted national traditions to celebrate the veterans and their cause.

But there was still to be no official recognition of the Australian International Brigaders. The Australian government had declined to be represented at the homecoming celebrations in 1939, and would not alter this position in later years. The enormity of the Second World War pushed the Spanish Civil War into the background. As peace returned a silence about the Spanish Civil War descended and lasted through the

Cold War years that followed. This official refusal to acknowledge Australia's premature anti-fascists avoided embarrassment for those who, in contrast to Dickinson, McNeill and their comrades, had appeased Europe's fascists. Menzies, for example, returned as Prime Minister in 1949, would scarcely have wanted to recognise those who had fought in Spain against the Condor Legion while he himself was praising Hitler.

Instead, if the bravery and commitment of the International Brigaders' anti-fascism was to receive any recognition in Australia, it was going to come from the left of the political spectrum. The few interruptions to the official silence mainly came from the CPA and often from McNeill himself who, in particular, seemed determined not to let the memory of his friend Dickinson's magnetic personality be lost. His efforts were part of what the historian Judith Keene described as a global process that saw the International Brigades "canonised by the international left as premature anti-fascists and living symbols of political solidarity and self-sacrifice".[9]

Having seen the utility of the International Brigade Association in Britain, in 1947 McNeill attempted to establish an equivalent organisation of Australian veterans. But it "failed to get on its feet" as people were "already bogged down with other work" and were either unable to be contacted or living too far from each other.[10] This effort was likely associated with a public appeal for £50 to support the publication of a memorial booklet for the Australian International Brigaders. People who wished to support the project were asked to send donations to McNeill.[11]

The appeal succeeded and in 1948 an updated and revised version of *Australians in Spain* was published by the CPA's Current Book Distributors. Billed as a memorial booklet, it was sub-titled *Our Pioneers Against Fascism* and explicitly linked the struggle against

---

[9] Judith Keene, 'The Spanish International Brigadier as Veteran and Foreign Fighter', *Contemporary European History*, 29, 2020, pp. 276-278.

[10] Letter from McNeill, dated 22 July 1965, in the Saffin Collection, State Library of Victoria, MS SEQ Box 15.

[11] *Tribune*, 4 July 1947, p. 1.

Franco's fascists with the recent war against Nazi Germany and Imperial Japan. The booklet placed Australian members of the International Brigades, both men and women, in "the great democratic traditions of Australia". They had fought for "something that is deep in the Australian way of life – freedom." The booklet asked why the Brigaders went to Spain, and answered:

> They went to Spain for the same reason as Australians a few years later went to El Alamein and Tobruk, to the Battle for Britain, to Syria and Singapore, Timor and Milne Bay and the Kokoda Trail, and so on to Bougainville and Balikpapan – because they saw a fight between freedom and tyranny, and they had to be on freedom's side.
>
> All that has happened since has made it clear that Spain was the first stage of an international war into which we would all be drawn sooner or later.[12]

McNeill himself wrote a chapter on how the legacy of the International Brigades should be understood:

> But greater than the military details was the importance of the International Brigade as a proof to the world that the unity of the Common People against tyranny was real – and ultimately victorious.
>
> It was something written in the blood of men of all countries who had died together in a new sort of war. Not a national war, but a war for the liberation of all men and women of all nations.[13]

Probably reflecting the input of McNeill, the section on Dickinson corrected the spelling of his name, provided more biographical information about his life in Australia, and omitted the detail about the top of his head being blown away, preferring the less graphic "fell dead". Dickinson's heroic death was said to be "typically Australian – a story we should never forget".[14]

---

[12] Palmer and Fox, *Australians in Spain*, p. 4.
[13] Ibid., p. 10.
[14] Ibid., pp.12-14.

By the time *Australians in Spain: Our Pioneers Against Fascism* was released, the veterans had already suffered another loss. On 26 June 1945 Franklyn, one of their most prominent number, was working on Sydney's wharves when he fell into the hold of a ship. Injured, he suffered pain in the stomach, chest, head and back, shuffled when he walked, and took giddy turns. A month later, having not returned to work, he went for a drink in the Fitzroy Hotel at Woolloomooloo with two other waterside workers. After the hotel closed, there was a melee outside on Dowling Street and Franklyn was found injured in the gutter. He was taken to the Sydney Hospital and died on 31 July, just days before the end of the war in the Pacific. An inquest determined that he died from a fractured skull and brain injury, accidentally caused by falling and hitting his head on the kerbing.[15] Carter believed that he had been struck while attempting to settle a domestic dispute.[16]

His funeral was a major event and featured four hundred unionists marching in columns ahead of his coffin. The obituary in *Tribune* noted that one of his happiest memories was tossing a bar of pig-iron onto the platform when Menzies spoke at a riotous public meeting in Kings Cross during the 1943 election campaign.[17] Menzies had been greeted with shouts of "Fascist" from boisterous groups that gave him the fascist salute.[18]

The McNeill family

A happier occasion for McNeill, who was working on the Sydney waterfront after his discharge, took place on 26 March 1945 when Mabel and Vanessa arrived in Sydney, part of a group of 47 wives and 32 children who received a welcome from repatriation officials at the Sydney Town Hall. McNeill saw a political dimension to the wartime relationships that had been formed. He stated that marriages

---

[15] NSW State Archives: NRS 345 [19/3736] Date: 27/08/1945.
[16] Joe Carter – Amirah Inglis, Amirah Inglis Collection, Noel Butlin Archives, Australian National University.
[17] *Tribune*, 9 August 1945, p. 7.
[18] *Daily Mirror*, 30 July 1943, p. 2.

between Australians and Englanders would do much "for greater unity between the workers of both countries". Mabel said she looked forward to resuming her party work.[19] She became involved in the Union of Australian Women, an organisation closely associated with the CPA that campaigned for affordable childcare and equality for women in the workplace.

Photo 27 – Reunited – McNeill with daughter Vanessa, wife Mabel, and mother Mary. (SEARCH Foundation/Illawarra Museum)

---

[19] *Tribune*, 29 March 1945, p. 3.

Photo 28 – Mabel McNeill (front right) marching with the Union of Australian Women. (Illawarra Museum)

The first task for the McNeills was to get settled. Australia's post-war housing shortage meant that this was not easily accomplished. Initially the couple shared a house with one of McNeill's brothers in Rockdale, in Sydney's south. Soon after, a series of pleading advertisements was placed in *Tribune*:

> WANTED
>
> *Jim McNeill, wife and daughter Vanessa (aged 2 years), require accommodation, furnished or unfurnished URGENT.*
>
> *Please phone MA 5663 or write Current Book Distributors, 695 George St., Sydney.*[20]

A permanent solution to the family's accommodation needs was the purchase in February 1946 of a home in O'Connor Street, Guildford, in Sydney's burgeoning western suburbs. The family's home was a

---

[20] The advertisement ran for four issues from 24 May to 5 June 1945.

modest, two-bedroom weatherboard and fibro cottage. The bedrooms were small, the toilet was in an outhouse in the backyard, hot water in the bathroom came from a chip heater, and the kitchen had a wood stove. The house sat on a large block and McNeill was able to develop a thriving vegetable garden which he enjoyed working in. It was to be the McNeills' home for the rest of their lives.[21]

Photo 29 – The McNeills' home in O'Connor Street, Guildford. (Illawarra Museum)

To support the family, McNeill worked in different jobs, including as a storeman for Colgate-Palmolive at Villawood and at the Insulwool factory at Camelia. Mabel spent most of her time on domestic duties, but did spend some years in the workforce as a typist and administrative assistant. Vanessa attended the Fowler Road Public School at Merrylands where Mabel applied her organisational skills as the secretary of the Parents and Citizens' Association. Vanessa remembered her childhood as "normal and loving".

> *I was not indoctrinated or brainwashed in any way. I'm sure that's what a lot of people think communists did to their children, but I*

---

[21] FORM Architects, *Heritage Significance Assessment of 11 O'Connor Street Guildford*, c 1990.

was never forced to do anything. The CPA ran the JELs, the Junior Eureka League, for the younger children, and the Eureka League for the teenagers, and I was never told or influenced in any way to do any of that stuff.

Where Vanessa did think her parents' communism influenced her childhood was in being afforded cultural opportunities, such as ballet classes and trips to the theatre.

> My mother, perhaps because she was a communist, felt that 'the people', all the people, should be able to go to the theatre. They gave me a very good upbringing, because that's what they felt everyone should have. Access to culture, access to music. They were also both voracious readers, and there were no libraries here so they bought their books. Compared with around here, I had a privileged upbringing.[22]

When not gardening, McNeill repeatedly read his favourite novel, Mikhail Lermontov's *A Hero of Our Time*. Set in the Caucasus, the novel recounts the escapades and conquests of Pechorin, the caddish anti-hero.

ASIO surveillance

Apart from an interest in Russian literature, in many ways the McNeills were no different from tens of thousands of other families living in simple fibro cottages across suburban Sydney, raising their children and working in manufacturing and administration. What did set the McNeills apart from their suburban peers was that they were under surveillance by Australia's security agencies. The Commonwealth Investigation Service opened McNeill's security file in 1946. Maintaining it became the responsibility of the Australian Security Intelligence Organisation (ASIO) after its establishment in 1949. ASIO penetrated the Merrylands/Guildford Branch of the CPA, which regularly met in the McNeills' living room. As a result of ASIO's diligence, it is possible to have an understanding of the

---

[22] Personal communication with Vanessa McNeill, 18 January 2023.

political attitudes and activity of McNeill and his close comrades in the post-war years.[23]

The security agencies took careful note of his participation in May Day marches and in the lectures hosted in the McNeills' home. These featured guest speakers of considerable standing and were a feature of the McNeills' party work over many years. One speaker in 1948 was Ernie Thornton, national secretary of the Federated Ironworkers' Association, who was facing a challenge to his control of the union from organised anti-communist forces. Other speakers included Len Fox, who had been an activist with the Spanish Relief Committee, and Charles Bresland, head of the Eureka League, who reported on his 1954 trip to the Soviet Union. Bresland was later dismissed from his post after an incident in the public toilets at Central Station. In the 1950s, and for years to come, the CPA's leadership did not accept homosexuality.[24]

An event at the McNeills' home was held several weeks after Stalin died in March 1953. Promoted as a memorial meeting, tea and refreshments were served. Attendees heard an address by Edgar Ross, editor of the Miners' Federation newspaper *Common Cause*, on "The Life and Work of Joseph Stalin". Ross was a hard-line Stalinist, and his speech would have been in rigid accord with the hagiographic coverage of Stalin's death in *Tribune* which proclaimed "Stalin's name is immortal" and that he was the "greatest man" of our time.[25]

By the early 1950s, with the Cold War raging, the CPA was already in steep decline. In 1949 the international communist movement achieved an epic victory of global consequence when Mao's communists won power in China, but this, together with the establishment of the Iron Curtain across Eastern Europe, the Soviet Union's acquisition of an atomic bomb, and the Korean War, only hardened anti-communist sentiment in Australia.

Domestically, the party had not helped itself with a string of

---

[23] NAA: A6119, 7669; NAA: A6119, 7670; and NAA: A9626, 1087.
[24] Mcintyre, *The Party*, p. 348.
[25] *Tribune*, 9 March 1953, p. 1.

strategically ill-judged strikes. Reckless industrial militancy inspired organised opposition from anti-communist Industrial Groups which, at their formation, enjoyed official endorsement from the Labor Party. Communists lost control of key unions and with these losses the power of the CPA was significantly weakened. One consequence of the loss of trade unions, and of a general decline in membership, was an increasingly parlous financial position. Marx House had to be sold and in 1949 the party moved into smaller headquarters. What became of the Spanish Civil War honour roll is not known.

With the CPA besieged from inside the labour movement, Menzies sensed a political opportunity to vanquish an old enemy. His government legislated the dissolution of the CPA. The law, extreme in its provisions, was challenged in the High Court. The advocate for unions affected was Dr H.V. Evatt, the Leader of the Labor Party. The Court disallowed the legislation. To correct the unconstitutionality of his legislation, Menzies held a referendum. The Labor Party, with immense divisions that heralded the greatest split in the party's history, advocated opposition to a constitutional amendment designed to dissolve the CPA. The Labor Party spoke against what it regarded as a violation of fundamental democratic principles.[26]

Though he lost the referendum Menzies won the political victory. Divisions over communism in the labour movement were stoked, not resolved, by the defeat of the referendum. A major split in the Labor Party followed which enabled Menzies to remain in power as Australia's longest-serving Prime Minister until his retirement in 1966.

Throughout all this, the CPA kept promoting McNeill's record of service in Spain and with the Australian Imperial Force. During the post-war years his anti-fascism and unqualified patriotism was clearly an asset for the party. On the tenth anniversary of the outbreak of the Spanish Civil War, McNeill published an article in *Tribune* titled "If the men who died in Spain came back today". He wrote again of Dickinson's "undying courage" and in memory of the "fallen Australians who lie in the valley of Jarama". He resolved to "carry on their fight till Franco has

---

[26] Mcintyre, *The Party*, pp. 251-257.

been overthrown, till the working people are united, till fascism in every country is defeated and ended for all time".[27]

In 1948, *Tribune* published McNeill's thoughts on Anzac Day. He argued that there had to be more than a day of commemoration if the peace were "really to be won". He wanted the problems around veterans' rehabilitation addressed and more attention given to housing, training, wages and prices. He was concerned by the anti-communism afoot in the Returned Soldiers' League and, as an advocate for worker-soldier unity, thought it a pity "to see some of our ex-service officials indulging in union-baiting and redbaiting. That sort of thing won't get us anywhere."[28] McNeill was proud of his military service and in the 1960s and 1970s regularly took part in the Anzac Day marches and commemorations.

His service in the International Brigades had formed part of a CPA attack on Frank Browne, the Democratic Party's candidate for Bondi in the NSW elections of May 1944. The Democratic Party was a short-lived entity formed by the merger of the United Australia Party and the Commonwealth Party. It was the main conservative party and one of the entities subsumed by the creation of the Liberal Party of Australia in October 1944.

Browne, who had fought as a professional boxer in America, was a prominent anti-communist. It was alleged by the CPA that he had claimed to have fought in the Spanish Civil War and worn a phony decoration called a "Comintern Star" to bolster his credentials. McNeill, Carter and Franklyn, along with other International Brigaders, signed a leaflet distributed to 10,000 Bondi homes which attacked Browne and questioned his credibility. The leaflet challenged Browne to "face International Brigade interrogators like a man".[29]

The CPA's effort may well have contributed to the narrow defeat that Browne, with 10,694 votes, suffered to Labor's Abe Landa MP, who won with 11,164 votes. Noted for his expertise in providing racing

---

[27] *Tribune*, 19 July 1946, p. 4.
[28] *Tribune*, 1 May 1948, p. 5.
[29] *Tribune*, 25 May 1944, p. 3.

tips as the greyhound reporter for the *Daily Mirror*, in the post-war years Browne became increasingly irascible and published a notorious scandal sheet, *Things I Hear*. In 1955, his journalism caused him and his publisher to become the first and only people in Australian history imprisoned for breaching parliamentary privilege.[30]

In 1951, at the request of their British intelligence counterparts, ASIO trailed McNeill around Sydney as he met James Cameron, who was believed to be a courier for the Communist Party of Great Britain. The pair met for a drink in the Gresham Hotel and Cameron stayed overnight in McNeill's home.

A newspaper seller

Whatever the truth of the Cameron episode, the main focus of McNeill's CPA activity seems to have been selling *Tribune*. He attended the *Tribune* Ball, grew vegetables for sale at the fundraising *Tribune* Fair, and established a regular routine that involved setting up a stand outside the Guildford Hotel each Friday afternoon and Saturday morning. He maintained this practice for 25 years and was regularly mentioned in competitions for the paper's most popular seller. A photograph of McNeill at his stand shows him in a crisply pressed suit, white shirt and wide brimmed hat, engaging in conversation with a customer while holding copies of *Tribune* headlined "Soviet Seeks New Life for UN". His stand holds a range of other CPA and Soviet publications.[31]

---

[30] Gavin Souter, "Browne, Francis Courtney (Frank) (1915–1981)", *Australian Dictionary of Biography*, National Centre of Biography, Australian National University, https://adb.anu.edu.au/biography/browne-francis-courtney-frank-12259/text21999, published first in hardcopy 2007, accessed online 7 January 2024.

[31] *Tribune*, 19 October 1960, p. 11.

Photo 30: McNeill selling *Tribune* at Guildford, c1960. (SEARCH Foundation/Illawarra Museum)

McNeill was not unique in his dedication. Driving circulation was a major priority for the party.[32] If nothing else, the CPA was a long-running fraternity of newspaper sellers. A *Tribune* Readers & Sellers' Conference was held in 1962 and attended by more than 150 people who discussed strategies to boost sales. McNeill gave the enthusiasts tips on increasing the profitability of *Tribune* stands by selling foreign language publications. He had sold 30 copies of a Russian medical book and

---

[32] Jim McIlroy in his 'Introduction' to Dianne Menghetti, *The Red North: The Popular Front in North Queensland*, 2018, p. 10.

told the conference "Our job is to convince every member that in some way or other they can sell one or more Tribunes."³³ His commitment was matched by other members, including the prominent communist playwright Dorothy Hewitt, who recalled in her autobiography:

> *I led out the South Sydney comrades on yet another Tribune drive. Nothing can stop me. Some terrible emptiness of the heart drives me out week after week to tramp the lonely, often hostile streets, with my newspapers and petitions.*³⁴

It was while selling *Tribune* that McNeill met Cecil Holmes, an intellectual filmmaker from New Zealand, who found McNeill to be a "a most mild-mannered fellow and our friendship was to last a long time". Holmes saw a "saintly quality" in McNeill and found the meetings of the Merrylands/Guildford branch to be a "kind of therapy" with like-minded people who planned little campaigns of leafleting and door-knocking with *Tribune*. Holmes appreciated the "genuine camaraderie, openness and acceptance" at the branch, but was unimpressed with the "boring and stultifying" senior officials of the CPA who "aped the Stalin style".³⁵

Other branch members who McNeill knew and worked with included the journalist Rupert Lockwood and a young activist, Jack Mundey, who both lived locally. Lockwood lived with his family on Fowler Road, around the corner from the McNeills, and had been in Spain as a war correspondent, making radio broadcasts from Madrid and providing detailed accounts of the conflict for Australian newspapers.³⁶ Mundey, who had moved from Queensland to play for the Parramatta rugby league club, was to lead the Green Bans that saved many of Sydney's heritage precincts, buildings and bushlands from destruction in the 1970s. He found McNeill to be a "delightful man" and joined

---

[33] *NAA:* 32538840; *Tribune*, 27 June 1962, p. 2.
[34] Dorothy Hewett, *Wild Card: An Autobiography 1923-58*, Ringwood, 1990, p. 189.
[35] Cecil Holmes, *One Man's Way*, Ringwood, 1986, pp. 39-40; Fox, *Broad Left*, p. 44.
[36] For the radio broadcasts see the *West Australian*, 23 June 1937, p.15. For examples of the newspaper articles see *The Herald*, 24 July 1937, p. 35 and *Sunday Mail*, 8 August 1937, p. 4.

him working the *Tribune* stand at the Guildford Hotel.[37]

By now McNeill had earned the nickname of "Gentleman Jim" and it was probably his positive qualities that Holmes wanted to capture in his film about the history of Australia's radical and working-class press, *Words for Freedom*. Starring McNeill on his *Tribune* round, the film featured the actor Leonard Teale providing a mellifluous narration of an uncredited script believed to have been written by Hewitt.[38] The film traced the history of the Australian labour movement from the diggers of the Eureka Stockade, to the Great Strikes of 1891, the anti-conscription campaigns, street brawls with the New Guard, and the role of *Tribune* in combatting the influence of the pulp and tabloid media during the Cold War.

McNeill, his dark hair now snowy white, was the star of the film. He was seen sitting with Vanessa on a sunny riverbank while rolling a cigarette at the 1954 *Tribune* picnic, then walking the quiet streets of Sydney's west, tall and thin in his suit and hat, knocking on doors and selling his papers. Teale's narration provided this commentary:

> *This man who sits in the sunlight on the grass is Jim McNeill. He fought in Spain, a modest kind of bloke who likes to down a schooner, have a yarn, enjoy a joke.*
>
> *An ironworker is Jim and things like freedom, bread and peace depend on men like him. He goes out and sells the Tribune in the streets, he pulls it from his pocket on the job.*
>
> *On Sunday mornings you can see him, lean and spare and grey, with a Tribune in his hand. You can imagine what he'd say: 'Would you like to buy the workers' paper, mate?'*

---

[37] Jack Mundey, *Green Bans & Beyond*, Sydney, 1981, p. 21.
[38] Deane Williams, *An Arc of Mirrors: Australian Post War Documentary Film*, Bristol, 2008, p. 69. *Tribune* attributed the script to Judith Wright, but this seems to have been an error.

Photo 31: A scene from *Words for Freedom* – McNeill and Vanessa at the 1954 *Tribune* picnic. (Estate of the late Robert Gowland)

Photo 32: A scene from *Words for Freedom* – McNeill walks the streets of Sydney's west. (Estate of the late Robert Gowland)

The 19-minute film premiered in October 1955 at the Bondi School of Arts during an evening that featured a concert by the Bushwhackers, the playing of a recorded speech that Paul Robeson gave in London, a recitation of works by Henry Lawson, and the novelist Frank Hardy reading his short story *Tommy Macnamara's Tribune Run*.³⁹

McNeill credited his commitment to selling *Tribune* to a conversation he had with Bill Young while the pair were resting in a *chabola*:

> *Bill and I discussed the difficulties of the Spanish Party with so many illiterates. Bill said, "How easy for us to sell the party press, we have a literate population, all we have got to do is find enough sellers." We decided if we got out alive, we would establish the best stand of literature and papers in Australia.*

> *Salud, Bill Young, your spirit lives on, especially in the hundreds of sellers of literature and the party press in work places, streets, pubs, railway stations, houses and elsewhere, and among those striving to establish your ambition, the best literature and Tribune stand in Australia.*⁴⁰

Spain and his former comrades in the International Brigades were never far from McNeill's mind. In 1945, he raised the mysterious case of Frank Ryan, an Irishman who had played a heroic role in rallying the shattered British Battalion at Jarama. McNeill had known friends of Ryan, and said there was "something very suspicious" about recent reports of his death from a stroke in a Dresden sanatorium. McNeill postulated that Ryan had actually been killed by forces acting for Franco or Hitler.⁴¹ The truth about Ryan's last years remains contentious. Some have suggested that, in pursuing the reunification of Ireland, he had lapsed into collaboration with the Nazis. It is generally accepted that, with his health seriously damaged from his time in Spain, his death in Dresden was from natural causes.⁴²

---

39   *Tribune*, 5 October 1955, p. 10. The National Film and Sound Archive of Australia kindly arranged a screening of this film. https://www.collection.nfsa.gov.au/search/query=Words%20for%20Freedom
40   *Tribune*, 7 December 1960, p. 6.
41   *Tribune*, 23 October 1945, p. 7.
42   Tremlett, *International Brigades*, pp. 528-9.

Cold War politics

ASIO recorded that McNeill wrote to the Governor of Pennsylvania in support of Steve Nelson, who had been a leading figure in the Abraham Lincoln Battalion. During the Cold War, many former International Brigaders faced persecution and discrimination in the USA. As a prominent member of the American Communist Party, Nelson was prosecuted on the grounds that his membership constituted proof that he was attempting to overthrow the American government. Found guilty, he was sentenced to twenty years imprisonment and ordered to pay a fine of $10,000 in addition to $13,000 in costs. The cases involved made their way to the Supreme Court of the United States, which considered competing federal and state laws, heard evidence of perjury from a prosecution witness, and ordered a new trial. In 1957 the government abandoned the cases.[43]

As time passed, McNeill settled into the role of a party elder. *Tribune* referred to him as a hero, and he instructed younger people about the lessons of the past. His concern to have the Spanish Civil War properly remembered remained constant. He gave a talk to the University of NSW Labour Club where he read an eyewitness account of Dickinson's capture and execution at Jarama. He told the students that while there was adventure and perhaps romance in getting to Spain, there was "no adventure or romance in the war itself, only horror and the degradation of mankind".[44]

A student at the University of Adelaide, John Playford, corresponded with McNeill in 1958 while researching his honours thesis on the history of the left-wing of the South Australian labour movement. McNeill said that his time in South Australia was "most hectic" and that the IWW "copped the spleen of the newspapers and ruling section".[45] In his thesis, Playford described Dickinson as "possessing a strong personality and being a vigorous and able speaker". His view was that, given Dickinson's

---

[43] NAA: 32538840 and Abraham Lincoln Brigade Archive, accessed 18 December 2023, https://alba-valb.org/volunteers/steve-nelson/

[44] The speech notes are in the McNeill Collection, Illawarra Museum.

[45] Letter from McNeill to Playford, 14 February 1958, McNeill Collection, Illawarra Museum.

oratory and organising ability, he could have risen high in the Labor Party had he ever been able to wed his "picturesque individuality to the requirements of the Party machine".[46]

Brian Aarons, who was a young CPA activist in the 1960s, remembers McNeill recounting his experiences at a party function:

> *Jim was a truly wonderful person – one of those "salt of the earth" blue-collar working class communist activists of that era, modest and self-effacing with it. One Saturday night at a local CPA function in our backyard in Fairfield, he enthralled people with his account of his life and experiences, including the Spanish Civil War.*[47]

McNeill was obviously proud to have fought in Spain, but not all his listeners were as enamoured as Aarons. One of ASIO's informants attended a combined meeting of the Fairfield, Merrylands/Guildford and Cabramatta branches and reported that McNeill spoke for some time on what was dryly described as his "favourite subject", the Spanish Civil War. The agent commented: "He's a fanatic."[48]

By the 1960s, McNeill's health was poor and he took a position in the Communist Party's bookshops, which involved only light duties. Described by ASIO as an "old man", he initially worked at the Pioneer Bookshop, then in 1964 transferred to the New World Booksellers, which was "a large, modern bookshop" that sold Eastern Bloc books, pamphlets, records, watches, perfumes and toys. McNeill's "sole duty appears to be opening incoming mail including assignments of new books". ASIO noted that the shop turnover was £1000 per week, and that McNeill was paid £16 per week, while the women he worked with received £14 per week.[49]

In April 1963, McNeill and Stan Moran, his friend since the Depression, travelled to the USSR. Articles in *Tribune* stated that the purpose of the trip was to receive medical treatment, although an invitation for a farewell party said it was to witness the May Day

---

[46] Playford, 'History', pp. 125–6.
[47] Personal communication from Brian Aarons, 20 October 2023.
[48] NAA: 32538840.
[49] NAA: 32538840.

parade.⁵⁰ It was likely both.

McNeill sent a letter to *Tribune* from his bed in a newly built hospital near Moscow. It revealed that McNeill still saw the Soviet Union through rose-tinted glasses, unaffected by Khrushchev's denunciation of Stalin in February 1956 and the USSR's brutal invasion of Hungary later that year. He contrasted the "tense, sometimes worried looks of a Pitt Street or George Street crowd, always in a hell of a hurry" with the "leisurely, content and smiling faces of a secure, happy people" in Moscow. Soviet women were fashion conscious, and wore smart stockings, while the men had panama hats and tussore silk coats.⁵¹ Mabel's enthusiasm for the Soviet Union matched her husband's. She made a trip to Europe in 1964 and reported that conditions for workers in England and Scotland were poor, but in Russia "all was good".⁵²

The McNeills imagined a communist idyll, but in the real world global communist unity was tottering and events were only to worsen through the 1960s. The Soviet Union's invasion of Hungary had disillusioned many CPA members. Among the ranks of those leaving was a teacher from Vanessa's school who came to the McNeills' home to advise that he had resigned his party membership.⁵³

A split between China and the USSR ended the solid ideological unity of the CPA. McNeill told the Merrylands/Guildford Branch that the crux of the dispute was that China wanted to keep the revolution "seething and boiling" until the entire world was communist, while Russia had cooled down and wanted to take a more peaceful line with the West. McNeill told his local branch that in some other branches 30 per cent of members were staying away because of the dispute. Meetings fell into disarray when members following the Peking line insisted on discussing the split and the merits of each country's approach to communism. McNeill's solution was not to have the matter discussed at branch meetings. Instead, he sought to devote the

---

50   *Tribune*, 3 April 1963, p. 12; *Tribune*, 9 April 1963, p. 3; NAA: 32538840.
51   *Tribune*, 19 June 1963, p. 9.
52   NAA: 32538840.
53   Personal communication from Vanessa McNeill, 18 January 2023.

Branch's energies to opposing the escalating war in Vietnam, with members invited to attend protests outside the American consulate.[54]

McNeill was also reading histories of the Spanish Civil War that began to be published in the 1960s. He had a 1962 edition of Hugh Thomas' *The Spanish Civil War*, a highly influential and popular account that was banned in Spain.[55] In his copy of Vincent Brome's 1965 work, *The International Brigades*, McNeill carefully marked the sections dealing with the Barcelona farewell and the fate that befell many of the leaders of the International Brigades in Stalin's purges:

> *The cadre of leaders who had gained military experience in Spain and in the Far East was almost completely liquidated… No veteran leader of the International Brigades in Eastern Europe was safe. The witch-hunt gradually spread its net until, as Hugh Thomas says, most of them were arrested and many shot.*[56]

He had also been given a Spanish language copy of the history of the Spanish Communist Party, personally signed by La Pasionaria. This was a treasured possession, obtained for McNeill by a friend active in the Australia-USSR Friendship Society who met La Pasionaria on a visit to Russia. The friend presented her with a copy of *Australians in Spain – Our Pioneers Against Fascism*. In return, she sent McNeill the history book, inscribed by her in Spanish:

> *To Comrade Jim McNeill,*
>
> *In memory of our unforgettable collective struggle for freedom and democracy in Spain.*
>
> *Cordially*
>
> *Dolores Ibarruri*
>
> *January 1962*[57]

---

54 *NAA*: 32538840.
55 Paul Preston, 'Lord Thomas of Swynnerton', *The Guardian*, 10 May 2017, accessed 20 December 2023 https://www.theguardian.com/books/2017/may/09/lord-thomas-of-swynnerton-obituary
56 Brome, *International Brigades*, pp. 276-8. McNeill's copy is in the possession of the writer.
57 WL interview. The frontispiece was detached from the book and is now part of the McNeill Collection, Illawarra Museum.

On the thirtieth anniversary of the commencement of the war, *Tribune* published a major article by McNeill, spread across two pages, which told the story of Jarama and again recounted Dickinson's execution.[58] McNeill followed this with a biographical profile of his friend, published in the December issue of the *Australian Left Review*, which covered their experiences in Adelaide and Dickinson's time in Britain and Spain. It was a deeply affectionate piece, with McNeill describing Dickinson as a man of "great humour and kindliness, yet still a tough and uncompromising fighter for the 'working stiff.'" Dickinson, he said, was an enthusiastic speaker, with tons of ability, who was "an unforgettable character".[59] The article appeared with a pencilled portrait of Dickinson by the artist Herbert McClintock, whose work is now held in major Australian collections, including that of the National Gallery of Australia. The portrait was drawn from the photograph taken with McNeill in the Adelaide Botanic Gardens in 1927.

Photo 33 – *Dickinson* by Herbert McClintock. Originally published in the *Australian Left Review* in 1966. (SEARCH Foundation and the Herbert McClintock Estate)

---

[58] *Tribune*, 6 July 1966, pp. 6-7.
[59] McNeill, 'Ted Dickinson', p. 45.

Czechoslovakia 1968

On the night of 20 August 1968, the Soviet Union and several of its Warsaw Pact satellites invaded Czechoslovakia. The tanks were ordered into Prague to bring an end to the liberalisation that had been sanctioned by the local leadership. Moscow regarded such actions in the Eastern Bloc as a threat to Soviet hegemony. The Soviet aggression, coinciding with the war in Vietnam which the CPA was vehement in denouncing, plunged the CPA into a major crisis, one that had a profound impact on McNeill and communists like him.

Since its establishment in the wake of the Bolshevik revolution, the CPA had been steadfast in its loyalty to the Soviet Union. It had supported every policy and policy reversal, accommodated and justified every action, including the murder of Lenin's contemporaries and the Nazi-Soviet Non-Aggression Pact. But on this occasion the response was different and an emergency meeting of the national executive condemned the invasion of Czechoslovakia.[60] This decision ended the CPA's subservient relationship to the Soviet Union and commenced a long running dispute between Australian communists that lasted until the dissolution of the party itself.

The national executive's position was not supported by a substantial minority of the CPA's membership who were intent on maintaining a dogged fealty to the USSR. McNeill immediately supported the national executive and became an active participant in the debate. ASIO noted that he and Mabel advised the Merrylands/Guildford branch that they would leave the CPA if it decided to support the USSR.[61]

McNeill attended a day-long meeting of the national executive called to discuss the Czech-Soviet issue. He wrote a letter to *Tribune* describing as "absurd" a suggestion that the paper should provide space for articles "justifying the invasion by a mighty nation of over 220 million of its small neighbour". He cited his branch's record in maintaining a *Tribune* stand at Guildford for twenty years and

---

[60] Mcintyre, *The Party*, p. 385.
[61] NAA: A6119, 7670

challenged the party's internal opposition to go out onto the streets and sell more papers.⁶² McNeill's view was, as he told his branch, that the party "should get back into harness and attend to work on local matters rather than persist with pointless arguments and debates about Czechoslovakia".⁶³

One who took a different view was Carter. Deploying his status as a veteran of the war in Spain, he wrote to *Tribune* suggesting that the CPA had been "too hasty in condemning the Soviet Union". In a position that was odd for an Australian International Brigader to adopt, he suggested that as the Soviet Union was part of Europe, it "MUST be in a better position to sum up the situation than we are".⁶⁴

While relations between the USSR and the CPA were strained, McNeill's status as a veteran of the International Brigades was still honoured. In January 1970 he accepted an invitation to attend a reception hosted by the Soviet Ambassador to celebrate the centenary of Lenin's birth. McNeill travelled to Canberra with other CPA members of longstanding, with ASIO tracing their movements from the Three Swallows Hotel at Bankstown to the Soviet compound. They travelled in a beige Volkswagen registered to Reg Wilding, a Wollongong communist. Afterwards, ASIO recorded an embassy official dictating an article for *Pravda* that noted the presence of McNeill, "the fighter of the International Brigade", at the event.⁶⁵

McNeill returned to the factional fray in 1970 with a joint letter signed with Jack Mundey, Brian Aarons and Noel Abello, a union activist in the metal industry. The letter was published ahead of the CPA's national congress, the party's supreme body. The four authors challenged the pro-Soviet opposition to public debates in front of unionists, anti-war protestors or party members.⁶⁶

The national congress decisively ratified the national executive's position

---

⁶² *Tribune*, 17 December 1969, p. 11.
⁶³ NAA: A6119, 7670.
⁶⁴ *Tribune*, 11 September 1968, p. 11.
⁶⁵ NAA: A6119, 7670.
⁶⁶ *Tribune*, 18 February 1970, p. 11.

on Czechoslovakia but the matter was still not settled. The debate would drag on, debilitate the party and eventually result in a formal split. About 800 members left the CPA in 1971 to establish the pro-Moscow Socialist Party of Australia.[67] Among the members to leave were many of McNeill's long-time friends and colleagues, including Stan Moran and Edgar Ross.

The dispute had intensified into a schism. Since its creation the CPA had strict rules of governance: unquestioning loyalty by party members to the leadership, sustained and reinforced by the unquestioning loyalty of the leadership to the Soviet Union. Members were now witnessing their leaders defy the USSR. Events, and reactions to events, unleashed anger and pain and were deeply traumatic for communists like McNeill who had given decades of political effort, alongside friends and comrades, to a cause that he now saw had betrayed its fundamental ideals.

McNeill and other Depression-era communists had joined the CPA at a moment of deep economic and social crisis. The Labor Party and trade unions had been overwhelmed by the scale of the crisis and been ineffectual in alleviating the Depression's misery. In contrast, the CPA provided a coherent world view that identified the cause of economic ruin as the capitalist system itself. Membership of the CPA was an unending education with a central part of the syllabus being that the capitalist system, not the unemployed, had failed. The party provided an explanation for their personal circumstances that gave comfort and justification. Party discipline and monolithic unity added an enduring sense of security.

The events of 1968 meant beliefs and practices that had sustained communists for a lifetime were now being shattered beyond repair. Life-long friendships ended and people's faith was broken. Vanessa remembers her parents as "sad and depressed" throughout the period.

> *Their life's work, if you like, and their network of friends collapsed around them. From being very active, involved people, to everything*

---

[67] Mcintyre, *The Party*, p. 402.

> *going pear-shaped. The collapse of their dream knocked the stuffing out of them. They changed after that and I don't think they would have been the only ones.*
>
> *They never spoke about it with me, but my mother just said she'd read "But the Dead Are Many" by Frank Hardy and my father read it as well.*[68]

Hardy's novel, published in 1975, is about a communist who loses his faith and suicides in a hotel in a fictional village outside Wollongong. It is based on the suicide of Hardy's close friend, the ex-seminarian Paul Mortier, a communist deeply affected by the invasion of Hungary. A cultural critic and full-time party functionary, Mortier had regularly spoken at the Merrylands/Guildford Branch's street meetings and was well known to McNeill. A minor character in Hardy's book is Albert Brink, a "ponderous" man who works at the CPA bookshop and "walks with a limp from an obscure knee injury". The characters in Hardy's works are usually based on real people, and McNeill may have been the inspiration for Brink.[69]

For the McNeills, the practical impact of the split was the collapse of the Merrylands/Guildford branch. With their branch defunct, they transferred their membership to the Parramatta Branch, but indicated that they would not be attending meetings regularly.[70] The split took a toll on personal relationships, as Vanessa recalled about an incident at a function.

> *My mother saw that there was going to be a cottage lecture and she was interested in that and so we went. But there was a woman there who just cut my mother dead. Zealots, fanatics. It was really horrible.*[71]

In 1970, McNeill published a series of articles in *Common Cause* which recounted episodes of Dickinson's political activity in Australia and Britain.[72] In 1974, McNeill again spoke admiringly of Dickinson

---

[68] Personal communication from Vanessa McNeill, 18 January 2023.
[69] *Tribune*, 5 July 1953, p. 7; Frank Hardy, *But the Dead are Many*, Sydney, 1975, p. 15; Mcintyre, *The Party*, p. 400.
[70] *NAA:* 32538840.
[71] Personal communication from Vanessa McNeill, 18 January 2023.
[72] They appeared in *Common Cause* on 2, 9, 23 & 30 May 1970.

in an interview recorded with Wendy Lowenstein, a social historian researching an oral history of the Depression. He told her that Dickinson was a "brilliant speaker and organiser and a real good working-class journalist".[73] McNeill's reminisces about Dickinson and their time in Adelaide were published in Lowenstein's successful 1978 book, *Weevils in the Flour: An oral record of the 1930s Depression in Australia.*

As an afterthought, the interview moved from the Depression to the Spanish Civil War. McNeill said that he felt that the war "never really struck a deep chord in Australia" as it was fought so far away. He told Lowenstein that he had made two major political mistakes in his life. These were, firstly, believing that the French would intervene if the Spanish Republic could hold on just a little longer, and secondly, believing in the Soviet Union:

> *I made a mistake in my analysis of the situation. I was carried away with the united front in France, the Popular Front, carried away with what I'd read in the Workers' Weekly and party propaganda. I thought that if Spain looked like fighting, then the Popular Front would march across the border and help. That sort of business.*
>
> *It was the one big political mistake I made, – apart from being sucked in by the Soviet Union for so long.*[74]

In 1975, the Australian Broadcasting Commission interviewed McNeill about his experiences in Spain for *Behind The News*, a current affairs program for schools. Both Jim and Mabel enjoyed the experience, with the film crew working busily in the McNeills' sunny back garden and old friends contacting them to let them know they had seen the broadcast.[75]

On 20 November 1975 Franco died in his hospital bed. With the dictator dead, a transition to democracy in Spain began. Earlier, when it was clear that the dictator was ailing, the CPA had established a fund to

---

[73] WL interview.
[74] WL interview.
[75] Letter from Mabel McNeill to Len Fox, 5 August 1976, Len Fox Papers 1852-2001, Mitchell Library, State Library of New South Wales, MLMSS 8085.

support the publication of *Mundo Obrero*, the newspaper of the Spanish Communist Party. McNeill contributed a $10 donation, a significant proportion of the couples' modest pension, which he said was made in memory of Dickinson, Morcom and Young.[76]

Early in 1976 McNeill underwent prostate surgery and spent a month in hospital. He recovered and was well enough to participate in Sydney's May Day march, but sickened again in late June. He died on 10 July 1976 in the Repatriation General Hospital at Concord. He had been seriously ill with his death certificate recording the cause of death as bronchopneumonia, a leaking aortic aneurysm, acute renal failure and chronic lymphatic leukaemia.[77]

His funeral oration was delivered by Ted Lipscombe, a veteran CPA member from Sydney's western suburbs, who hailed McNeill as being "among Australia's first pioneers against fascism".[78] Hec Chalmers, a Labor Party member who had known McNeill since the 1920s, wrote to *Tribune* to tell of his "admiration" for "what he was and what he did". Others made donations to the *Tribune* press fund in McNeill's memory while Lloyd Edmonds, another veteran of the Spanish Civil War, said that he was an "exemplar of the battler".[79]

After being ill for two years, Mabel died on 9 October 1981, aged 69. Her obituary in *Tribune* remembered her as a "dedicated communist and an efficient organiser" who lived a down to earth life with a "wry twist of humour".[80] The McNeills' ashes were placed in the family plot at Waverley Cemetery, where McNeill's parents and three infant brothers were buried.

---

[76] *Tribune*, 4 March 1975, p. 2; In March 1975 the aged pension partnered rate was $1339 per annum, or $25.75 a week. https://guides.dss.gov.au/social-security-guide/5/2/2/10

[77] Death certificate for James Vincent McNeill, NSW Registry of Births, Deaths and Marriages, 19 July 1976.

[78] *Tribune*, 21 July 1976, p. 11.

[79] *Tribune*, 4 August 1976, p. 2; *Tribune*, 15 September 1976, p. 10; *Tribune*, 25 August 1976, p. 6.

[80] *Tribune*, 18 November 1981, p. 14.

Carter in Wollongong

Carter lived in Wollongong and spent the rest of his working life on the Port Kembla wharves. He earnt several nicknames, including "The Kid from Spain" and "Casanova Carter".[81] He remained an avid boxing fan and continued to be a proud communist, contributing regularly to the party's press fund. After he retired from the wharves, he campaigned for improvements to the aged pension. ASIO maintained a file on him, collecting such titbits as his selling *Tribune* to seamen when their ships pulled into Port Kembla and that his 1954 model blue Holden utility was used in Wollongong's 1956 May Day march. ASIO had informants at meetings of the South Coast District of the CPA through the 1970s and their reports regularly noted Carter's attendance and his status as "an old Spanish Civil War fighter".[82]

Photo 34 – Joe Carter (L) campaigning for an increase to the aged pension with Bill McDougall, 1975. (From the collections of the Wollongong City Libraries and the Illawarra Historical Society – P09094)

---

[81] *Tribune*, 2 April 1940, p. 4. Released in 1932, *The Kid from Spain* was a musical comedy starring Eddie Cantor.
[82] NAA: A9626, 1083 and NAA: A367, C49308.

Carter married Lyla Whitehead, had no children and outlived his wife. By the 1970s his status as an International Brigader began to be recognised. In 1973 he spoke on a platform alongside Manuel Azcarate, the leader of the Spanish Communist Party and a veteran of the war, when he visited Australia on a speaking tour.[83] Carter's experiences began to be of interest to historians and he gave at least five oral history interviews. Journalists sought him out and his story was told in feature articles in the *Illawarra Mercury* and *Sydney Morning Herald*. Invited by a journalist to nominate what he saw as the major issues of the day, he replied: "The environment and the bomb. And they aren't separate issues. If we lose either it could mean that we are done for."[84]

In 1986, to mark the fiftieth anniversary of the commencement of the Spanish Civil War, *Tribune* conducted a long interview with Carter. Of McNeill, Carter said: "I'd safely say he'd be one of the greatest men ever I struck, the most honest, naturally he was a communist and [if there's] a gentleman's gentleman, he was it."[85] Looking back on his time in Spain, he said:

> *It was a tremendous experience and I met some of the finest and bravest people alive. I remember with affection Jack Franklyn, one of the truest and most humorous of mates.*
>
> *[I went] because I was a communist. I wanted to help the Spanish people beat fascism and build a socialist society.*[86]

Carter was celebrated in Wollongong with local CPA members holding a birthday party for him in 1987. He died of renal failure in Bulli Hospital on 30 December 1993. An obituary in the *Illawarra Mercury* described him as "just a working man" with a political and social consciousness that took him to a country far from Wollongong to fight for a cause. George Murray, who played the bass drum in the band that welcomed McNeill and Carter back to Wollongong in 1939 and had later become the president of the South Coast Labour Council, said that Carter

---

[83] *Tribune*, 21 January 1975, p. 9.
[84] *Sydney Morning Herald, Good Weekend*, 23 April 1983, pp. 1 - 2.
[85] *Tribune*, 8 October 1986, p. 14.
[86] *Tribune*, 16 July 1986, p. 16.

was "a humble man who simply hated injustice".[87] His funeral heard a message sent by Lloyd Edmonds, who had met Carter at Ripoll, which praised his courage, steadfastness and capacity for mateship.[88]

---

[87] *Illawarra Mercury*, 5 January 1994, p. 4.

[88] Laurie Aarons archive, Mitchell Library, State Library of New South Wales, MLMSS 7924 Box 5.

18

Afterlife

The stories about Dickinson that McNeill had written for *Common Cause* were republished in 1977 in an anthology of stories about the 1930s edited by Len Fox. In his introduction to *Depression Down Under*, Fox recalled McNeill as a "softly-spoken man" who had lived through exciting times in Adelaide, before battling the New Guard and then fighting in Spain. He was a "fine person", a "warm and generous friend", "quiet and down to earth" and to "think of him is to the think of the fight against fascism". Fox noted that McNeill's reminiscences were not about himself and his own actions, but were modestly centred on Dickinson, who emerged as a handsome and heroic figure, a "great and colourful" character.[1]

Theatrical productions

McNeill would surely have been delighted to know that his stories were the starting point for a theatrical depiction of Dickinson's life.[2] The play, *Dickinson*, was written by David Allen, directed by David Young and performed by the Troupe Theatre Company at The Space in Adelaide's Festival Centre in 1978. It told the story of Dickinson's life and included some fictional episodes, such as an imagined upbringing in the mining town of Broken Hill, alongside more factual, and celebratory, retellings of his escapades in Adelaide. Reeve appears as Dickinson's mentor and inspiration, but McNeill doesn't feature, his

---

[1] Len Fox, (Ed), *Depression Down Under*, Potts Point, 1977, pp. 54, 61, 65; Fox, *Broad Left*, p. 44.
[2] Personal communication from David Young, 22 April 2023.

role being subsumed into that of another Wobbly.

In England, Dickinson loses his job at an oil company after challenging one of Mussolini's ministers to a duel, then brawls with fascists at his fish stall, clubbing a Blackshirt with a large fish.

> MYRTLE: *I didn't realise selling fish was so dangerous.*
>
> TED: *Depends on your customers.*
>
> MYRTLE: *You enjoyed it?*
>
> TED: *I enjoy a scrap.*

The turning point of the play is when Dickinson meets Orwell at a rally of the British Union of Fascists. Dickinson and Orwell pepper Mosley with challenging questions. As Blackshirt violence threatens, Orwell steps in with advice that keeps Dickinson unharmed. Afterwards, in the play's crucial scene, their conversation convinces Dickinson to travel to Spain, and also suggests his fate:

> MYRTLE: *Ted's for action.*
>
> ORWELL: *(Light irony) Is that what he was looking for in the meeting just now? That seemed more like attempted suicide.*
>
> MYRTLE: *Let me tell you mate, Ted knows what action is all about.*
>
> TED: *It's alright love, he's right. That kind of disorganised stirring achieves nothing, worse than nothing. If it hadn't been for him, I'd have been done over by the Blackshirts... and somehow, I think that's what I wanted.*
>
> MYRTLE: *No, Ted, no. That's not you. You fight to win.*
>
> ORWELL: *Hurling yourself at the likes of Mosley and his thugs is only right and proper, but ultimately it's like treating small-pox by picking the scabs. Capitalism, fascism are international diseases – their treatment must be international; it's too late for nationalist solutions – I suspect it always was...we must band together, seek out the virus and exterminate it. Then the scabs will drop off*

	on their own accord.
MYRTLE:	*You're talking about Spain, aren't you?*
ORWELL:	*The first step, yes…If you're interested in battlefields, then there's the test: the clear-cut confrontation between left and right.*
TED:	*Democracy and fascism.*
ORWELL:	*There are shades of democracy of course.*
TED:	*Observer, will you be going?*
ORWELL:	*I think so.*

The production was staged with research assistance from Bill Ivey, a former Adelaide Wobbly, and John Playford, the student who had written to McNeill in 1958 and had since become a prominent academic. The production included visual slides of the unemployed riots in Adelaide, Mosley in full cry, and fighting in the Spanish Civil War. The play was promoted with an image of Dickinson's head, bullet-blasted, with a bolt of lightning bursting from his mouth. The program notes described Dickinson as "an almost 'classic' hero of the left" and said his life "strongly and simply exemplifies the continuing struggle between the 'haves' and the 'have-nots.'"[3] The production found its audience and set a box office record for the venue. Such was the demand an additional matinee was added to the production's run. The impact of the play attracted the attention of the Premier of South Australia, Don Dunstan (Labor), who provided Troupe with sufficient funding to become fully professional.[4]

The critics were also favourably impressed, with Alan Roberts in the *Advertiser* seeing Dickinson as "a romantic. He believed in people". Roberts found the production to be "funny, witty, mad; full of life, energy and guts". Another critic, Peter Farrell, saw Dickinson as a "romantic figure in a romantic play", and praised Young's direction, "which obviously consisted of a large slice of his heart". Farrell did offer the criticism that the audience didn't "really learn very much about

---

[3] Program for Space Theatre's production of Dickinson, by David Allen with David Young and Henry Salter, 1980, State Library of South Australia, Record: b2159431.

[4] Personal communication from David Allen, 4 April 2023.

Dickinson the man" who was portrayed as an "Everyman of the left, an honest if naïve figure". In his review in *Tribune*, Don Sutherland said the play was "unashamedly working class" and captured the realities of class struggle. He hailed Dickinson as a "dedicated anti-fascist" and an "exciting 'character.'"[5]

In 1980, the play was staged in Brisbane by the La Boite Theatre company. In the program notes David Allen located Dickinson "in the best Australian tradition, a stirrer".[6] One reviewer, Veronica Kelly in *Theatre Australia*, saw Dickinson as a "charismatic agitator" struggling against a "predatory and bloodthirsty capitalism" while the *Courier Mail*'s David Rowbotham saw the play as "a lesson about the past that is relevant today".[7] Incredibly, more than 50 years after Dickinson had been imprisoned, his story again attracted the attention of the police. As the director Malcolm Blaylock explained:

> *Particularly with the major plays - Dickinson, Traitors – but generally most plays unless there was a fluffy one they didn't care too much about...the police would turn up in Sexton Street in a marked police car usually on preview night so they wouldn't have to pay... They would sit in the front row, two or three of them, and watch it and leave. And nothing ever happened but they were there and I had to know they were there and there would be a file on me.*[8]

---

[5] *Advertiser*, 2 December 1978, p. 27; An undated clipping provided by David Young in an email to the author, 12 April 2023; and *Tribune*, 29 November 1978, p. 8.

[6] Program for the La Boite Theatre's production of *Dickinson*, 1980, Len Fox Papers 1852-2001, Mitchell Library, State Library of NSW, MLMSS 8085.

[7] *Theatre Australia*, August 1989, p. 53; *Courier Mail*, 30 June 1980, p. 2.

[8] Christine Anne Wilmington Comans, 'La Boite Theatre 1925 to 2003', Queensland University of Technology PhD thesis, 2006, p. 163.

Jim McNeill and his mates in the Spanish Civil War

Photo 35: Anthony Phelan in *Dickinson* by David Allen, directed by Malcolm Blaylock, at the La Boite Theatre, Brisbane, 1980. (Image provided courtesy of QPAC Collections)

Historical interest

The staging of the play prompted familial interest in Dickinson's story. With Dickinson's mother and brother both dying in the 1970s, a nephew, Ross Dickinson, made an appeal in *Tribune* for material that could assist him in writing a biography of his uncle. Unfortunately, this project did not proceed.[9] Several years later, Young, director of the Adelaide production, travelled to Bendigo to meet Myrtle and her daughter. Both were very proud of Dickinson. Myrtle made it clear that she had supported his political activity in Adelaide and England. Myrtle also observed that he was the sort of man who should never have married. Like Ted's nephew, his daughter said she was proposing to write a biography. If it ever eventuated, it has not been traced.[10]

In 1978, the South Australian academic Ray Broomhill published

---

[9] *Tribune*, 13 December 1978, p. 10; Personal communication from Rafe Dickinson 22 May 2023.

[10] Personal communication from David Young, 12 April 2023 and 17 December 2023.

Unemployed Workers: A Social History of the Great Depression in Adelaide that made mention of the IWW's efforts to campaign among the unemployed. There was no mention by name of Dickinson, McNeill or Morcom, and Broomhill concluded that neither the IWW nor the CPA managed to achieve a large membership. The "revolution, of course, did not materialize".[11] In 1981, Broomhill wrote the entry for Dickinson in the *Australian Dictionary of Biography* which stated that he was a "stirring, enthusiastic and fiery speaker" and noted reports from Spain that he was a "born leader".[12]

In the 1980s, more than four decades after the commencement of the Spanish Civil War, interest in the participation of Australians in the conflict began to awaken. In 1981, Diane Menghetti's *The Red North: The Popular Front in Queensland* was published with chapters on the men who left the cane fields around Innisfail, Ayr, and Ingham to fight with the International Brigades and the supporting efforts made by local communities to raise money for the Republic's cause.[13]

Also in 1981, Elizabeth Burchill, an Australian nurse, published her autobiography, *The Paths I've Trod*, which provided an account of her medical service with the Southern Spanish Relief Committee. Burchill was based in Almeria and spent most of her time tending to the needs of refugees. She regarded herself as a politically neutral nurse, carrying out a humanitarian mission, "intent only on caring for innocent victims of war".[14] In 1983, Arthur "Bluey" Howells published his memoir, *Against the Stream*, which detailed his time in the Labor Party, anti-fascist activities in Australia, and a visit he made with his wife to the Spanish Republic in October 1938.[15]

---

[11] Broomhill, *Unemployed*, pp. 166-9.

[12] Ray Broomhill, 'Dickinson, Edward Alexander (Ted) (1903–1937)', Australian Dictionary of Biography, National Centre of Biography, Australian National University, https://adb.anu.edu.au/biography/dickinson-edward-alexander-ted-5976/text10197, published first in hardcopy 1981, accessed online 10 January 2025.

[13] Menghetti, *The Red North*, pp. 51-66.

[14] Elizabeth Burchill, *The Paths I've Trod: Autobiography of an Australian Nurse*, Richmond, 1981, p. 55.

[15] Howells, *Against the Stream*.

In 1985, the first book that dealt exclusively with the participation of an Australian in the conflict was published. *Letters from Spain* was a collection of the letters that Lloyd Edmonds had sent home to his family.[16] It was edited by Amirah Inglis, who as an eleven-year-old attended a Spanish Relief Committee meeting in Melbourne and donated ten shillings to the Republican cause. A dedicated member of the CPA from the late 1940s to the early 1960s, Inglis had a close family interest in the conflict. One of her Jewish uncles had fought in the International Brigades as a member of the Polish Dabrowski Battalion.[17]

In 1986 the fiftieth anniversary of the outbreak of the Spanish Civil War was marked with a conference held at Sydney University. Films were shown, an exhibition of photographs was displayed, a Spanish-themed dinner was held and Joe Carter and Lloyd Edmonds addressed the attendees. The Australian Broadcasting Corporation marked the anniversary by broadcasting a television documentary series on the war and both Carter and Edmonds were interviewed by the *Sunday* current affairs program.[18]

In 1987, Inglis published the first full-length historical study of Australia's involvement in the war. Her book, *Australians in the Spanish Civil War*, was a comprehensive account of the attitudes and actions taken by different interests in Australia, including the media, churches, unions and political parties. It provided an overview of the motivations of the Australian volunteers, and included accounts of Dickinson's fate.

Her work strove for objectivity and sought to tell all sides of the story, but her sympathies were clear. She gave her position in the preface, which stated that those "who went to fight for the Republic

---

[16] Lloyd Edmonds, edited by Amirah Inglis, *Letters from Spain*, North Sydney, 1985.
[17] Inglis, *Australians,* p. xiv.
[18] *Tribune*, 5 November 1986, p. 7; Eureka Youth League National Conference Papers, Mitchell Library, State Library of New South Wales, MLMSS 11167, DC 136, VT 5778. The Australian Broadcasting Commission became the Australian Broadcasting Corporation in 1983.

were on the right side".¹⁹ Inglis' work signalled a resurgence of interest in the Australians who served in Spain. The Australian Broadcasting Corporation broadcast a radio documentary, *A Poet's War*, about Australians and the Spanish Civil War, and an academic historian at the University of Sydney, Judith Keene, published *The Last Mile to Huesca*, the annotated diary of Agnes Hodgson, an Australian nurse who had volunteered her services to the Spanish Republic.²⁰ Keene had earlier published a scholarly article detailing Bull's service for Franco, and another on Aileen Palmer, an Australian communist poet and linguist, and her experiences working with the Republic's medical services.²¹

Despite this research and scholarship, there remained no official recognition of Australia's International Brigaders and their pioneering role in fighting fascism. Perhaps the nearest to official recognition came in 1988 when the National Gallery of Australia acquired James Cant's 1938 painting, *Returning Volunteer*. It is a powerful image of a maimed International Brigader standing alone in a desolate, washed-out landscape with purple sand dunes in the distance. His left leg has been amputated at the knee; his left hand is missing. He stands with the aid of a crutch; his footsteps are dots and dashes. His mouth is agape in a silent scream as he gives the International Brigades' clenched fist salute. It is a defiant, unsettling and accusing image.²²

Cant had studied in Sydney before moving to London in 1934 where he exhibited alongside artists of the calibre of Ernst, Klee and Bacon. In 1936 he set off for Spain where he met Miro, Picasso and Magritte. Not fully comprehending what he was witnessing in Barcelona, he understood that he was influenced by the war simply because he saw it:

> I couldn't understand the chaps that were getting around the streets in Barcelona carrying obviously loaded rifles, ready to take a shot at you, whatever you might be doing.²³

---

[19] Inglis, *Australians*, p. xv.
[20] Keene, *The Last Mile to Huesca*.
[21] Keene, 'An Antipodean Bridegroom'; Judith Keene, 'A Spanish Springtime: Aileen Palmer and the Spanish Civil War', *Labour History*, Vol. 52, May 1987, pp. 75-87.
[22] The painting can be viewed: https://searchthecollection.nga.gov.au/object/90973
[23] Jean Campbell, *James Cant and Dora Chapman*, Sydney, 1995, p. 30.

On his return to London, he found the International Brigades were at "the fore of the art and literary minds", and set about producing a number of Spanish-themed pictures. One, *The Merchants of Death*, is obviously influenced by Picasso's *Guernica*, and is held in the Art Gallery of South Australia. The art historian Ron Radford noted that Cant moved away from surrealism after associating its irrationality with the irrationality of fascism. Cant returned to Australia, enlisted in May 1941 and served as a warrant officer on islands in the Torres Strait, apparently using his artistic skills to paint camouflage, until being medically discharged in 1944. He joined the CPA and established, with his wife and collaborator Dora Chapman, the Studio of Realist Art and took to exhibiting his art in factories and at street gatherings.[24]

The National Gallery's acquisition of Cant's artwork was a rare moment of recognition by Australia's cultural institutions of the International Brigades. Benjamin Britten's *Ballad of Heroes*, prefiguring his more famous *War Requiem*, was written in honour of the International Brigades and is performed regularly around the world, but does not appear to have ever been part of the repertoire of an Australian orchestra.[25] Instead, the eventual commemoration of the men and women who fought fascism in Spain was left to a handful of enthusiasts and a surviving International Brigader.

An unofficial memorial

The genesis of the idea to have a national memorial came in a letter from John Longstaff, a British International Brigader who had fought at the Battle of Ebro. He wrote to Prime Minister Bob Hawke pointing out that there were many memorials to the International Brigades in England, Ireland and Scotland and asked why there was no such memorial in Australia. He urged Hawke to raise one. The Australian government decided not to erect a memorial, but officials in the Prime

---

[24] Campbell, *James Cant*, p. 10; and NAA: B884, N270270.
[25] Email from the Sydney Symphony Orchestra to the author 18 December 2023. Searches through Trove and Google have not identified the work ever being performed in Australia. Any information to the contrary would be welcomed.

Minister's Department did refer the matter to Amirah Inglis.[26]

With the Cold War over and the CPA having wound itself up in 1991, the timing was finally favourable. In 1992 a committee composed of Inglis, Keene, Labor Party activist Netta Burns, Lloyd Edmonds and Len Fox, was formed to raise funds for the erection of a memorial to honour those who went to Spain. A public appeal was launched:

> *Memorials have been raised in Spanish towns and villages, in Britain, the United States and other countries, but no memorial exists to our Australian volunteers. We feel that the time has come to remind Australians of this neglected part of their heritage and to honour the brave Australian women and men who went from 'the other end of the earth' to offer their lives in the fight against fascism.*[27]

Contributions were received from trade unions, Labor MPs, members of the Spanish community and the general public. A sum sufficient to erect a memorial was collected. The Committee wrote to the Australian War Memorial, but was told that the *Australian War Memorial Act 1980* confined the institution to matters related to "operations in which Australians have been on active service", with active service defined as "war or warlike operations by members of the Defence Force". The Director, Brendon Kelson, advised that the legislation "wouldn't allow us to have a memorial or display specifically related to Spain".[28]

The Australian War Memorial's position is not matched by Britain's Imperial War Museum. This institution, which has a representative of the Australian government on its governing board of trustees, takes a wider approach and aims to be "a leader in developing and communicating a deeper understanding of the causes, course and consequences of war".[29] A consequence of this broader and more inclusive approach is that the Imperial War Museum holds one of Carter's oral history interviews in

---

[26] Letter from Inglis to Thurley, 2 December 1992, Amirah Inglis Collection, Noel Butlin Archives, Australian National University.

[27] Amirah Inglis Collection, Noel Butlin Archives, Australian National University.

[28] Letter from Kelson to Inglis, 23 November 1992, Amirah Inglis Collection, Noel Butlin Archives, Australian National University.

[29] Imperial War Museum, *Annual Report and Accounts 2022-2023*, p. 6.

its collection; the Australian War Memorial does not.

After receiving Kelson's rebuff, the Committee worked with Bill Wood MLA, a minister in the Labor government of the Australian Capital Territory, to secure a site in Canberra's Lennox Gardens, across Lake Burley Griffin and not in sight of the Australian War Memorial. There a memorial was erected. It is a masonry wall, on which a brass relief map of Spain, sculpted by Dr Ross Bastiaan, shows the main battlefields where the Australians served. Another brass panel, in English and Spanish, explains the historical background and states that the monument honours those who defended the cause of the Spanish Republic.

> *The Australian writer Nettie Palmer, who was in Barcelona when the uprising occurred, said of those who supported the Republic, 'though they were few in number and not powerful and seemed often to be shouting against the wind, theirs was a truly brave chapter in Australia's history.'*

Carter was too ill to attend the dedication of the monument, which was performed by Edmonds on 11 December 1993. The Spanish Ambassador to Australia, whose father had been a pilot in the Republican Air Force, planted a row of olive trees beside the memorial. The unveiling ceremony began with the well-known International Brigades anthem, *Jarama Valley*.[30]

Bull, the only Australian to have fought for fascism in Spain, is not honoured by the memorial. The invitation for the dedication included the names of 65 volunteers that were to be memorialised; Bull's name was not among them. His life is however formally acknowledged in Canberra.

The Australian War Memorial maintains two memorial rolls to honour Australians who died in war. The most well-known is the Roll of Honour, bronze panels above the Pool of Reflection, which list the names of more than 100,000 members of Australia's armed forces who died in war, warlike service or certain peacetime operations. The second

---

[30] Recording of the unveiling ceremony for the Spanish Memorial, Lennox Gardens, Amirah Inglis Collection, Noel Butlin Archives, Australian National University.

memorial roll is the Commemorative Roll, a leather-bound volume that lists those Australians who died in the same circumstances as those included in the Roll of Honour, but who were not members of Australia's armed forces.

Bull is honoured in the Commemorative Roll as he was killed in the Second World War while flying for the RAF. Dickinson, Morcom, Young and the other Australians who died in Spain fighting against the fascist forces of Hitler, Mussolini and Franco, are excluded from Australia's national remembrance.[31]

In 1996 Spain passed the *Democratic Memory Law* which granted members of the International Brigades Spanish citizenship. It was legislation that fulfilled the promise that Negrin had made to the volunteers at the Las Masies farewell in 1938, - that Spain would be theirs. But by then, none of the Australian volunteers were alive to accept the honour of being made citizens of a democratic Spain.

In 2006 the town of Morata erected a memorial to the International Brigaders. It honours those who "in solidarity fought for freedom in the Battle of Jarama". Placed atop a quiet battlefield hill that is covered in clumps of low grasses and honeycombed by trenches, tunnels and dugouts, the monument depicts a pair of clasped hands, russet in colour, set on a large concrete plinth. The memorial has, on several occasions, been vandalised by fascist sympathisers.

During the course of this research, McClintock's portrait of Dickinson that accompanied McNeill's 1966 article of remembrance was located. It was offered as a gift to both the Australian War Memorial and the National Portrait Gallery.

The donation was politely declined by both collecting institutions.

---

[31] A search of the Commemorative Roll was undertaken on 10 January 2024.

Appendix 1

The Ripoll photograph

Along with McNeill, Carter and Franklyn, the photograph features two Australians, Lloyd Edmonds and Kevin Rebbechi, and two New Zealanders, William Murn Macdonald and Herbert Bryan.

Born in London in 1907, **Lloyd Edmonds** migrated to Australia with his family in 1912. Edmonds attended the Socialist Sunday School, where he learnt the Ten Commandments of Socialism. He graduated from the University of Melbourne in 1927, worked as a teacher and served on the executive of the Victorian teachers' union. During the 1930s he was active in the Labor Party until expelled in a dispute over the appropriate response to Mussolini's invasion of Abyssinia.

Photo 36 – Lloyd Edmonds, 1939.
(Australian National University Archives Centre)

At the outbreak of the Spanish Civil War, Edmonds was in London, intending to study at the London School of Economics. Instead of study, he decided to go to Spain. He was introduced to the recruiting centre by Professor Harold Laski and arrived in Spain on 16 June 1937. He joined the Spanish Communist Party three months later. In letters home he told his father how Spain was "notoriously backward" with carts pulled by donkeys and ploughs by mules. He found the Spanish girls "most attractive", the food excellent, but the barracks "dirty and insanitary" and the houses "filthy". He joined the International Brigades as a driver and was unimpressed with Spanish drivers who drove too fast on the winding roads. He met Hemingway and remembered him for his store of limericks and his generosity with cigarettes, oranges and imitation whisky.[1]

> *Hemingway was big and burly and he had a red moon face and a deep voice. He was 38 then, in the prime of life, and splendidly alive.*[2]

Edmonds served at Brunete, Madrid, Aragon and the Ebro. While waiting to be repatriated from Ripoll, Edmonds became ill with jaundice and was unable to join the departure of the British Battalion. He was admitted to a Carmelite convent that was functioning as a hospital in the ancient city of Vic and was treated with diluted condensed milk and a single pill. He recovered, but was left to make his own way back to Britain. As Barcelona fell to the fascists, he began walking the 150 kilometres to the French border and was strafed while doing so:

> *After Barcelona fell the three main roads leading from that city to France were covered with a dense moving mass of combatants and non-combatants, escaping from the terrors of Franco's fascism.*
>
> *The fascist 'planes flew above the roads machine-gunning the refugees indiscriminately, whether they were troops or not.*
>
> *I saw the corpses of many non-combatants who had been brutally*

---

[1] 545/6/127/36-39; Palmer and Fox, *Australians in Spain*, pp. 49-50; Edmonds, *Letters from Spain*, pp. xii and 92; *Sydney Morning Herald, Good Weekend*, 23 April 1983, p. 1.

[2] *Sydney Morning Herald, Weekend Magazine and Book Reviews*, 13 August 1966, p. 18.

*murdered.*³

Edmonds was without food, weak and exhausted, but survived to be haunted by memories of the diving Stukas for the rest of his life.⁴ On arrival in the border town of Puigcerdà, he met the British journalist Sefton Delmer who provided him with the financial assistance to return to England.⁵

In February 1939, he was repatriated by the Australian government and boarded the *Moreton Bay* for the trip home. On arrival he spoke for the Spanish Relief Committee at events in Perth, Melbourne and Sydney. During the Second World War he married and began a family. He took a job as an industrial welfare officer with the Department of Labour and National Service and in 1942 enlisted in the Volunteer Defence Corps.⁶

During the post-war years Edmonds worked in the public service and kept up a wide range of social and political interests, duly recorded in the extensive files that ASIO maintained on him. He was a dedicated member of the Essendon Branch of the CPA and campaigned for improved municipal services. He was active in the Victorian National Parks Association, worked for the environmental protection of the Mornington Peninsula, agitated for more protections for kangaroos and planted hundreds of trees in the Organ Pipes National Park. He also served as the secretary/treasurer of the Melbourne Branch of the Australian Society for the Study of Labour History.⁷ He expressed despair in 1991 when, as the USSR was disintegrating, the CPA recognised the futility of its own existence and dissolved itself.

---

3   *Workers' Weekly*, 4 April 1939, p. 3.
4   *Sydney Morning Herald, Good Weekend*, 23 April 1983, p. 1; Peter Love, 'Edmonds, Frederick John Lloyd (1906–1994)', *Australian Dictionary of Biography*, National Centre of Biography, Australian National University, https://adb.anu.edu.au/biography/edmonds-frederick-john-lloyd-27616/text35031, published online 2019, accessed online 17 June 2024.
5   *Sydney Morning Herald, Weekend Magazine and Book Reviews*, 13 August 1966, p. 18.
6   NAA: B884, V371467.
7   Peter Love, 'Lloyd Edmonds 3 July 1906 – 18 September 1994', *Labour History*, No. 67, November 1994, pp. 1-3; Lloyd Edmonds interview with Laurie Aarons, Mitchell Library, State Library of New South Wales, MLOH 80.

Edmonds died in September 1994, the last of the Australian veterans of the International Brigades. A memorial ceremony at Melbourne's Trades Hall was attended by hundreds. In an obituary, the historian Amirah Inglis said he was "astonishingly modest" and a dedicated activist to the very end of his life. She recalled him valiantly distributing *Tribune* even when the CPA had declined to no more than a rump of old faithfuls.[8]

Kevin Francis Jas Rebbechi was described by Edmonds as "an existential hero, with little hope but determined to try" and by others as being of the "quiet, thoughtful type".[9] Rebbechi's father, Jas Augustine (Gus), was active in the labour movement and became the secretary of the Victorian branch of the Federated Clerks' Union in late 1924. Kevin was born in 1917 and, along with his two brothers, lost his mother in 1925 when Margaret Alice Rebbechi (nee O'Callaghan), died at the age of 33. At 15, Rebbechi left his home in Gordon Street, West Brunswick, Melbourne, and travelled widely across Australia. Appalled by the poverty and degradation caused by the Depression, he settled his idealism upon the Soviet Union and stowed away in an attempt to see this workers' paradise for himself. He ended up in Britain but struggled to find work.

Rebbechi eventually got a berth as a crew member on a ship that was evacuating refugees from the north coast of Spain. The ship was attacked and on its return to England Rebbechi decided to go back to Spain to join the International Brigades. Described as tall and slim, he left London's Victoria Station with Jack Jones and George Wheeler, two English volunteers associated with the Labour Party.[10] He walked over the Pyrenees with McNeill and at the age of 21 enlisted and was placed in No. 4 Company of the British Battalion. He trained alongside McNeill and received a gunshot wound to the leg during the first week of the Ebro offensive. His injury was made worse when the

---

[8] Amirah Inglis, 'Lloyd Edmonds', *Labour History*, No. 67, November 1994, pp. 4-5.
[9] *Tribune*, 8 October 1986, p. 14.
[10] Wheeler, *To Make the People Smile Again*, p. 38.

mule transporting him slipped and crushed him. He had no political affiliation on arriving in Spain, but to the officers of the International Brigades he seemed a "good soldier in the lines". He was judged to be a "consistent anti-fascist" who had demonstrated that he "had acquired some knowledge politically of the Spanish situation" and intended to join the CPA on his return to Australia.[11]

Rebbechi was too ill to join the rest of the British Battalion on the train back to London and was admitted to the same hospital as Edmonds. After his leg injury, he had, as McNeill said, "never got too strong". He was ill with fever and did not recover. He died of typhus on 1 January 1939 and was buried in the Vic municipal cemetery.[12] Of the members of the British Battalion to die in Spain, he is one of the few with a known grave.[13]

As a failed bank robber, New Zealand's **William Murn Macdonald** made for colourful company. In 1933 he armed himself with a revolver and walked into the Palmerston North branch of the Union Bank of Australia. He demanded £200 from the teller who produced his own revolver and started shooting at the fleeing would-be bandit. Captured soon after, the apprentice mechanic's lawyer told the court that the 19-year-old Macdonald had "always been highly strung, somewhat reckless in spirit and had an exaggerated idea of his capabilities".[14] The failed robber served two years and four months of a four-year sentence in a borstal and left New Zealand after his release. In 1936 he was working in the kitchen of London's Union Club. He arrived in Spain on 17 January 1937 and joined the Abraham Lincoln Battalion. He was injured in the Battle of Jarama with a gunshot wound to his shoulder.

While recovering, he wrote home to his family making it clear that he was not a communist, but an anti-fascist fighting for the government of Spain. He was impressed that New Zealand's reputation for progressive social programs was recognised in the International Brigades:

---

[11] Palmer and Fox, *Australians in Spain*, pp. 23-24; RGASPI 545/6/68/219-225.

[12] *Workers' Voice*, 4 February 1939, p. 2; Inglis, *Australians*, p. 176.

[13] *IBMT Newsletter*, No. 43/3 – 2016, p. 16.

[14] *Pahiatua Herald*, 16 September 1933, p.5; *Taranaki Daily News*, 16 September 1933, p. 7.

> *People who have never heard of Phar Lap, the Waitomo Caves, or the All Blacks can tell you the history of our old age pensions and free schooling.*[15]

After recovering, he became a driver in the transport section of the International Brigades. In a ludicrously comedic development, the former bank robber was entrusted with collecting the battalion's payroll. Perhaps predictably, he reported that the payroll had been stolen from his hotel room. He was arrested for negligence, not theft, and suffered a demotion, but recognised that he had been treated very leniently. In addition to his service at Jarama, he fought at Brunete, Caspe and the Ebro. In October 1937 he asked to be repatriated to England. Despite this request not being granted, he remained disciplined and loyal to the cause, and welcomed the increasingly professional organisation of the Republic's military forces. He had been at the front for a total of 17 months when the order to withdraw was received. On departing, his only criticism of the Republican government's program was that it was too liberal, especially regarding the foreign ownership of property.[16]

Macdonald was made a sergeant-major in an anti-tank unit of the New Zealand Expeditionary Force that was raised in Britain on the outbreak of the Second World War. He thought the British troops did not understand how well they were treated: "Their conditions are incomparably better than anything we had in Spain."[17] He used his Spanish Civil War experiences to lecture British troops on anti-tank tactics:

> *The sudden appearance of tanks can be terrifying, but determined infantry can halt them. Another efficacious method is to lie flat on the ground, under the tank's line of fire, and to throw grenades – under the tank, where there is usually a vulnerable spot.*[18]

---

[15] Mark Derby, (ed), *Kiwi Companeros: New Zealand and the Spanish Civil War*, Christchurch, 2009, p. 68.

[16] Derby, *Kiwi Companeros*, p. 66 – 70; RGASPI 545/6/68/161-170.

[17] *Daily Telegraph*, 22 December 1939, p. 3.

[18] *Daily Telegraph*, 14 December 1938, p. 3.

Macdonald served in Egypt and was transferred into the British Army in 1941. He became a commando with the Special Services and was remembered as "boldly courageous in action". As a proud New Zealander, he would react with disgust when called a "colonial".[19] He took part in the disastrous Operation Agreement raid on Tobruk in September 1942. Captured after the attack collapsed, he was held in various prisoner of war camps in Italy, Austria and Germany. After attempting to escape from the Modena camp, he was to be transferred to Germany, but succeeded in escaping by jumping from a train near Salzburg. He was recaptured after five days and remained a prisoner of war until April 1945. His service was recognised by being mentioned in despatches.[20]

After the war Macdonald accepted a Colonial Office posting in Libya, which the British were administering ahead of its independence. He had a French wife and was the District Commissioner for the district around Souk El Giuma, responsible for mediating local disputes, collecting taxes and managing the response to a locust plague. The Americans were constructing an airbase nearby and this led to Macdonald becoming the subject of a long profile in the *New Yorker*, which described him as a "slight, slim unpretentious man of thirty-eight, with a philosophical twist in his eyes" who enjoyed holidaying on the French Riviera with his wife.

He told the American magazine that he had gone to Spain to become a pilot. It was an ambition unfulfilled, although in some consolation he was, while soaking in a bath, served a drink by Hemingway. Of his time in Spain he said that he was so immature that he didn't know what the word immature meant. His political views were no longer militant and had taken on a jaundiced hue. He recalled:

> *The commissars were always talking of ideals when they addressed the troops, but then they would go back to Madrid, where they ran around with women and I don't imagine had much time to worry about*

---

[19] Gordon Landsborough, *Tobruk Commando*, London, 1956, p. 27.
[20] United Kingdom National Archives WO 373/102/825.

ideals.[21]

Described as a complex and troubled character, Macdonald suicided in Lisbon, Portugal, in 1968.[22]

Herbert "Bert" Bryan had also spent time in custody in New Zealand, but not for armed robbery. Like Dickinson, Bryan had been convicted and gaoled for publishing seditious literature.

Bryan was born in Timaru, New Zealand, on 18 October 1908 and received an elementary education. He went to sea as a teenager and in 1925 was working as a deck boy on trips between New Zealand and Australia. He worked as a labourer and seaman and joined the Communist Party of New Zealand in 1932 and became a member of the party's central committee and the editor of *The Red Worker*, the party's official paper.[23]

He and other members of the party spent six months in the Mount Crawford Prison after publishing a pamphlet, *Karl Marx and the Masses*, which was held to encourage lawlessness and violence. Bryan told the magistrate the booklet had been published in Britain and Australia and was not held to be seditious in those countries. He went on to state that he "did not expect to get justice in this court" and that the police had taken "Hitler-like action" against him.[24] He worked his way to Britain as a seaman and, through the offices of the Communist Party of Great Britain, arrived in Spain in March 1938. He said he had come to help defeat international fascism and was soon trying to do so on Hill 481.[25]

Asked by the International Brigades what lessons he would take home, he wrote:

---

[21] Joseph Wechsberg, 'Twilight in Souk El Giuma', *New Yorker*, 5 April 1952, pp. 109-123.

[22] Derby, *Kiwi Companeros*, p. 70.

[23] RGASPI 545/6/68/35-53,

[24] Derby, *Kiwi Companeros*, pp. 79-82; *New Zealand Herald*, 15 August 1933, p. 8; *New Zealand Herald*, 15 August 1933, p. 8.

[25] RGASPI 545/6/68/35-53.

> *I have learnt that it is vitally necessary to establish as speedily as possible a people's front of all democratic, progressive and peace-loving people against the fascist war mongers.*

He thought any delay would be fatal. He was assessed as being well-disciplined and a good soldier, although it was noted that he drank too much.[26]

Bryan was repatriated by the government of New Zealand and undertook a speaking tour organised by the New Zealand Spanish Medical Aid Campaign. In his address he said that 2700 volunteers from the British Empire had fought for the Republic.

> *I consider that these Britishers have at least done something to save humanity, and to save England from the shame which the Chamberlain government has brought upon the country.*[27]

He was proud of his Spanish service and in 1947 wrote to the *Evening Star* defending the Spanish Republic from an accusation that it had been anti-Catholic. He wrote how he had gone into action under Lewis Clive and listed other prominent supporters of the International Brigades, including Paul Robeson and Charlotte Haldane:

> *They were proud fighters against oppression, and it was my humble honour to have the privilege to march in such distinguished and gallant company.*[28]

Returning to civilian life was not easy for him. A friend believed he suffered from guilt about accidentally shooting a fellow soldier. He became an alcoholic and was remembered as being "a little pitiful". He died in Dunedin in 1961.[29]

---

[26] RGASPI 545/6/68/35-53.
[27] *King Country Chronicle*, 8 May 1939, p. 5.
[28] *Evening Star*, 16 June 1947, p. 9.
[29] Derby, *Kiwi Companeros*, p. 82.

Appendix 2

The *Maloja* photograph

The journey home on the *Maloja* was made by six International Brigaders: McNeill, Carter, Franklyn and three Charlies - Charlie McIlroy, Charlie Walters and Charlie Riley.

It is not certain who **Charles McIlroy** truly was. He told the International Brigades that he had been born in Derby, Western Australia, on 12 March 1913. The Western Australia register of births has no record of such a boy.[30] He stated that he had been educated at the decidedly non-proletarian Geelong Grammar, a private school in Victoria popular with wealthy Australian families. A review of the school's records and magazines found no evidence of his enrolment or attendance.[31] He claimed he joined the CPA in 1932 at Spring Hill, Brisbane, was involved in anti-eviction struggles, and spent June 1933 in Boggo Road gaol for having incited riotous behaviour. A review of prison's *Register of Male Prisoners Admitted* for May, June and July 1933 finds no entry for Charles McIlroy.[32]

---

[30] Searches of the index were made on 15 February 2024: https://www.wa.gov.au/organisation/department-of-justice/online-index-search-tool.

[31] Personal communication from Darren Watson, Archivist, Geelong Grammar, 12 February 2024.

[32] Queensland State Archives, Item ID ITM341019.

Photo 37: Charlie McIlroy, 1938.
(Australian National University Archives Centre)

On returning to Western Australia, he claimed he was a nurse at the St. John of God Hospital at Bunbury for four years, before deciding to travel to Spain to fight fascism. He claimed to have stowed away on a boat, leaving Australia on 6 September 1937. He climbed over the Pyrenees and arrived in Spain in March 1938. He endured the fighting on the Ebro and the retreats through the Pandols and Cavalls and was assessed as being a hard worker and reliable in battle, but with a tendency to be drunk and disorderly when away from the lines. A photograph in the archives of the International Brigades, taken while in Spain, shows a clean-shaven young man, looking boyishly handsome and happy.[33] McIlroy was remembered for his "gaiety and cheerfulness" but also for his "bravery in dragging in wounded men under fire".[34]

After completing a July 1939 speaking engagement for the Spanish Relief Committee in Perth, McIlroy seems to vanish from the historical record. McNeill believed that during the Second World War he served with the Australian military's medical services in New Guinea, but

---

[33] RGASPI 545/6/68/175-201.
[34] Inglis, *Australians*, p. 54.

there are no enlistment records to support this belief. Post-war, ASIO, which was assiduous in monitoring the activities of CPA members, did not maintain a file on Charles McIlroy.

Charles Walters was born in Lewes, Sussex, England on 5 October 1898. In 1921 he enlisted with the British Army's Royal West Kent Regiment. He was garrisoned in Ireland and would later say that this experience prompted a political awakening. He resolved to leave both Britain and its army as soon as he could.[35]

Photo 38: Charlie Walters,1938.
(Australian National University Archives Centre)

He arrived in Australia as Ernest Walters, a passenger on the *Bendigo* which landed in Adelaide on 2 April 1923. Working as a fur trapper across South Australia and Tasmania, he played football for a team in Blyth, South Australia. Described as a "slim, fair, good-looking young man", he joined the CPA in 1932 and was active in the Movement Against War and Fascism. During the Depression he became a leader

---
[35] Personal communication from Max Haldane Walters, 23 February 2024.

of anti-eviction protests and was charged after being involved in the "confiscation" of an empty house in Hobart. He read about the war in Spain, and felt that as "the only single man in the [Tasmanian] party it was my duty to come". He worked his way from Tasmania to Europe aboard the *Port Sydney*, a "hell ship" carrying 32,000 cases of apples and pears to Britain. His "greatest ambition" was to continue his political education in the Soviet Union.[36]

In a Paris café Walters was befriended by two Frenchmen. These new friends were actually fascists who were planning to lure him to a lonely spot and despatch him with a knife. Two Germans pulled him aside and warned him of the political leanings of his new friends. With the Germans, who were genuine anti-fascists, he made it to Spain, arriving in August 1937.[37] He trained at Albacete and in December was at the plaza in Mondejar when Attlee inspected the British Battalion. The visit from the future Labour Prime Minister was a great success. Attlee delivered an inspirational speech and the men responded by staging a dramatic torchlight procession.[38] The day after the visit, Walters wrote home:

> *A man thinks a lot out here. I think I wouldn't mind dying for democracy.*
>
> *Please send us food and clothes. It is so cold.*[39]

Walters didn't die, but was seriously concussed at Teruel and appears to have had a psychological breakdown. He spent months in hospital with "neurasthenia, gastritis and general debility". In February 1938 he was in hospital at Benicasim and sent pitiful letters to his superiors pleading to be repatriated as he had a mouthful of bad teeth and was in a "very poor condition physically and also in regard to nerves". Walters said that the Communist Party had told him that he could leave Spain after

---

[36] NAA: A2910, 433/1/85 PART 1; Playford, 'History', p. 144; *The Mercury*, 26 June 1934, p. 11; *Workers' Weekly*, 22 February 1939, p. 2; Website - Sussex International Brigaders Remembered accessed 20 February 2024 https://blogs.brighton.ac.uk/sussexbrigaders/2021/03/06/charles-edward-walters/.

[37] *Workers' Weekly*, 24 February 1939, p. 2.

[38] Brome, *International Brigades*, p. 234.

[39] *Workers' Weekly*, 8 February 1938, p. 1.

serving for six months.

While in hospital he met Egon Kisch, the multi-lingual Czechoslovakian journalist that the Australian government was so determined to block from entering Australia that the literacy test all immigrants faced was given in the obscure language of Scottish Gaelic. Kisch attempted to thwart the bureaucratic obstruction by literally jumping ship, breaking a leg in doing so. His case went to the High Court which ruled that Scottish Gaelic was not a living language and not a fair test of literacy.

It was an early and humiliating defeat for Attorney-General Menzies, who said that the case was about "the right of every civilized country to control the terms upon which foreigners shall enter it".[40] Having won his case, the gregarious Kisch, who revelled in the limelight, undertook a high-profile speaking tour to warn Australians of the dangers of fascism. To mock the government's ham-fisted efforts, Kisch was serenaded by Gaelic pipe bands when he toured the NSW coalfields.

A recuperating Walters enjoyed the company of Kisch who possessed an "amazing knowledge of Australia" and proved to be "one of the boys". Walters' requests for repatriation were eventually successful and he arrived in England on 18 October 1938.[41]

Walters returned to South Australia with the intention of working as a rabbit-trapper at Myponga. He maintained a correspondence with the Haldanes as he worked in Adelaide with the Spanish Relief Committee to raise funds for Republican refugees. By 1941 he was in Melbourne, where he married Charlotte Evelyn Shaw, an artist and the secretary of the Collingwood Branch of the CPA. In 1942, the couple was living in Sydney, with Walters working in the by-products section of the Homebush abattoir while also picking up some work on the waterfront. The couple had a son, Maxwell Haldane Walters.

The proud father wrote to Professor Haldane informing him of the naming honour that had been bestowed on him. The Professor, by then enjoying a world reputation for his scholarship, was working

---

[40] *Hansard*, House of Representatives, 11 November 1934.
[41] RGASPI 545/6/68/242-216; Palmer and Fox, *Australians in Spain*, p. 49.

with the Royal Navy and undertaking physiological studies on former International Brigaders to research how submariners could escape from their vessels in an emergency. Haldane replied:

> *Many thanks for your letter of May 20, and for the honor done me in calling your son after me.*
>
> *I hope he will continue to be as sturdy as he looks from the photograph, and that by the time he grows up it won't be necessary for him to do the sort of thing you did.*
>
> *However, if it is necessary, he looks as if he might be prepared to do a job, like his father, for freedom.*[42]

The marriage to Evelyn failed and the couple separated in 1945. Evelyn would later say that she had "escaped".[43]

Throughout his life Walters remained proud of his service in the Spanish Civil War. He had his International Brigader lapel badge gold-plated, presumably as an expression of its value to him. He retired to Dora Creek, NSW, and died there in 1979. An obituary in *Tribune* stated that he had retained his socialist beliefs.[44]

Charles Riley, born in 1894, was originally a Londoner and at 15 had joined the Royal Field Artillery and later went to sea. On one voyage across the Atlantic, his ship steamed through the floating debris left by the *Titanic*. During the Great War he re-joined the British Army, and served in the 3rd (Prince of Wales's) Dragoon Guards. He fought for two years on the Ypres sector of the Western Front and was injured while bayoneting a German soldier. After the war he moved to New Zealand, where he studied engineering at the University of Canterbury. Suffering a breakdown, he abandoned his studies and worked as a goldminer.[45]

---

[42] *Tribune*, 25 November 1943, p. 3.
[43] Evelyn Healy - Shirley Kingsford McLeod, Fairfield City Library.
[44] https://www.infinite-women.com/women/evelyn-healy/ and *Tribune*, 7 November 1979, p. 14.
[45] Derby, *Kiwi Companeros*, pp. 53-59.

Photo 39: Charlie Riley, 1938.
(Australian National University Archives Centre)

During the Depression he moved his political allegiance from the Labour Party to the Communist Party and began organising among the unemployed in Christchurch. His political activities led to a succession of charges and the police secured his conviction for being an "idle and disorderly person". The police told the court his pockets were crammed with communist pamphlets. On entering the witness box, he was defiant and said he would "take a communist oath".[46] In 1934, he faced charges of dealing fraudulently with the sale proceeds of leather bags that he had taken on commission. He pleaded guilty and was sentenced to six months hard labour.[47]

On release, he left New Zealand and went to Australia where he worked with explosives as a shotfirer in the Rising Sun gold mine at Tennant Creek in the Northern Territory. The progress of Hitler's Nazis alarmed him sufficiently that in December 1937 he decided to go to Spain:

---

[46] *Press*, 4 December 1931, p. 9.
[47] *Evening Star*, 23 January 1934, p. 5.

"Adolph the Butcher had got right under our skins." He walked and hitched his way to Darwin, where he met a group of Chinese workers who, on hearing about his mission, pitched in for his fare aboard the *Merkur* to Sydney. From there he made his way to Port Kembla and joined the *Anglo-Australian*, a decrepit freighter, and worked his passage to Britain.[48]

He arrived in Spain on 18 March 1938 and, with his experience in the British Army and of handling explosives in the mines, was assigned to train other soldiers. In circumstances that remain uncertain he was seriously wounded. Records of the International Brigades state that he was wounded in an incident at the rifle range, while Riley described how he was hit by bullets and shrapnel during the Battle of the Ebro:

> *After being wounded in the head, face and left jugular artery, both shoulders and arms, I must have presented a pretty sight. One side of my face was a mass of congealed blood, the khaki beret which I held to neck being saturated with the thick bloody mass....*[49]

The Spanish Civil War saw several innovations in the medical science of blood transfusions. A nurse donated her blood at the Valls Hospital and his right arm was saved from amputation. Injured and underweight, he left Spain in late October 1938 aboard a Red Cross train to Paris. His superiors in the International Brigades appraised him as being "disciplined and steady".[50]

After arriving back in Australia, a medical report established that Riley was suffering from what was described as "mental strain" and "nervous tension". The Spanish Relief Committee paid for Riley's first-class fare to New Zealand.[51] Like McNeill, he ignored the Comintern's position that the Second World War was an imperialist one and should be opposed. He was keen to again fight fascism and was quick to enlist. He took seven years off his age and somehow, given the seriousness of

---

[48] Inglis, *Australians*, p. 117; *Workers' Weekly*, 21 February 1939, p. 2.
[49] RGASPI 545/6/68/226-231; Derby, *Kiwi Companeros*, p. 57.
[50] Derby, *Kiwi Companeros*, p. 58; RGASPI 545/6/68/226-231.
[51] Minutes of the Spanish Relief Committee, 8 March 1939 and 16 March 1939, Phil Thorne Collection, Noel Butlin Archives, Australian National University.

his Spanish injuries, passed a medical examination and joined the New Zealand Expeditionary Force to participate in his third war. He fought in North Africa and Greece, and in 1942 was wounded in the foot, an injury that finally brought his fighting days to an end.[52]

Returning to New Zealand, Riley married again, (his first marriage had failed during the Depression years) and lived quietly in Naenae, Lower Hutt. His socialist principles were intact and he kept in touch with the International Brigade Association in Britain, reflecting in one letter to its secretary Nan Green:

> *The real heroes and honourable men and women – the salt of the earth – are those noble folk like yourself that carry on amidst disappointment, monotony and with very little material rewards – to do good and endeavour to organise people and try and raise the level of culture, living conditions, and bring cheer and hope to their neighbours.*[53]

Riley worked on his autobiography and lodged the manuscript in the Alexander Turnbull Library, now part of the National Library of New Zealand. An oral history interview followed, at the conclusion of which he said:

> *Yes, I've been a bit unlucky. And lucky. Could have been worse.*[54]

He died in 1982.

---

[52] Derby, *Kiwi Companeros*, p. 59.
[53] Inglis, *Australians*, p. 207.
[54] Derby, *Kiwi Companeros*, p. 59.

Appendix 3

Another one

Jim McNeill was one of the very few Australians who fought fascism on three separate occasions. Another was Jack Alexander.[55]

Alexander was born in Alice Street, Rosalie, in Brisbane on 26 January 1918 to Maurice Sydney Alexander and Caroline Ethel Mary Alexander (née Belcher). He had two older siblings, Dorothy and Cyril.[56] Both his parents were English immigrants and his father, who worked on the railways, had recently joined the Australian Imperial Force.

Alexander's childhood was tragic. His father deserted the family and his mother returned to England in September 1923 with her three young children. She left the children there and became a ship steward, working on the *Borda* during its voyages between England and Australia. She became involved with the ship's assistant butcher, 19-year-old Leonard Edwin Smith. She died after an illegal abortion was performed on her in a Darlinghurst flat by two ship's doctors. The case was sensationally covered in the Sydney newspapers with Smith and the doctors charged with having feloniously slain her. The accused were tried and acquitted.[57]

It is not known who Alexander's guardian was, but they appear to have been living in Grays, a town in Essex, England, and presumably were relatives or friends of his mother. He attended Grays School for his primary education and then went to Palmer's College for his high schooling. Established in 1706, Palmer's College was a grammar

---

[55] Except as noted, this biography of Alexander is drawn from his records held in the Australian War Memorial (AWM65 33 Alexander Jack 4233932), the National Archives of Australia (NAA: A9301, 423393) and RGASPI 545/6/90/1, 545/6/91/146 and 545/6/856/17-18.

[56] Queensland Registry of Births, Deaths and Marriages.

[57] *Truth* 28 February 1926, p. 11; *Daily Telegraph*, 9 February 1926, p. 1.

school described by Lord Strang, a diplomat and prominent former student, as "one of the leading grammar schools in the county".[58]

At fifteen and with his schooling complete, Alexander went to sea and spent several years seeing the world. He worked the coasts of South America and spent six months as a cow-puncher in Argentina. It was here that he met some Spaniards, an association that created an affinity that would help him decide to go to Spain. Returning to England he was living in Bethnal Green in London's East End and in 1936 joined the Young Communist League at nearby Limehouse. His first anti-fascist activity came through the League's confrontations with Mosley's Blackshirts.

He left for Spain in August 1937, trained at Taragona and Albacete, and then served with the Thalmann Battalion of the XIth International Brigade on the Jarama Front. Named after Ernst Thalmann, the leader of the German Communist Party imprisoned by Hitler, this unit was centred around staunch anti-Nazis who had fled their homeland. Hardened by their experiences in Germany, these were tough, disciplined and brave men who could provide inspiration and leadership.[59]

In January 1938 he transferred into the British Battalion, giving his occupation as a motorcycle tester. Alexander fought in the Battle of Teruel and was promoted to lieutenant having given outstanding service in the battle and the subsequent disastrous Aragon retreat. He was captured after being caught in an explosion that left him with shrapnel wounds to his head and legs. Knocked senseless and almost buried alive, he was revived by Italian rifle butts and led to a nearby wall to be executed with five others. A staff officer intervened and ordered the group be spared so they could be used in a prisoner exchange. Alexander, described as a Londoner, was one of 200 men taken prisoner east of Alcaniz. An announcement from Franco's official chronicler described the men as "Almost exclusively manual

---

[58] Lord Strang, *Home and Abroad*, London, 1956, p. 26.
[59] Tremlett, *International Brigades*, p. 188.

labourers and of Jewish extraction."[60]

Alexander then became an inmate in the notorious San Pedro de Cardena concentration camp. Located in an old monastery near the town of Burgos, conditions were horrific. Mistreatment and torture were routine. Alexander was beaten with sticks, fists and leather thongs, and saw how the Gestapo and its Italian counterpart, the *Opera Vigilanza Repressione Antifascismo* (Organization for Vigilance and Repression of Anti-Fascism), set about their work. He was court martialled and sentenced to death, being psychologically scarred by being taken to his place of execution, then returned to barracks. The 600 prisoners were denied medical attention, given no washing facilities and issued with only meagre rations. Alexander would later say the conditions were "indescribable" with all the men suffering from dysentery.

The prisoners maintained their morale by establishing what they called the "San Pedro Institute of Higher Learning". Experts among the men gave classes and Alexander improved his fluency in German and Italian. A camp magazine, the *Jaily News*, was produced with the text written on cement bags. Songs were written and sung, and an Indian volunteer told fortunes by reading palms.[61]

Bizarrely, the prisoners were subjected to a pseudo-scientific study that measured their skulls and limbs. They were photographed and records of their physical attributes were supplemented with a detailed questionnaire about their sexual histories. The study concluded that a third of the English prisoners were "mental retards", another third were "schizoids, paranoids or psychopaths", while the remaining 29 per cent had become Marxists because they were "social imbeciles".[62]

Alexander was transferred to the Vinalta Concentration Camp near Palencia. This was a camp administered by the Italian military and while conditions were still harsh, there was less ill-treatment than at

---

[60] *Halifax Evening News*, 2 April 1938, p. 6; *Portsmouth Evening News*, 2 April 1938, p. 8.
[61] Tremlett, *International Brigades*, p. 466.
[62] Ibid., p. 468.

the San Pedro de Cardena camp. His wounds began to heal, although he was still suffering from nightmares and fevers. In October 1938 he was taken to Irun and marched over the bridge and released into France as part of a prisoner exchange.[63] He returned to England and stayed there until December 1939, returning to Australia by working his way home aboard a Shaw, Savill and Albion liner.

He took a job at the Garden Island dockyard and, as the president of the Mortlake Branch of the Labor Party, spent much of 1940 campaigning for the election of Curtin as Prime Minister. He also enrolled at the University of Sydney, where he spent two years studying economics and political science. He joined the Sydney Journalists' Club and the Yugoslav Club. He enjoyed football and cycling.

In November 1941, while working as an Assistant Superintendent in the stores department of the Cunard-White Star Line shipping company, he applied to join the RAAF. In his application, he did not disclose that he had fought in Spain. On one form he left the section that asked about previous service blank; on another he stated that his previous military service was nil. After being accepted and trained, his service with the International Brigades was no longer kept secret and Alexander wrote to his headquarters:

> *I had hoped that as an air gunner I could continue the fight against Fascism that I had begun in Spain.*

He trained at Bradfield Park, Parkes and Evans Head, and received his air gunner's badge in December 1942. He left Australia in January 1943 aboard the troop ship *West Point* bound for San Francisco. He crossed America by train and sailed for England, arriving on 17 March 1943. In Britain he underwent aircrew commando training and was promoted to Flight Sergeant.

During the first week of April he took private leave and attended a conference convened by the International Brigade Association to call for the speedy release of all International Brigaders who were still being held in camps, prisons and labour battalions across North Africa.

---

[63] *Daily News*, 25 October 1938, p. 15.

Alexander addressed the Conference and compared the situation to his own imprisonment:

> *Even there we were not as badly off as many of our comrades still interned. At least we were recognised as prisoners of war and eventually exchanged for a batch of Italians the Republicans had captured.*[64]

His service was promoted by both the RAAF and the CPA. In October 1943 the RAAF issued a publicity bulletin titled "Australian Airman Wears Medal of International Brigade: Man Who Faced Firing Squad" which gave a detailed account of Alexander's experiences in Spain. The bulletin said that he had enlisted to take "up the fight against fascism again". It also noted that he was the only member of the RAAF entitled to wear the military medal of the International Brigades, a reference to the lapel button he had acquired. Photographs were issued of Alexander proudly wearing his International Brigades button on his RAAF uniform and the story was published in numerous Australian newspapers.[65]

Photo 40: - Jack Alexander in his RAAF uniform wearing his International Brigader lapel badge, 1943. (Australian National University Archives Centre)

---

[64] *The Volunteer for Liberty*, Vol. 4, No. 3, 1943, p. 4.
[65] *Daily Mirror*, 16 October 1943, p. 8; *Courier Mail*, 18 October 1943, p. 3.

The CPA, in its phase of providing full-throated support for the war, claimed Alexander as one of its own in articles saturated with enthusiasm for his bombing escapades. One article was based on a letter that Alexander had sent to Stan Moran, a former housemate:

> *We are dropping bombs on Germany and when I go over I think: 'Here's one for Spain; and one for you, Stan; and one each for Comrades Miles and Sharkey.'*[66]

Another article reported he had taken part in "mass raids on the Ruhr and Rhineland" and seen planes hit, burst into flames and spin to the ground.

> *Fascists who twice sentenced Australian International Brigader Jack Alexander to death amid the ruins of Spain are sorry they didn't carry out the sentence.*
>
> *In a Lancaster bomber, Flight-Sergeant Jack Alexander, with the clenched-fist medal of the International Brigade on his chest, contributed his avenging bombs to the Nazi factories which supplied the weapons for Spanish democracy's assassination.*
>
> *As Essen, Ludwigshafen, Mannheim, Munich flamed up beneath his Lancaster, Jack Alexander could remember those better Germans who lay beneath Spanish soil.*[67]

None of this was true. He had not flown any bombing sorties over Germany, and had only completed one nickel run to drop copies of *Le courrier de l'air*, a French-language propaganda leaflet, over occupied France. The reality was that Alexander's ordeal in Spain had left him so damaged, both physically and psychologically, that his flying career was terminated before it had properly begun.

Alexander was suffering from headaches, dizzy spells, nightmares and airsickness. He had also developed a fear of enclosed spaces and darkness. The Senior Medical Officer at RAF Base Winthorpe recommended that Alexander be removed from all air crew duties:

---

[66] *Tribune*, 11 November 1943, p. 4.
[67] *Tribune*, 16 March 1944, p. 3.

> *He is heavily disposed to nervous breakdown and has not fully recovered from his experiences in Spain where he was blown up, held in a concentration camp for 7 months and subject to brutal treatment during a period of under nourishment and intercurrent infection. It is probable that he suffered a basal skull fracture.*
>
> *He is over-conscientious and, in my opinion, has made every effort to overcome his fear of flying.*

The case was submitted to the Air Ministry with the request that it be given sympathetic consideration. Before he departed Britain, Alexander wrote to RAAF Headquarters asking to be considered for other duties so that he could, in another capacity, "still render service in this war against Hitlerism". He suggested that with his language skills and university studies he could be engaged in intelligence work, but this entreaty was not taken up by the authorities.

He returned to Australia and was discharged from the RAAF on 25 May 1944, receiving the war pension at a 20 per cent rate.

In 1948, *Australians in Spain: Our Pioneers Against Fascism* reported that Alexander had settled at Bronte, a beachside suburb in Sydney.[68] Details of his life beyond this date are not known and during the years of the Cold War he did not come to the attention of the ASIO.

---

[68] Palmer and Fox, *Australians in Spain*, p. 52.

Acknowledgements

I would like to thank the following people for their essential contributions:

- Vanessa McNeill: who shared with me her father's Spanish Civil War artefacts and story, including his enduring admiration for Dickinson.
- Martie Lowenstein: who retrieved, digitised and shared the oral history interview her mother conducted with McNeill in 1974.
- Judith Keene: who first suggested that the stories of McNeill and Dickinson be told together.

I would also like to thank Seve Montero and Dr Almudena Cross (acrossmadrid.com) for guiding me across the Jarama battlefield. Thanks also to Alan Warren (pdlhistoria.wordpress.com) for escorting me around the sprawling Ebro battlefield and for reviewing several chapters of this text.

Rodney Cavalier provided detailed comments on an earlier draft. Milton Cockburn kindly volunteered to review the final draft and made some valuable suggestions.

A Labour councillor and antiquarian book dealer in Manchester, Richard Gold, generously provided me with a copy of Dickinson's *The Black Plague*. This was very much appreciated as I could not locate it in an Australian library.

I relied on Mark Derby's *Kiwi Companeros: New Zealand and the Spanish Civil War* for the biographies of the volunteers from New Zealand and I thank him for his assistance.

The SEARCH Foundation provided access to the records of the CPA held in the Mitchell Library, State Library of New South Wales.

Jane Ferguson listened to countless monologues on McNeill and Dickinson and I thank her for her endurance.

Many other people provided valuable advice and responded to queries. These included Brian Aarons, David Allen, David Young, Max Haldane Walters, Rafe Dickinson, Pauline Dickinson, Chris Sumner, Luke Whitington, Paul Daley, John Hughes, Katrina Samaras, Simon Drake, Tony Fox, Darren Watson, Hugh Robertson, Paul Willoughby, Brent Gowland, Helen Sims, Susan James and Sue Tracey.

Len Fox's poem, *Return of the International Brigades*, appears with the kind permission of the Trustees, Castlemaine Art Gallery & Historical Museum.

I made use of the resources of the following libraries and archives and thank the staff of these institutions for their professional assistance: State Library of New South Wales, University of Wollongong Archives, Butlin Archives at the Australian National University, NSW State Archives Collection, Australian War Memorial, National Library of Australia, National Archives of Australia, National Film and Sound Archive of Australia, State Library Victoria, State Library of South Australia, University of Massachusetts Amherst Libraries, National Archives (United Kingdom), National Library of Scotland, New York University Tamiment Library and Wagner Labor Archives, Marx Memorial Library and Workers School, New York Public Libraries, Russian State Archive for Social-Political History (RGASPI), State Library of Pennsylvania, Mitchell Library (Glasgow), Wollongong City Libraries, Working Class Movement Library, Inner West Council Library, Fryer Library - University of Queensland, University of New England Archives and Heritage Centre, Fisher Library – University of Sydney, City of Newcastle Library, National Library of New Zealand, Modern Records Centre at the University of Warwick, and the Imperial War Museum.

None of these individuals or institutions are responsible for this text and any errors are entirely my own.

List of illustrations

1 — Jim McNeill (L) and Ted Dickinson (R) in Adelaide, 1927. (Illawarra Museum)

2 — The front page of *Direct Action* that resulted in Dickinson being gaoled for sedition. (State Library of NSW)

3 — The unemployed march for beef, King William Street, Adelaide, 1931. The march turned into a riot. (State Library of South Australia, B 60882)

4 — Hitler and Franco inspect a guard of honour at the Irun railway station, Spain, October 1940. (National Digital Archive, Poland)

5 — Eric Campbell, Leader of the New Guard, Sydney, 1931. (Fairfax Photographic Archive)

6 — Wollongong's 1938 May Day march with a banner of La Pasionaria. (University of Wollongong Archives, collection D22/12/04/01)

7 — Wollongong's 1938 May Day march. Placards read: "Barry and Dickinson – Two Australians Sons —Died in Spain for Freedom". (University of Wollongong Archives, collection D22/12/04/06)

8 – Joe Carter, 1938. (Australian National University Archives Centre)

9 — "Farewell, Comrade!" The *Workers' Weekly* illustrates the news of Dickinson's execution. (SEARCH Foundation/State Library of NSW)

10 - To get to Spain, McNeill stowed away on the *Melbourne Star*. (Harry Issell, State Library of Victoria)

11— Jim McNeill in Spain, 1938. (Illawarra Museum)

12 – Jim McNeill in Spain, 1938. (Illawarra Museum)

13 – Bill Young's prison record. (Museums of History New South Wales - State Archives Collection)

14 – Jack Franklyn, 1938. (Australian National University Archives Centre)

15 — McNeill (centre, no cap) at the Montblanc training base, 1938. (Tamiment Library and Robert F. Wagner Labor Archives, New York University)

16 — Bert Bryan and Jack Franklyn (obscured) fighting on Hill 481. (Australian War Memorial, AWM2023.312.1)

17 - International Brigaders from Australia and New Zealand at Ripoll, awaiting repatriation from Spain, 1938. Top L-R: Kevin Rebbechi, Lloyd Edmonds, William Murn Macdonald, Joe Carter; Bottom L-R: Jack Franklyn, Bert Bryan, Jim McNeill. See Appendix 1. (Alexander Turnbull Library, Wellington, New Zealand)

18 - Jack Franklyn, Jim McNeill and Tommy Bloomfield (L-R) in London, c1938. (Illawarra Museum)

19 - Attorney General Menzies (aka Pig-iron Bob) in Wollongong, January 1939. (Fairfax Photographic Archive)

20 - Returning home on the *Maloja* are (L-R) Jim McNeill, Charlie McIlroy, Charlie Riley, Charlie Walters, Jack Franklyn and Joe Carter. See Appendix 2. (State Library of Western Australia b2377462_1)

21 - Informal group shot on the *Maloja*. Standing (L-R) are Joe Carter, Charlie Walters and Jim McNeill. Sitting (L-R) are Jack Franklyn, Charlie McIlroy and Charlie Riley. (Illawarra Museum)

22 - The returning International Brigaders are welcomed at Perth's railway station. (State Library of Western Australia b2377462_6)

23 - 1st Forestry Company, Royal Australian Engineers. (Illawarra Museum)

24 - Mr and Mrs McNeill. (Illawarra Museum)

25 - Jim and Mabel McNeill with daughter Vanessa. (Illawarra Museum)

26 - McNeill leads the International Brigades veterans in Sydney's 1944 May Day march. (Illawarra Museum)

27 - Reunited – McNeill with daughter Vanessa, wife Mabel, and mother Mary. (SEARCH Foundation/Illawarra Museum)

28 - Mabel McNeill (front right) marching with the Union of Australian Women. (Illawarra Museum)

29 - The McNeills' home in O'Connor Street, Guildford. (Illawarra Museum)

30 - McNeill selling *Tribune* at Guildford, c1960. (SEARCH Foundation/Illawarra Museum)

31 - A scene from *Words for Freedom* – McNeill and Vanessa at the 1954 *Tribune* picnic. (Estate of the late Robert Gowland)

32 - A scene from *Words for Freedom* – McNeill walks the streets of Sydney's

west. (Estate of the late Robert Gowland)

33 - *Dickinson* by Herbert McClintock. Originally published in the *Australian Left Review* in 1966. (SEARCH Foundation and the Herbert McClintock Estate)

34 - Joe Carter (L) campaigning for an increase to the aged pension with Bill McDougall, 1975. (From the collections of the Wollongong City Libraries and the Illawarra Historical Society – P09094)

35 - Anthony Phelan in *Dickinson* by David Allen, directed by Malcolm Blaylock, at the La Boite Theatre, Brisbane, 1980. (Image provided courtesy of QPAC Collections)

36 – Lloyd Edmonds, 1939. (Australian National University Archives Centre)

37 – Charlie McIlroy, 1938. (Australian National University Archives Centre)

38 – Charlie Walters, 1938. (Australian National University Archives Centre)

39 – Charlie Riley, 1938. (Australian National University Archives Centre)

40 - Jack Alexander in his RAAF uniform wearing his International Brigader lapel badge, 1943. (Australian National University Archives Centre)

Bibliography

Archives

Laurie Aarons archive, Mitchell Library, State Library of New South Wales, MLMSS 7924 Box 5

Guy Aldred Collection, Mitchell Library, Glasgow

Communist Party of Australia Records, Mitchell Library, State Library of New South Wales, MS 5021 Box 5. Accessed with kind permission from the Search Foundation.

Courts SA, Transcripts

David Crook's diary, Marx Memorial Library, SC/VOL/DCR/1

Len Fox Papers, 1852-2001, Mitchell Library, State Library of New South Wales, MLMSS 8085

Amirah Inglis Collection, Noel Butlin Archives, Australian National University

International Brigade Collection, Russian State Archive for Social-Political History, Moscow (RGASPI)

McNeill Collection, Illawarra Museum

National Archives of Australia (NAA)

Aileen Palmer collection, 6759, National Library of Australia

Saffin Collection, State Library of Victoria

Oral History Interviews

George Aitken – Judith Cook, Imperial War Museum, IWM 10357

Joe Carter – Amirah Inglis, Amirah Inglis Collection, Noel Butlin Archives, Australian National University

Joe Carter – Glen Mitchell, Illawarra Stories, Wollongong City Libraries

Joe Carter – John Clements, Imperial War Museum, IWM 3812

Joe Carter – John Shipp, Wollongong University Archives, B16

Joe Carter – Laurie Aarons, Mitchell Library, State Library of New South Wales, MLOH 628/5

Frederick Bayes Copeman – Margaret A. Brooks, Imperial War Museum, IWM 794

John Peter Cowan Dunlop - Conrad Wood, Imperial War Museum, IWM 11,355

John Peter Cowan Dunlop – B.G.Kiernan, Imperial War Museum, IWM 823

Lloyd Edmonds – Wendy Lowenstein, Wendy Lowenstein Collection, access courtesy of Martie Lowenstein

Lloyd Edmonds – Address - Laurie Aarons interviews with and addresses by members of the Communist Party of Australia, MLOH 80 – Item 67, Mitchell Library, State Library of New South Wales

Evelyn Healy – Shirley Kingsford McLeod, Fairfield City Library

John Longstaff – Conrad Wood, Imperial War Museum, IWM 9299

George Leeson – Bill Williams, Imperial War Museum, IWM 803

Bill McDougall - Unknown, Wollongong University Archives, B80

Jim McNeill – Wendy Lowenstein, Wendy Lowenstein Collection, access courtesy of Martie Lowenstein (WL interview)

James Maley – Conrad Wood, Imperial War Museum, IWM 11947

Charles Francis Riley – Raymond Frank Grover, National Library of New Zealand, OHColl-0021/1

Phil Thorne – Baiba Irving, Wollongong University Archives, B2

Newspapers and Journals

The main Australian newspapers used were the *Illawarra Mercury, South Coast Times, Workers' Weekly,* and *Tribune*. These and other titles as noted in the footnotes were accessed through Trove (trove.com.au) except *Workers' Weekly Herald* and the *Workers' Voice* which were accessed from the newspaper collection of the National Library of Australia.

New Zealand newspapers as noted in the footnotes were accessed through Papers Past (paperspast.natlib.govt.nz).

The main British newspaper used was the *Daily Worker*. Other British titles as noted in the footnotes were accessed through:

- British Newspaper Archive
- UK Press Online
- British Library Newspapers Parts IV, V and VI (Gale)
- *Times* Digital Archive 1785-2019 (Gale)

Novels, Plays and Literature

Allen, David, *Dickinson*, Typescript, 1978, Fryer Library, University of Queensland

Fox, Len, *Gumleaves and Memories*, Self-published, Potts Point, 1990

Hardy, Frank, *Tommy Macnamara's Tribune Run*, Typescript, c1955, National Library of Australia, Frank Hardy Papers, Box 111

Hardy, Frank, *But the Dead are Many: A Novel in Fugue Form*, Bodley Head, Sydney, 1975

Hemingway, Ernest, 'On the American Dead in Spain', *New Masses*, Vol. XXX, No. 8, 14 February 1939, p. 1

Holmes, Cecil, *Words for Freedom*, film, 1955

Lermontov, Mikhail, *A Hero of Our Time*, Foreign Languages Publishing House, Moscow, 1947

Loftus, John, *Remember Pedrocito*, typescript, c1938, New Theatre Collection, State Library of New South Wales, MLMSS 6244, Series 4, Boxes 107, 139, 147X

Maley, Willy and John, *From the Calton to Catalonia*, Calton Books, Glasgow, 2014

Roland, Betty, 'War on the Waterfront', *Communist Review*, February 1939, pp. 110-114

Books, Articles and Theses

Aarons, Mark, *The Family File*, Black Inc., Melbourne, 2010

Amos, Keith, *The New Guard Movement 1931-35*, Melbourne University Press, Melbourne, 1976

Baxell, Richard, 'The British Battalion of the International Brigades in the Spanish Civil War 1936-39', PhD thesis, London School of Economics and Political Science, 2001

Baxell, Richard, *Forged in Spain*, The Clapton Press, London, 2023

Beevor, Antony, *The Spanish Civil War*, Cassell, London, 1999

Bowers, Claude G., *My Mission to Spain: Watching the Rehearsal for World War II*, Victor Gollancz, London, 1954

Brome, Vincent, *The International Brigades: Spain 1936-1939*, Heinemann, Great Britain, 1965

Broomhill, Ray, *Unemployed Workers: A Social History of the Great Depression in Adelaide*, University of Queensland Press, St Lucia, 1978

Burchill, Elizabeth, *The Paths I've Trod: Autobiography of an Australian Nurse*, Spectrum Publications, 1981

Burgmann, Verity, *Revolutionary Industrial Unionism: The Industrial Workers of the World in Australia*, Cambridge University Press, Cambridge, 1995

Cain, Frank, 'Biography and Ideology in the Industrial Workers of the World in Australia 1911-1922', Paper to the 2011 Australian Society for the Study of Labour History Conference

Calvo, Javier M. and Montero, Severiano, *International Brigade Sites in Madrid: Battles of Jarama and La Coruna Road*, Asociacion de Amigos de las Brigadas Internacionales, 2015

Campbell, Eric, *The New Road*, Briton Publications, Sydney, 1934

Campbell, Eric, *The Rallying Point: My Story of the New Guard*, Melbourne University Press, Carlton, 1965

Campbell, Jean, *James Cant and Dora Chapman*, The Beagle Press, Sydney, 1995

Cervello, Josep Sanchez, and Micola, Pere Clua, *The Battle of the Ebro: A River of Blood*, Consorci Memorial dels Espais de la Batalla de l'Ebre, 2018

Chadwick, Justin, 'The 'men behave well and are a credit to Australia': Australian Forestry Companies in the UK during WW2', *Sabretach*, Vol. LIX, No. 2, June 2018, pp. 32-37

Charlton, Peter, *The Thirty-Niners*, Macmillan, South Melbourne, 1981

Childe, V. G., *How Labour Governs: A Study of Workers' Representation in Australia*, Labour Publishing, London, 1923

Clarke, Michael, *My War 1939-1945*, Michael Clarke Publishing, Toorak, 1990

Comans, Christine Anne Wilmington, 'La Boite Theatre 1925 to 2003', Queensland University of Technology, PhD thesis, 2006

Cook, Judith, (ed), *Apprentices of Freedom*, Quartet Books, London, 1979

Copsey, Nigel, *Anti-Fascism in Britain*, Palgrave, New York, 2000

Corcoran, John, 'Fighting the Good Fight: The Rev Robert Martin Hilliard', *Saothar*, Vol. 3 (2006), pp. 55-62

Crook, David, *Hampstead Heath to Tian An Men — The Autobiography of David Crook*, 1990: davidcrook.net

Dickey, Brian, *Holy Trinity Adelaide 1836-2012: The History of a City Church*,

Trinity Church Trust, Adelaide, 2013

Edmonds, Lloyd, (edited by Amirah Inglis), *Letters from Spain*, George Allen & Unwin, North Sydney, 1985

Edwards, John, *John Curtin's War: The Coming of War in the Pacific and Reinventing Australia*, Penguin Random House, Melbourne, 2017

Evans, Richard J., *The Third Reich in Power*, Allen Lane, London, 2005

Evans, Richard J., *The Third Reich at War*, Allen Lane, London, 2008

Fox, Len, (ed), *Depression Down Under*, Self-published, Potts Point, 1977

Fox, Len, *Broad Left, Narrow Left*, Self-published, Chippendale, 1982

Fox, Len, *Australians on the Left*, Self-published, Potts Point, 1996

Friedlander, Saul, *Nazi Germany and the Jews: The Years of Persecution 1933-1939*, Harper Collins, New York, 1997

Graham, Helen, *The Spanish Republic at War 1936-1939*, Cambridge University Press, Cambridge, 2002

Gray, Daniel, *Homage to Caledonia: Scotland and the Spanish Civil War*, Luath Press, Edinburgh, 2008

Gurney, Jason, *Crusade in Spain*, Faber and Faber, Great Britain, 1974

Healy, Evelyn, *Artist of the Left: A Personal Experience 1930s -1990s*, Left Book Club, Sydney, 1993

Hemingway, Ernest, 'Milton Wolff', in Davidson, Jo, *Spanish Portraits*, Georgian Press, New York, c1939

Henry, Chris, *The Ebro 1938: Death Knell of the Republic*, Osprey Publishing, Oxford, 1999

Hewett, Dorothy, *Wild Card: An Autobiography 1923-58*, McPhee Gribble, Ringwood, 1990

Hochschild, Adam, *Spain in Our Hearts: Americans in the Spanish Civil War 1936-1939*, Macmillan, London, 2016

Holmes, Cecil, *One Man's Way*, Penguin, Ringwood, 1986

Hopkins, James, K., *Into the Heart of the Fire: The British in the Spanish Civil War*, Stanford University Press, Stanford, 1998

Hoskins, Sir Cecil, *The Hoskins Saga*, Self-published, Sydney [?], 1969

Howells, A.F., *Against the Stream: The Memories of a Philosophical Anarchist 1927-1939*, Hyland House, Melbourne, 1983

Hughes, Ben, *They Shall Not Pass! The British Battalion at Jarama*, Osprey Publishing, Oxford, 2011

Hyndman, Tony, 'Volunteer in Trouble' in Cunningham, Valentine (ed) *Spanish Front: Writers on the Civil War*, Oxford University Press, Oxford, 1986

Inglis, Amirah, *Australians in the Spanish Civil War*, Allen & Unwin, North Sydney, 1987

Inglis, Amirah, 'Lloyd Edmonds', *Labour History*, No. 67, November 1994, pp. 4-5

Jackson, Angela, *At the Margins of Mayhem: Prologue and Epilogue to the Last Great Battle of the Spanish Civil War*, Warren & Pell, Pontypool, 2008

Jump, James R., *The Fighter Fell in Love: A Spanish Civil War Memoir*, The Clapton Press, London, 2021

Keene, Judith, 'An Antipodean Bridegroom of Death: An Australian with Franco's Forces in the Spanish Civil War', *Journal of the Royal Australian Historical Society*, Vol. 70, Part 4, April 1985, pp. 251-269

Keene, Judith, 'A Spanish Springtime: Aileen Palmer and the Spanish Civil War', *Labour History*, Vol. 52, May 1987, pp. 75-87.

Keene, Judith, *Fighting for Franco*, Leicester University Press, New York, 2001

Keene, Judith, 'The Spanish International Brigadier as Veteran and Foreign Fighter', *Contemporary European History*, Vol. 29, 2020, pp. 276-278

Keene, Judith, *The Last Mile to Huesca: An Australian Nurse in the Spanish Civil War*, (Revised Edition), The Clapton Press, London, 2023

Lacey, Robert, *The Queens of the North Atlantic*, Sidgwick & Jackson, London, 1973

Landsborough, Gordon, *Tobruk Commando*, Cassell & Co, London, 1956

Lockwood, Rupert, *War on the Waterfront: Menzies, Japan and the Pig-iron Dispute*, Hale & Ironmonger, Sydney, 1987

Long, Gavin, *To Benghazi*, Australian War Memorial, Canberra, 1961 (revised edition)

Love, Peter, 'Lloyd Edmonds: 3 July 1906 – 18 September 1994', *Labour History*, No. 67, November 1994, pp. 1-3

Lowenstein, Wendy, *Weevils in the Flour: An Oral Record of the 1930s Depression in Australia*, Scribe, Brunswick, 1998

MacDougall, Ian, *Voices From the Spanish Civil War: Personal recollections of Scottish volunteers in Republican Spain 1936-39*, Polygon, Edinburgh, 1986

Macintyre, Stuart, *The Reds: The Communist Party of Australia from Origins to Illegality*, Allen & Unwin, St Leonards, 1998

Macintyre, Stuart, *The Party: The Communist Party of Australia from Heyday to Reckoning*, Allen & Unwin, Crows Nest, 2022

McNeill, James, 'Ted Dickinson', *Australian Left Review*, No. 4, December 1966, pp. 41-45

Maley, Willy (ed), *Our Fathers Fought Franco*, Luath Press, Edinburgh, 2023

Martin, Sylvia, *Ink In Her Veins: The Troubled Life of Aileen Palmer*, UWA Publishing, Crawley, 2016

Menghetti, Diane, *The Red North: The Popular Front in North Queensland*, Resistance Books, 2018

Merritt, J.A., 'A History of the Federated Ironworkers' Association of Australia 1909-1952', Australian National University, PhD thesis, 1967

Merritt, J.A., 'The Federated Ironworkers' Association in the Depression', *Labour History*, No. 21, 1971, pp. 48-61

Miles, Patricia, 'War Casualties and the Merchant Navy', Office of Environment and Heritage, New South Wales Government

Moore, Andrew, *The Secret Army and the Premier: Conservative Paramilitary Organisations in New South Wales 1930-32*, New South Wales University Press, Kensington, 1989

Moss, Jim, *Sound of Trumpets: History of the Labour Movement in South Australia*, Wakefield Press, Cowandilla, 1985

Moulds, Francis Robert, *The Dynamic Forest: A History of Forestry and Forest Industries in Victoria*, Lynedoch Publications, Richmond, 1991

Mundey, Jack, *Green Bans & Beyond*, Angus & Robertson Publishers, Sydney, 1981

Orwell, George, *The Road to Wigan Pier*, (1937), Penguin Books, Hammondsworth, 1982

Orwell, George, 'Clink', in Orwell, George, *The Collected Essays, Journalism, and Letters of George Orwell* (Edited by Sonia Orwell & Ian Angus), Volume 1, *An Age Like This*, London, Secker & Warburg, 1968

Orwell, George, *Homage to Catalonia*, (1938), Bibliotech Press, 2018

Orwell, George, 'Spilling the Spanish Beans', in Orwell, George, *The Collected Essays, Journalism, and Letters of George Orwell* (Edited by Sonia Orwell & Ian Angus), Volume 1, *An Age Like This*, London, Secker & Warburg, 1968

Orwell, George, 'Looking Back on the Spanish War', in Orwell, George, *The Collected Essays, Journalism, and Letters of George Orwell* (Edited by Sonia Orwell & Ian Angus), Volume 2, *My Country Right or Left*, London, Secker & Warburg, 1968

Overy, Richard, *Russia's War*, Penguin, Great Britain, 1998

Playford, John, 'History of the Left-wing of the SA Labor Movement 1908-36', BA thesis, University of Adelaide, 1958

Plowman, Peter, *Across the Sea to War*, Rosenberg Publishing, Dural, 2003

Prest, Wilfred (ed), *The Wakefield Companion to South Australian History*, Kent Town: Wakefield Press, 2001

Preston, Paul, 'Lord Thomas of Swynnerton', *The Guardian* (online), 10 May 2017

Preston, Paul, *A People Betrayed: A History of Corruption, Political Incompetence and Social Division in Modern Spain 1874-2018*, William Collins, London, 2020

Richardson, Len, *The Bitter Years: Wollongong during the Great Depression*, Hale & Ironmonger, Sydney, 1984

Romilly, Esmond, *Boadilla*, (1937), Macdonald & Co, London, 1971

Santamaria, B.A., *Against the Tide*, Oxford University Press, Melbourne, 1981

Silver, Lynette and Young, Billy, *Billy: My Life as a Teenage POW*, Sally Milner Publishing, Binda, 2016

Smith, Elaine R., 'But What Did They Do: Contemporary Jewish Responses to Cable Street', in Kushner, Tony and Valman, Nadia (Eds) *Remembering Cable Street: Fascism and Anti-Fascism in British Society*, Portland, London, 2000

Steinacher, Gerald, *Nazis on the Run: How Hitler's Henchmen Fled Justice*, Oxford University Press, Oxford, 2011

Strang, Lord William, *Home and Abroad*, Andre Deutsch, London, 1956

Taffrail, *Blue Star Line at War 1939-1945*, Foulsham, Slough, 1973

Thomas, Hugh, *The Spanish Civil War*, Eyre & Spottiswoode, London, 1962

Tilles, Daniel, 'Jewish Decay against British Revolution: The British Union of Fascists' Antisemitism and Jewish Responses to it', PhD thesis, Royal Holloway, University of London, 2011

Tremlett, Giles, *The International Brigades: Fascism, Freedom and the Spanish Civil War*, Bloomsbury Publishing, London, 2020

Wait, R.N., 'Reactions to Demonstrations and Riots in Adelaide 1928 to 1932',

MA thesis, University of Adelaide, 1973

Walker, Bertha, *Solidarity Forever: A part story of the life and times of Percy Laidler – the first quarter of a century*, National Press, Melbourne, 1972

Ward, Russell, *A Nation for a Continent: The History of Australia 1901-1975*, Heinemann, Richmond, 1977

Wechsberg, Joseph, 'Twilight in Souk El Giuma', *New Yorker*, 5 April 1952, pp. 109-123

Wheeler, George, *To Make the People Smile Again*, Zymurgy Publishing, Newcastle upon Tyne, 2003

White, Jon, 'The Port Kembla Pig Iron Strike of 1938', *Labour History*, No. 37, November 1979, pp. 63-77.

Williams, Deane, *An Arc of Mirrors: Australian Post War Documentary Film*, Intellect, Bristol, 2008

Wintringham, Tom, *English Captain*, Faber and Faber, London, 1939

The Book of the XV Brigade: records of British, American, Canadian, and Irish volunteers in the XV International Brigade in Spain, 1936-1938, Newcastle, 1975. A photo reprint of the 1938 ed. published by the Commissariat of War, XV Brigade, Madrid.

Pamphlets, Ephemera and Objects

Russell, Archer, *The Truth About Spain*, Current Book Distributors, Sydney, 1945

Form Architects (Australia) Pty Ltd, *Significance Assessment: 11 O'Connor Street, Guildford*, Holroyd City Council

Dickinson, E.A., *The Black Plague: An Exposure of Fascism*, Legion of Blue and White Shirts, Fulham, 1936

Franklyn, Jack, *An international brigader speaks!* Legal Rights Committee, Sydney, 1942

Howells, A.F. and M.J., *We Went to Spain*, Spanish Relief Committee, Melbourne, 1939

Isaacs, Isaac, *Australian Democracy and Our Constitutional System*, Horticultural Press, Melbourne, 1939

Palmer, Nettie, *Australians in Spain*, Spanish Relief Committee, [Sydney, 1938?]

Palmer, Nettie, and Fox, Len, (with the help of McNeill, Jim and Hurd, Ron), *Australians in Spain: Our Pioneers Against Fascism*, Current Book Distributors, Sydney, 1948

Program for the La Boite Theatre's production of *Dickinson*, 1980 in the Len Fox Papers 1852-2001, Mitchell Library, MLMSS 8085.

Program for Space Theatre's production of *Dickinson*, by David Allen with David Young and Henry Salter, 1978, State Library of South Australia, Record number: b2159431

Websites

Australian War Memorial: https://www.awm.gov.au

Abraham Lincoln Brigade Archives: https://alba-valb.org/

Australian Dictionary of Biography: https://adb.anu.edu.au/

Richard Baxell: https://richardbaxell.info/

International Brigades Memorial Trust: https://international-brigades.org.uk/

Willy Maley: https://willymaley.scot/

People Australia: https://peopleaustralia.anu.edu.au/

Spanish Civil War: A Virtual Museum: https://www.vscw.ca/en

Index

Aarons, Brian 261, 266
Aarons, Sam 197
Aitken, George 109, 127
Aldred, Guy 57, 58
Alexander, Jack 305-11
Allen, David 275, 278-9
Attlee, Clement
    challenged to a duel 59
    support for the International Brigades 154, 184, 299
    support for the Spanish Republic 93, 190
Azana, Manuel 70, 213
Baeza, Ricardo 125, 210
Baillieu, Clive 95
Barry, Jack 91-2, 160
Bastiaan, Ross 285
Blackburn, Maurice 94, 207
Blaylock, Malcolm 278
Bloomfield, Tommy 117, 127, 185-6
Bourke, Percival 42-3
Bourne, Harry 167
Bradman, Don 131
Briskey, Bill 108, 110, 114
Britten, Benjamin 283
Brome, Vincent 263
Broomhill, Ray 280
Browne, Frank 253-4
Bryan, Herbert (Bert) 177, 181-2, 294-5
Bull, Nugent 221-2, 285-6
Burchill, Elizabeth 280
Burns, Netta 284
Butler, Richard 31-32, 37, 40
Cameron, Archibald 206

Cameron, James 254
Campbell, Eric 81-2
Cant, James 282-3
Carter, Joe 13, 141, 171, 246, 253
    arriving home 200-1, 203, 208-10, 213-4
    battle of the Ebro 160-8
    in London 184-187
    journey to Spain 129-33, 219
    leaving Spain 171, 176-7, 180-2
    life before Spain 97-99
    life in Wollongong 271-3
    on Czechoslovakia 266
    remembering Spain 281, 285
    training in Spain 156-7
Chamberlain, Neville 155, 175, 182, 184, 193, 198, 205, 295
Chapman, Dora 283
Childe, V.G. 19
Churchill, Winston 72, 227, 230
Clive, Lewis 163. 295
Colahan, Colin 237
Conway, Kit 107, 110, 114
Copeman, Fred 108, 111-4, 128
Crook, David 105-7
Curtin, John 93-4, 217, 236, 240-1, 308
Dickinson, Edward Alexander (Ted) 13, 15, 73-5, 146, 160, 186, 197, 281, 286
    arrest, trial and imprisonment 40-7
    battle of Jarama 110, 114-5
    breaks with the Australian left 58
    captured and executed 115-8
    departure from Australia 47-50
    duel challenge 59-61
    early life and political actions 17-25

first days in Spain 101, 104-8
free speech campaign 26-29
International Freedom League 55-7
Legion of Blue and White Shirts 61-5
play about Dickinson 275-80
poem about Dickinson 204
reaction to death 120-6
remembered by McNeill 203, 206, 230, 244-5, 253. 260-1, 264, 268-70
reviving *Direct Action* 33-8
unemployment campaign 30-32
Wollongong's May Day 91-2

Dickinson, Myrtle (nee Ankers) 49, 55, 123, 124, 279
Dunlop, John 167
Duhig, James 94
Eden, Anthony 121, 228
Edmonds, Lloyd
  at Ripoll 181-3
  biography 287-91
  Canberra memorial 284-5
  on McNeill 270
  on Carter 273
  publishes letters 281
Elias, Phil 116
Esmond, Romilly 172
Evatt, H.V. 236, 252
Fanelli, Captain 59-60
Fox, Len 173, 194, 251, 275, 284
Francis, William 42
Franco, Francisco 1, 16, 69-72, 74, 94-5, 108-9, 117, 125, 149, 151-2, 161, 165-6, 168, 172-3, 177, 182, 189-90, 198, 203, 213, 221-2, 238, 245, 253, 259, 269, 282, 286, 288, 306
Franklyn, Jack 13, 154, 159, 253
  arriving home 199-203

battle of the Ebro 161-7
death 246
departure from Spain 181-3
farewell to Spain 177
in London 184-7
life before Spain 146-8
non-payment of passage 213-4
remembered by Carter 272
Second World War 240-2

Fry, Harry 101-2, 104-5, 107, 110-1, 114-6, 120, 128
Gallacher, Willie 136
Gandhi, M.K. 56-7
Garden, Jock 50, 58
Garcia, Jack 145-6
Gilroy, N.T. 94
Gosling, Mark 83
Grant, Donald 210-1
Green, Annie 36
Green, Nan 304
Gurney, Jason 73, 102-6, 116, 127
Haldane, Charlotte 154, 186-7, 295
Haldane, J.B.S. 186, 300-1
Halifax, Edward 43
Hawkins, Sheila 237
Hardy, Frank 258, 268
Healy, Jim 214
Hemingway, Ernest 221, 288, 293
Hewitt, Dorothy 256-7
Holmes, Cecil 256-7
Hill, Lionel 32, 48-9, 51-2
Hills, Tom 130, 133
Hilliard, Robert 103
Hitler, Adolf 14, 59, 61, 64, 71-2, 82, 84, 89, 91, 129, 137, 151-3, 168, 175-6, 181, 187, 190-1, 193, 197-8, 215-8, 221-2, 239-41, 244, 259, 286, 294,

303, 306, 311
Hodgson, Agnes 282
Howells, A.F. 197, 280
Hughes, Billy 208
Hurd, Ron 121, 125-6
Hyndman, Tom 112-3
Ibárruri, Dolores (La Pasionaria) 91-2, 178, 213
Inglis, Amirah 281, 284, 290
Isaac, Isaacs 193
Jones, Jack 137, 290
Jump, James 156
Keene, Judith 244, 282, 284
Kelson, Brendon 284-5
Kerrigan, Peter 107, 229
King, Gordon 99, 206
Lang, Jack 50, 58, 80, 84
Lazzarini, Bert 88
Lockwood, Rupert 256
Loftus, John 172
Long, Gavin 220
Longstaff, John 283
Lowenstein, Wendy 269
Lyons, Joe 95, 185, 193, 198, 205
Macartney, Wilfred 107
McClintock, Herbert 264, 286
McDonald, Paddy 90
Macdonald, William Murn 181-2, 291-4
McHenry, Pat 89-90, 218
McIlroy, Charles 184-5, 199-200, 202-3, 296-8
McNeill, James Vincent (Jim) 5, 50, 97, 124, 143, 146, 152, 214, 239, 241, 290, 291, 297, 303, 305
  arriving home 199-209
  at Port Kembla 87-8
  battle of the Ebro 161-71
  confronting the New Guard 82-5
  Czechoslovakia and its impacts 265-8
  death 270
  departure from Spain 179-82
  Dickinson's trial 42-7
  early life 15-7
  enlisting in the 2nd Australian Imperial Force 218-221
  family life 246-50
  free speech campaign 25-9, 57
  in England 228-30
  in London 184-7
  in Scotland with the 1st Australian Forestry Company 231-8
  joins the CPA 76-80
  leaving for Spain 99, 129-31
  marriage to Mabel 233-5
  memorialisation of the International Brigades 242-5, 252-3, 360, 264, 269, 275, 286
  not dead 189-90
  reading about the Spanish Civil War 263
  remembered by Carter 272
  reviving *Direct Action* 33-4
  selling *Tribune* 254-6, 259
  stowaway voyage 133-9
  training and convoy to Britain 223-6
  training in Spain 157-60
  travels to the USSR 261-2
  unemployment campaign 29-31
  withdrawal of the International Brigades 175-9
  Words For Freedom 257-8
McNeill, Mabel (Mabel Kendall) 233-5, 246-9, 262, 265, 269-70
McNeill, Vanessa 235, 246-50, 257-8, 262, 267-8

McPhee, Kenneth 210-1
McPhillips, Jack 165
McWilliams, Bob 129-30
Maley, James 118-9
Marty, Andre 102-3, 171, 180
Menghetti, Diane 280
Menzies, R.G.
    Communist Party of Australia 218, 252
    Dalfram dispute 192-4, 246
    Kisch affair 300
    National Register 214
    Second World War 233-4
    Spanish Civil War 95
    Views on Hitler 198, 215, 244
Meredith, Bill 115
Miles, J.B. 99, 181, 206
Miller, Margot (Margot Bennett) 144-5
Mola, Emilio 71
Moran, Stan 82, 165, 261, 267, 310
Morcom, William Arthur (Bill) 13, 144, 197, 219, 270, 280, 286
    death 162, 164-5
    journey to Spain 130-2
    life before Spain 52-3
    training 155-6
Morgan, Charles 111
Morrison, Richard 208
Mosley, Oswald 61-3, 82, 102, 276-7
Mundey, Jack 256, 266
Murray, George (Judge) 42, 44-5,
Murray, George (Unionist) 272
Mussolini, Benito 14, 17, 34, 59, 61, 71-2, 81-2, 84, 91, 132, 151. 181, 190, 193, 233, 276, 286-7
Nalty, Jack 139, 170
Negrin, Juan 174, 176, 2132

Nehru, Indira 160
Nehru, Jawaharial 160
Nelson, Steve 260
Newman, James 124-5
Norton, Rev. Dr 94
Olorenshsaw, Arthur 138
Orr, Bill 87, 130
Orwell, George 61, 68, 74, 79, 102, 179, 276-7
Overton, Bert 108, 110, 114-5, 127,
Page, Earle 223
Palmer, Aileen 282
Palmer, Nettie 124, 173, 205, 285
Pearce, George 95
Pitcairn, Frank 179
Playford, John 260, 277
Pollitt, Harry 74, 121, 136, 170, 187, 189
Pugh, James 121
Pulford, Reg 49
Radford, Ron 283
Rae, Arthur 50
Rebbechi, Kevin 137, 181-3, 290-1
Reeve, Charles 20, 22-3, 25, 28, 36, 61, 78, 124, 197, 211, 275
Renton, Donald 107, 117, 120
Richthofen, Wolfram von 229
Riley, Charles 184, 199, 200, 203, 206, 301-4
Roach, Ted 190, 192, 218
Robeson, Paul 154, 258, 295
Roland, Betty 191, 216
Ross, Edgar 206, 251, 267
Russell, Archer 238
Rutherford, James 120, 128
Ryan, Frank 259
Salazar, António de Oliveira 71
Santamaria, B.A. 94

Shaw, Charlotte Evelyn 300-1
Shirer, William L 64
Skitch, Cecil 53
Slessor, Kenneth 227
Springhall, Dave 103
Stalin, Josef 52, 69, 89, 143, 164
    and the CPA 79, 251, 256
    and McNeill 80, 251, 262
    and the International Brigades 103, 107, 263
    Nazi-Soviet Non-Aggression Pact 215-6
    Support for the Spanish Republic 72-4, 152
Standish, Fred 45-6
Stevens, John 116
Stieglitz, Herman 174
Thomas, Hugh 263
Thompson, Thomas 35
Thornton, Ernie 58, 251
Tomalin, Miles 118-9
Tunnah, John 113
Walters, Charles 184, 200, 203, 242, 298-301
Walters, Maxwell Haldane 300
Whateley, Dick 172-3
Wheeler, George 137, 290
White, Ted 131
Wild, Sam 229
Wintringham, Tom 107-8, 113-6, 127, 229-30
Wood, Bill 285
Young, Bill 98, 197, 259, 270, 286
    leaving for Spain 129-133
    life before Spain 140-3
    stowaway voyage 143-5
    in Spain 155, 159

battle of the Ebro 162-5
Young, David 275, 277, 279
Young, Keith William 140-3, 164-5

www.ingramcontent.com/pod-product-compliance
Lightning Source LLC
Chambersburg PA
CBHW052057300426
44117CB00013B/2160